ZANY'S

NEW YORK CITY APARTMENT GUIDE

2001

ON YOUR OWN PUBLICATIONS • NEW YORK

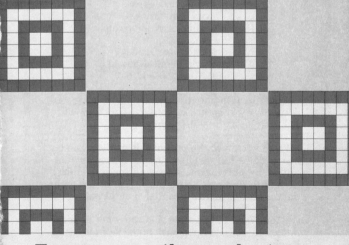

**Zanys.com—the easiest way
to find a NYC apartment**

PUBLISHER
Jeff Brauer

EDITORS IN CHIEF
Courtney Andrialis, Janet Beard

DESIGN
Greg Evans

ART
Julie Rofman

PRODUCTION
Pas Niratbhand

COPY EDITORS
Carla Sapsford, Imogen Rose-Smith

STAFF WRITERS
**Imogen Rose-Smith, Katherine Moon,
Reginald James**

ON YOUR OWN PUBLICATIONS, LLC
**Corporate Address:
Building #3, 6th Fl. Brooklyn Navy Yard
Brooklyn, NY 11205**

**Tel: 718.875.9455
Fax: 561.673.2436
www.zanys.com
E-mail: oyobooks@yahoo.com**

© December 2000
On Your Own Publications, LLC
IBSN 1-929377-12-6

For information about corporate orders or special editions of this book, contact On Your Own Publications at the address above.

All rights reserved. No part of this publication may be reproduced, stored in a retrieval system or transmitted by any means, electronic or mechanical, except brief excerpts for the purpose of review, without the express written permission of the publisher.

On Your Own Publications, LLC does not have any interest, financial or personal, in the locations listed herein.

CONTENTS

WHERE DO YOU WANT TO LIVE IN NYC?

BACKGROUND

WWW.ZANYS.COM
Find a NYC apartment now!

ZANY'S TOP LISTS

HOTTEST NEIGHBORHOODS
1. Williamsburg
2. Nolita
3. Chelsea
4. Park Slope
5. East Village

ONES TO WATCH
1. Harlem
2. Downtown
3. Clinton
4. Jersey City
5. Fort Greene

BEST KEPT SECRETS
1. Dumbo
2. Inwood
3. Prospect Heights
4. Morningside Heights
5. Roosevelt Island

BEST BANG FOR YOUR BUCK
1. Morningside Heights
2. Jersey City
3. Prospect Heights
4. Clinton
5. Lower East Side

BEST PLACES FOR ARTISTS/ALTERNATIVE LIFESTYLES
1. East Village
2. Chelsea
3. Greenwich Village
4. Williamsburg
5. Long Island City

BEST PLACES TO FIND PEACE AND QUIET
1. Upper East Side
2. Park Slope
3. Gramercy Park
4. Battery Park City
5. Brooklyn Heights

BROOKLYN'S BEST
1. Park Slope
2. Brooklyn Heights
3. Williamsburg
4. Fort Greene
5. Carroll Gardens

BEST PLACES FOR THE RICH AND FAMOUS
1. Central Park West
2. Tribeca
3. Upper East Side
4. Soho
5. Greenwich Village

BEST PLACES TO RAISE KIDS
1. Upper East Side
2. Tribeca
3. Park Slope
4. Yorkville
5. Forest Hills

WHERE DO YOU WANT TO LIVE IN NYC?

INTRODUCTION

◆◆◆◆◆◆◆◆

Why use a guidebook and a website to find an apartment in New York? Because unless you know what you're doing, finding a place to call home can be brutal, exhausting, fruitless and outrageously expensive. That's why.

The Big Apple is notorious for scalping unsuspecting newcomers who show up expecting the residential market here to be like it is in Des Moines. Think again. The bottom line is: to have a hope of finding the dream place in the most exciting city in the world—one that satisfies your heart but doesn't empty your bank account—you're going to need some help.

That's where Zany's NYC Apartment Rental & Sales Guide and www.Zanys.com comes in. We wrote the book and maintain the website because we've all been there, scrambling to find a place on short notice with little money or time, which in New York is a recipe for disaster. We'll tell you what somebody with experience should have told us when we first arrived: where to look, what details to consider and where to turn for help. And our website will help you find the best apartment at the right price.

Rather than spending days on end hoofing it all over town and asking all the wrong questions of all the wrong people, Zany's provides the answers to questions you didn't even know to ask. What neighborhoods are for you? Should you buy or rent? What about pets? Roommates? Doorman or not?

All the answers are here. In the end, Zany's will save you dozens of hours, thousands of dollars and worlds of frustration in your journey to the dark heart of the most unforgiving but ultimately satisfying real estate market in the world. Your peace of mind and precious free time will make Zany's a reliable companion throughout the process of renting a NYC apartment.

As they say in Manhattan, nobody's born lucky—you get smart, then you get lucky. Zany's and Zanys.com will help you get lucky in New York.

DISCLAIMER

New York City is one of the most racially and ethnically diverse cities in the world. Diversity is a fact of life here. Ethnically speaking, the United Nations has nothing on your average street in Brooklyn. In this book we discuss the racial and ethnic populations of the city's neighborhoods, since this contributes to intangibles like a neighborhood's "character," and often factors into many people's decision where to live. In doing this, we want to make it clear up front that we are not implying any connection between certain aspects of neighborhoods—positive or negative—and their racial or ethnic makeup.

"Man always assumed that he was more intelligent than dolphins because he had achieved so much— the wheel, **New York**, wars, and so on—while all the dolphins had ever done was muck about in the water having a good time. But conversely, the dolphins had always believed that they were far more intelligent for man—for precisely the same reason."

-Douglas Adams

WWW.ZANYS.COM
Find a NYC apartment now!

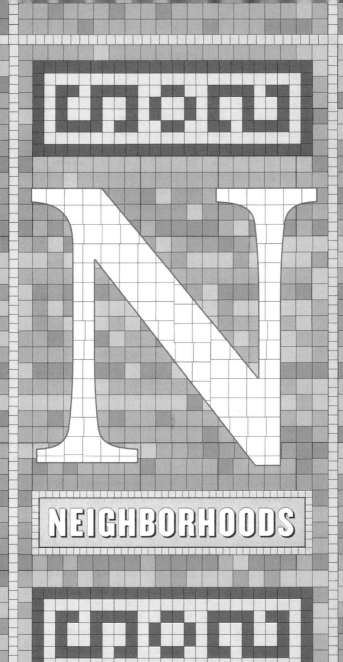

NEIGHBORHOODS

ASTORIA
• QUEENS •

The fact that Queens is looked down upon by Manhattanites, mainly because the borough remains a predominantly working class area, is good news for would-be bargain hunters in the housing game. This prejudice has meant that the surprisingly quaint neighborhood of Astoria has yet to be clobbered by the housing boom that has hit most of Brooklyn's boroughs. Consequently, if you venture out to Astoria you can still get a sizeable bang for your buck.

Astoria has a rich history. In 1652, William Hallett, an Englishman, purchased 1,500 acres of land from the Dutch governor, Peter Stuyvesant. Though the region's natives did not relish in this sale, they were coaxed by beads, seven coats, four kettles, a blanket and a bit of Hallett's smooth talking into a peace treaty with the Englishman. By the 1830s, this small community had been elevated to the status of a village and named Hallett's Cove. In 1839, a local fur trader named Stephen A. Halsey, who dreamt of making Hallett's Cove an affluent and bustling sector, proposed that this site be called Astoria in an attempt to lure the wealthy John J. Astor into investing in this developing community. Astor was not impressed by Hallett's sycophantic attitude and contributed nothing to Astoria's development; nevertheless, the name stuck.

Bound by the East River in the North and the West, Grand Central Parkway, the Brooklyn-Queens Expressway, and LaGuardia Airport in the East, and 35th Avenue and Sunnyside in the South, most of Astoria's charm has to do with its proximity to Manhattan and its reputation for being a safe yet sprightly neighborhood. The area can boast two major claims to fame: first, the penchant of Hollywood film makers for featuring this friendly neighborhood and second, the fact that Astoria, often referred to as "Little Athens," houses the largest concentration of Greeks outside of Greece itself. Moreover, Astoria has bragging rights as the birthplace of the Steinway piano, Hellman's mayonnaise, and the first Xerox copier.

In addition to the estimated 80,000 to 100,000 Greeks living in this area, Italian, German and Polish Americans have been residing in Astoria for decades. The recent infusion of immigrants from Bangladesh, Ireland, Philippines, Colombia, India and China means Astoria now plays host to a rich and eclectic medley of cultures. The neighborhood has a suburban feel. Astoria is not really known for its aesthetic allure but more for its practicality. Parks and recreation facilities do exist in this traditionally family oriented community, but you'll have to look hard to find them. In the residential areas, trees and gardens line the streets in an attempt to naturalize the cluster of low-rise tenements and brick row houses. Dark-suited older men retire to the benches lining the sidewalks, and mingle and socialize with their acquaintances. Greek pastry shops and cafes around 31st street and Ditmars Boulevard beckon any passerby with goodies, pastries and some strong 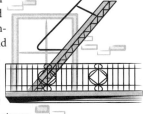 Greek coffee. Although you do not have to be Greek (or Italian) to fit in here, it doesn't hurt since there are quite a few exclusive social clubs and many of the shops are lined with alphabets foreign to the American reader.

Astoria may be proud of its roots and cultural heritage, but it is by no means unwelcoming or xenophobic. The people are always ready to lend a helping hand, and once settled, one cannot help but love the community feel of Queen's little treasure.

Zanys.com user comments: "Lots of professionals, amenities everywhere," but "not entirely clean—it ain't the upper Westside, here, but it's not awful." "Starbucks is coming, a sure sign that the neighborhood is being ruined." Also, the "N (Never) and R (Rarely) trains are a big reason

THE PEOPLE

POPULATION	140,000
AGE	
0-17	18%
18-44	45%
45-64	22%
65+	15%
ETHNICITY	
White	78%
Black	9%
Asian	13%
Spanish speaking	27%
Family households	59%
College educated	22%
HOUSEHOLD INCOME	
Below $25,000	43%
$25-75,000	52%
$75-150,000	4%
$150,000+	1%

I want to move." The neighborhood is "cool, if a little dirty," but "very safe." In short, "If Astoria were 15 min. closer to Manhattan I would love it."

Noise: The busiest avenues get their share of traffic, but most of the residential streets have a suburban feel. This is a working neighborhood, so anyone who wishes to rock out late into the night should be prepared for some hostile responses.

Parking: Most Astoria residents have cars, and street side parking is still generally available during the day. Although this is a relatively safe area, car owners should be weary of leaving their vehicles near the East River.

Kids & Families: This is a real family community. Kids and parents will find terrific neighborhood services including good schools, playgrounds and daycare.

Safety: Most streets in Astoria are residential, but those in the industrial areas are best avoided at night. One wrong turn can leave you feeling vulnerable on a deserted street.

Entertainment: If you want the more traditional city nightlife, this is not the place for you, but Astoria does have some recreational highlights. The American Museum of the Moving Image has a year round calendar of retrospective film screenings. There is a good selection of local drinking holes on Broadway and Steinway. An increasing number of more fashionable places are springing up on some of the out of the way streets that appeal to the die-hard trendies who can't afford Manhattan rents. Expect to pay Manhattan prices for a mixed drink though.

> "New York is a small place when it comes to the part of it that wakes up just as the rest is going to bed."
>
> **P.G. WODEHOUSE**

Restaurants: You'll do all right here so long as you like seafood, lamb or pasta. As the ethnicity of the community would suggest, the Greek and Italian food here can be exceptional. The legendary Elias' Corner has some of the freshest seafood imaginable, and if you want to snack on pizza, pick up a piping hot slice from John's Pizzeria on Astoria Boulevard.

Shopping: Most of the stores are fairly basic and generic. However, Astoria does boast a large selection of used furniture shops and imported food stores. So, if you're looking to kit out your new pad on the cheap, or fancy making something

THE NEIGHBORHOOD

AVERAGE RENT

Studio		$700-975
1	br	$850-1,400
2	br	$1,000-1,700
3	br	$1,400-2,000

AVERAGE SALE PRICE

Studio		$50,000-80,000
1	br	$50,000-100,000
2	br	$55,000-120,000
3	br	$70,000-150,000

COMMUTING

The N train stops at Ditmars Boulevard, Astoria Boulevard, 30th Avenue, Broadway and 36th Avenue. Buses are helpful for connections to the N and R lines.

DISTANCE

Time to midtown	15-30 min
Time to downtown	25-45 min

a little out of the ordinary for dinner, you're onto a good thing.

Parks & Gardens: Astoria has a surprisingly high number of open and cultivated spaces. The Isamu Noguchi Garden Museum, with its three galleries and outdoor Japanese garden, shows the works of internationally revered sculptor Noguchi, who died in 1988. Socrates Sculpture Garden dramatically displays gargantuan junk sculptures and contemporary works against the Manhattan skyline; the more run of the mill Astoria Park extends from 19th Street to the waterfront.

Final Words: It pays not to be a snob. Astoria is

still a great deal for those who want to be close to Manhattan but don't wish to live in a closet for the privilege. Just by stepping over the Queensboro Bridge you can have a garden, live in a comparably spacious abode and still pay less rent than many of your friends.

BATTERY PARK CITY
• MANHATTAN •

Battery Park City is Manhattan without Manhattan. It is a suburban enclave within a city—a planned community that was ambitiously designed to nurture the best tidbits of New York, while weeding out the other more distressing and obnoxious aspects of the Big Apple.

Built in 1979, Battery Park City is a relative newcomer to Manhattan. To this day, many native New Yorkers don't even know that it exists. The hole dug for the World Trade Center's foundation generated a million cubic yards of earth, which in turn was dumped into the Hudson River to produce the 23-acre base of this neighborhood. Governor Nelson A. Rockefeller envisaged this area as an almost utopian residential and commercial sector of New York.

In the midst of the Financial District, Battery Park City was planned to exhibit a less hectic and more nature-oriented existence. The plan worked, maybe a little too successfully. Residents tend to fall into two camps. They either love the area, praising its "quiet" and "peaceful" atmosphere. Or they hate it, damning the community for being "dead" and "sterile."

Located between West Street and the Hudson River, this upscale neighborhood has become a magnet for young professionals working downtown, as well as thirty and forty somethings who want to get away from the hustle and bustle of urban life.

You won't even feel like you are truly in Manhattan if you live in Battery Park City. The neighborhood appeals to out-of-towners who want the conveniences of living in the big city without actually having to partake of the urban environment. Those who like to be in the thick of it all would not enjoy the quiet and calm of this area after the workday is done.

With a mile long, beautifully landscaped esplanade, a marina for seafaring yachts, and one third of its 92 acres devoted to parks, plazas and gardens, onlookers can easily forget that they are still in Manhattan. The wide streets lined with trees are hardly ever congested or filled with the honking chaos that characterizes other New York streets. Officers in green uniforms patrol the five parks, plazas, and gardens, giving residents a sense of security, although for others it is uncomfortable to live in an overly policed environment.

> "Crossing the street in New York keeps old people young—if they make it."
>
> **ANDY ROONEY**

The surrounding waterfront is really what gives this neighborhood its appeal. Each shiny new skyscraper has its own laundry facilities, gym and in some cases, convenience stores, video rental places and other amenities. Ideal if you don't like straying too far from home for your creature comforts.

Battery Park itself is not that impressive, being overrun by tourists wearing Statue of Liberty hats, eager to trace their ancestral heritage on Ellis Island. But the surrounding parkland is gorgeous, painstakingly landscaped and exquisitely maintained. The cool breezes that permeate this rather sedate setting come off the Hudson River, and keep the neighborhood a good ten degrees lower then the rest of the island. This might seem like an asset in the sweltering summer heat, but come winter you'll be cursing.

Because all of the condos are new, maintenance costs are minimal, but you will be paying out a pretty penny for

THE PEOPLE

POPULATION	4,000
AGE	
0-17	8%
18-44	65%
45-64	20%
65+	7%
ETHNICITY	
White	70%
Black	11%
Asian	13%
other	16%
Spanish speaking	12%
Family households	36%
College educated	57%
HOUSEHOLD INCOME	
Below $25,000	18%
$25-75,000	42%
$75-150,000	17%
$150,000+	23%

the pleasure of an apartment here. The views over lower Manhattan are spectacular, and many residences have balconies so you can sit out and enjoy your own private show. Don't expect much architectural diversity—one modern apartment looks very much like another. Conformity is the rule amongst homeowners, too. The advantage to such uniformity is that there is little friction in the neighborhood. Residents more or less keep to themselves and go about their own business. The focus is very much on work, and there is no sense of a tightly-knit community.

Noise: Hardly any. The neighborhood is extremely quiet with very little traffic.

Parking: None, unless your building offers it.

Kids & Families: Battery Park City is good for young kids, since it is safe and offers lots of open space. There are very few school facilities, though, but if you live here you can afford to send them off to Andover, right?

Safety: The area is extremely safe and well patrolled. It does get quiet at night, though, and anyone venturing beyond the peripheries of the community should be wary.

Entertainment: There is very little excitement here outside of the occasional open air concert. However, you

THE NEIGHBORHOOD

AVERAGE MONTHLY RENT

Studio		$2,000-2,400
1	br	$2,300-2,900
2	br	$2,800-3,600
3	br	$3,400-4,800

AVERAGE SALE PRICE

Studio		$160,000-175,000
1	br	$250,000-450,000
2	br	$350,000-700,000
3	br	$600,000-1,000,000

COMMUTING

The N and R trains stop at Whitehall and the 4, 5 and 6 trains stop at Bowling Green.

DISTANCE

Time to midtown	15-35 min
Time to downtown	5-10 min

may want to visit the African Burial Ground, one of the city's more harrowing cultural heritage spots, where over 20,000 skeletons were discovered in a mass grave.

Restaurants: There is little exceptional dining around. The restaurant at the top of the World Trade Center will give you a spectacular view, and there are some upscale eateries in the World Financial Center. If your culinary skills are limited to pasta and ramen noodles, take-out and delivery are going to be your best bets.

Shopping: Except for the pricey boutiques in the World Trade and Financial Centers, there is little to choose from. Century 21 is only a short walk away and offers plenty of discount bargains for the less extravagant shopper.

Final Words: Battery Park City is not for everyone. If you want the ease and security of a planned community, then you will be enamored by its attributes. But if all this homogeneity sounds too much like the Stepford Wives meets American Psycho, stay well away.

BAY RIDGE
• BROOKLYN •

Just as pinstripes means Yankees to any true New Yorker, Bay Ridge means working class and lots of space. Come to Bay Ridge for an affordable existence where food is inexpensive and housing costs are still reasonable. It also recalls the meaning of a true neighborhood existence, something that is increasingly rare as New York grows and grows.

Bay Ridge was originally named Yellow Hook for the yellow clay in its soil, but when New York underwent a bout of yellow fever in 1853, the color lost its appeal. Noting the neighborhood's eye-catching panorama overlooking the New York Bay and a glacial ridge running along Ridge Boulevard, Yellow Hook residents prudently altered the name to Bay Ridge.

Throughout the late 19th century, this area was known as a haven for affluent Manhattanites who wanted to relax by the Bay and admire the scenery. However, with the development of the 4th Avenue subway in 1915, the neighborhood lost its elitist and exclusive air. The new public transportation facility allowed poorer folk access to this scenic spot. Performing a form of gentrification in reverse, the working and middle classes moved into the area and have more or less set the standard for the neighborhood ever since.

Bay Ridges stretches from 65th street to 101st street and from Belt Parkway to Fort Hamilton Parkway. By anyone's standards, it is gargantuan. Bring your sneakers and be forewarned: however much your tootsies throb at the end of a hard day's pounding the streets, you'll leave this neighborhood knowing that there is still so much more to see.

The ambiance clearly reflects the middle-class and family-oriented feel of the people residing here. A sense of community pervades the neighborhood. Many residents actively participate in the Bay Ridge Community Council, a body that includes PTA's, civic, trade and block associations. These groups and others try hard to maintain the upkeep of the streets. Mucky pups beware; Bay Ridge even has designated cleanup days.

Like many of the neighborhoods in Brooklyn, this sector is ethnically and socially diverse. During the 19th and 20th centuries, many Norwegian and Danish sailors immigrated to Brooklyn, and the Nordic heritage is still prevalent in certain sections. Lately there has been an influx of Irish, Middle-Eastern, Greek, Asian and, most recently, Russian immigrants. Just walking down Third Avenue you will be awed by the unique medley of restaurants, each a reflection of life in the old country, or somewhere along life's random, multi-cultural path.

Apartment houses that have been converted into co-ops are plentiful here, and there are also quite a few condominiums. The majority of residences are designed for one or two families, with some three to six family buildings also available. If you are looking to relocate the whole brood to the New York area, and can't stomach the idea of

WWW.ZANYS.COM
Find a NYC apartment now!

being cooped up in a Manhattan apartment, Bay Ridge might be a good option.

As one might expect, along with such family friendly accommodations comes a sizable host of recreation facilities. Areas such as Owl's Head Park overlooking the harbor are good places to relax and enjoy the view, or for those with a more active lifestyle, running, biking, or roller-blading on the Shore Parkway Promenade provides

THE PEOPLE

POPULATION	115,000
AGE	
0-18	23%
18-64	60%
65+	17%
ETHNICITY	
White	85%
Black	5%
Asian	10%
Spanish speaking	7%
Family households	44%
College educated	23%
HOUSEHOLD INCOME	
Below $25,000	48%
$25-40,000	17%
$40-60,000	16%
$60,000+	19%

a two and a half mile long stretch and ample scenery. A point of cultural interest, though privately owned, is the Gingerbread House at 82nd street and Narrows Avenue. Like something out of a children's fairy story, the home's unique appearance has earned it a verity of names, from the rather trippy Mushroom House to the more sinister Witch's House—an oblique reference to the Hansel and Gretel fable.

It is difficult to believe that Hansel and Gretel could have gotten into so much trouble if they'd lived in the charming neighborhood of Bay Ridge. If you like a com-

THE NEIGHBORHOOD

AVERAGE MONTHLY RENT

Studio		$500-900
1	br	$700-1,800
2	br	$1,000-2,500
3	br	$1,400-1,700

AVERAGE SALE PRICE

Studio		$80,000-90,000
1	br	$90,000-110,000
2	br	$100,000-150,000
3	br	$120,000-200,000

COMMUTING

The R train stops at Bay Ridge Avenue, 77th, 86th and 95th street. The N train stops at 61st street and 8 Avenue

DISTANCE

Time to midtown	70-90 min
Time to downtown	55-60 min

munity feel, well-kept streets and a quiet place to come home to after a long days work, Bay Ridge is a prime location. But if you want everyone to stay out of your business or if you enjoy playing punk rock into the early hours, don't expect to win any popularity contests at the Bay Ridge Community Council's AGM.

Noise: There's a bit of a racket on the thoroughfares. Otherwise, the noise level matches that of any suburban town—it's there but not overbearing.

Parking: Side street parking is available, but you may

WWW.ZANYS.COM
Find a NYC apartment now!

find it hard to find a space at night.

Kids & Families: Due to the plentiful amount of parks and recreational areas, parents who want to raise their kids outside of the smog and clutter of the big city will love it here. Kids often fly kites and ride bikes along the promenade, and they'll have plenty of space to romp and frolic.

Safety: The residents here say they feel secure, though they still lock their doors at night and take the necessary precautions. This is not a particularly dangerous neighborhood. However, the suburban feel can lull you into a false sense of security and it is always better to keep hold of your big city street smarts savvy.

Entertainment: There is a movie theatre and a bowling alley, but Bay Ridge is not exactly a happening locale in terms of an insane nightlife. Still, there is always Kings Square Dancing, if you're looking for some alcohol-free, squeaky clean, country fun.

Restaurants: 3rd Avenue is the place to be. Along the 25 block long walkway, you will have no problems finding something good in all flavors, from the cross section of little eateries to eclectic restaurants.

Parks & Gardens: The spot where Miss Norway is crowned each year, Leif Ericson Park is a tribute to the neighborhood's Norwegian heritage. Owl's Head Park and Shore Road Park are popular places to picnic and enjoy the scenery and the cool breezes from the harbor. The Shore Parkway Promenade is a great place to get outside and burn some of those calories that you gained from the good food nearby.

Shopping: Brand name shops are cluttered on 86th Street. For a little more local color, the shops on 5th Avenue are smaller and cozier with a more eclectic selection.

Final Words: Those who enjoy the hustle and bustle of urban life should probably look elsewhere. This is not a fast, classy or pompous neighborhood and is very community-oriented. On the other hand, Bay Ridge is definitely the right place for would-be suburbanites who want to live by the waters, feel the cool breeze sweep over their skin as they stroll through the parks, and enjoy some picturesque views.

BEDFORD-STUYVESANT

● BROOKLYN ●

A graffiti mural that, until recently, featured prominently in the district of Bedford-Stuyvesant read: "Live or Die in Bed-Stuy." This sentiment neatly sums up the area. Home to the largest African-American community in New York, the neighborhood of Bedford-Stuyvesant is often regarded by residents simultaneously as a neighborhood to be proud of and a cross to be born. Located in northern Brooklyn, Bedford-Stuyvesant is bounded by Classon Avenue on the west, Williams Place on the east, Flushing Avenue to the north and Park Place to the south.

The name Bedford-Stuyvesant first came into popular use in the 1930s when an effort was made to join the traditionally working class neighborhood of Bedford with its more middle class neighbor Stuyvesant Heights. Maybe out of a desire to indulge in all New Yorkers self-decreed license for perversity, or in a genuine display of neighborhood pride, there are still those who to this day refuse to acknowledge the union.

The ambivalent response that this neighborhood evokes finds its routes in the district's checkered past. Originally one of the only areas in the city where African Americans could purchase land, by the mid-nineteenth century the area housed not only blacks but Irish, German, Jewish, Scottish and Dutch immigrants in its grand apartment buildings. The dawn of the new century saw the neighborhood at the height of its popularity.

The opening of the Brooklyn Bridge in 1883 and the construction of the A train resulted in a massive influx of

> "You have to run ahead of people sometimes and try to kill them."

MELISSA ZEGANS ON CATCHING CABS IN MANHATTAN

WWW.ZANYS.COM
Find a NYC apartment now!

African-Americans. Simultaneously, Stuyvesant Heights developed as an upper-middle class neighborhood. Amongst the affluent who saw fit to call the area home was dime store king J. W. Woolworth. During the early part of the twentieth century, the community of Bedford-Stuyvesant was one of few successful examples of mixed race living in the country.

Neither the harmony nor the grandiose appearance would survive. In the 1940s, with the expansion of the Brooklyn Navy Yard, there was a rapid flood of homeless black workers who wanted to settle in the area, creating an air of competitive and intense housing pressure. Racist tactics utilized by shady realtors helped frighten the white population into leaving their homes in search of "safer" neighborhoods. With the riots that were characteristic of the times and the growing animosity between the whites and the blacks, the white population left, taking the funding for many of the community services with them. This was the start of the neighborhood's decline, as neglect and economic depression began to take its toll. Public housing projects did little to improve conditions, and soon the name Bed-Stuy was synonymous with ghetto.

Yet the residents of Bedford-Stuyvesant have never passively accepted the decay of their once glorious neighborhood, and there are ongoing attempts at urban revival. In recent years, notable efforts have been made to restore the hallmark houses of Stuyvesant Heights, and potential renters will be struck by the beauty of these tree-lined streets. Most residents live in either limestone or brick row houses or one of the handful of large apartment buildings, most of which are now under government control. Given the rundown nature of the area, repair costs can be steep, so make sure to include this factor in your budget if you decide to move here.

If you're looking for a sneak preview of Bed-Stuy, Spike Lee's *Do The Right Thing* was shot on location here. The film gives an idea of the architectural splendor, deep passions and underlying poverty of the area, though it exaggerates the presence of racial tensions. Whether or not you decide to live in Bedford-Stuyvesant, one thing is clear: this is a community struggling to pull itself back on track, and only a die-hard cynic could fail to be impressed.

Many of the local schools and churches have received a much needed make-over; and the importance of both of these institutions to the community at large demonstrates the determination of this bruised area to come back swinging. Certainly, crime and poverty still prevail. This is far from a safe area, and the housing prices and rents are low for this very reason. But conditions have much improved, and people are mostly optimistic for the future.

> "There is more sophistication and less sense in New York than anywhere else on the globe."
>
> **DON HEROLD**

Zanys.com user comments: "Inexpensive with good size apartments and transportation everywhere…" but "sketchy depending upon which block you live on," though safer "closer to the train." Also, "more white faces than ever…" and "loud in the summertime."

Noise: You'll be sure to get your full share of the urban orchestral experience here. One unanimous complaint is the constant racket. From car alarms to police sirens, children crying and music blaring, there's never a dull moment.

Parking: Street side parking is available throughout the day. Security can be an issue and most residents chose not to leave anything swankier than a station wagon unprotected. Reasonably priced garages are readily available.

Kids & Families: Kids are everywhere, but poverty and crime makes it a tough neighborhood in which to raise a family.

Safety: This is considered one of the worst crime neighborhoods in Brooklyn, so be alert at all times and don't take any unnecessary risks.

Entertainment: Most of the local entertainment is of the blue collar variety. Bowford Avenue has an old school bowling alley with old school prices, and the brave can take their pick from several of the area's corner dive bars. During the summer, Bed-Stuy proudly celebrates its heritage during the African Street festival, and the area erupts into a five day carnival of food, music and dancing.

Restaurants: Soul food is the dish of choice around here, and many restaurants will serve you up some good collard greens. There is also some Ethiopian cuisine available.

Parks & Gardens: This is not a lush neighborhood. However, Bed-Stuy does boast the Brooklyn version of Tompkins Square Park. Other possible destinations if you're craving the sight of a blade of grass are the well-maintained Brower Park, Saratoga Square Park and Herbert Von King Park.

THE PEOPLE

POPULATION	62,000
AGE	
0-17	22%
18-44	47%
45-64	19%
65+	12%
ETHNICITY	
White	14%
Black	85%
Asian	1%
Spanish speaking	13%
Family households	32%
College educated	13%
HOUSEHOLD INCOME	
Below $25,000	42%
$25-75,000	50%
75-150,000	7%
150,000+	1%

Shopping: Most of your choices will be limited to what you can find in struggling local retail stores. Residents have grown accustomed to making do with whatever is on the shelves. Many stores stock household hardware, which will come in handy in any maintenance crisis.

THE NEIGHBORHOOD

AVERAGE MONTHLY RENT
Studio		$400-700
1	br	$500-900
2	br	$600-1,200
3	br	$800-1,400

AVERAGE SALE PRICE
Studio		$50,000-85,000
1	br	$90,000-150,000
2	br	$100,000-170,000
3	br	$120,000-200,000

COMMUTING
Although Bed-Stuy is not easily accessible from Manhattan, the G, M, J, A and C trains serve the area. Drivers utilize the convenient Brooklyn or Manhattan bridges.

DISTANCE
Time to midtown	30 min
Time to downtown	20 min

Final Words: Despite its best intentions, Bed-Stuy remains one of the least desirable places to live in Brooklyn. Unless you can find a colossal loft space at a rock bottom price, it is difficult to come up with enough positives to justify moving here.

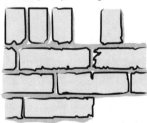

WWW.ZANYS.COM
Find a NYC apartment now!

BENSONHURST
● BROOKLYN ●

Who says you can't find Little Italy in New York any longer? Anyone who spouts such rumors has clearly never wandered into Bensonhurst. Brooklyn's own slice of *la dolce vita*, Bensonhurst has hardly changed at all since John Travolta danced his way out of it with *Saturday Night Fever*. The local teenagers may not be wearing white suites any longer, but this is still very much a hard-core traditional Italian community.

Originally part of the Dutch settlement of New Utrecht, the area retained its Dutch temperament and farmlands into the 19th century. The neighborhood was named after the Bensons, a family of potato and cabbage farmers. Though Bensonhurst began as an agricultural community, the area went through a brief spree as a seaside resort.

Bensonhurst-by-the-sea was to be a middle class alternative to the bawdy fun of Coney Island, and for a while the area's natural beauty pulled in quite a crowed. With the extension of the N and R trains in 1915, Bensonhurst became a retreat for the Italian and Jewish communities, who were clustered and congested in Manhattan's Lower East Side. To this day, there remains a longstanding Jewish presence along with a recent infusion of Irish, Polish and, most recently, Asian and Russian peoples, to bolster the predominantly Italian population. It was not until the 1950's, with the second wave of Italian immigration, that the community's present day character began to take hold.

Bounded by 7th Avenue to the northwest, 61st Street and MacDonald Avenue to the northeast, Avenue U and 26th street to the southeast, and Gravesend Bay to the southwest, Bensonhurst also claims the historic New Utrecht area and a triangle of land on Avenues O and P as its own. The district is a bit of a trek from Manhattan, and many residents live and work within the neighborhood's perimeters. However, the intrepid commuter will find the trip into the Big Apple, via the N/R, quite feasible.

The people here are well acquainted with one another, bonded by their shared interests in church, community-organized festivals, and sports leagues. A neighborhood that is not out to please tourists, this hamlet seems to cater to the finicky and particular tastes of its residents. Finding a place to live in this area is not difficult, but your best bet is to find a local who can keep an eye out for a vacant apartment. This kind of community does not feature prominently in the Village Voice, and local brokers handle most of the purchasing.

Despite the overwhelming Italian influence, there has been an infusion of Asian, and especially Russian, culture in recent years. Just like in the days of Greased Lightning, the younger generations of Italian-Americans often feel stifled by such a traditional community and are itching to get away. Older residents lament that the glory days of Bensonhurst are over, and if the ethnic statistics continue to change the way they have, this area could soon lose its Italian aroma.

The houses are mainly multi-family dwellings and were built for functionality more then aesthetic value. Many have brick, staccato or stone façades and include backyards or gardens. Bensonhurst streets offer plenty of shade and fresh air. These pleasant conditions are a result of the thoughtful legacy of green-fingered James Lynch, who planted over 5,000 trees in the neighborhood in the 19th century.

Walk around the neighborhood and you will doubtlessly be reminded of an Italian village; absorb the seductive pull of family, religion, and food that saturate the environment. You cannot but help to breathe in the stifling nuptial air exuded by the omnipresent bridal shops and wedding halls. At any hour of the day, elderly men and women squat in chairs, people-watching, and chatting away in Italian. In numerous local coffee shops, you will spy people sipping espressos and chomping on biscotti. Food is an integral social component of this community and you can expect a real taste of Italy when

WWW.ZANYS.COM
Find a NYC apartment now!

dining in any of the countless Italian restaurants, cafes, and groceries. Religious festivals are always large events, as locals decorate Bensonhurst with extravagance, pride and love for their religious convictions.

THE PEOPLE

POPULATION	160,000
AGE	
0-18	21%
18-64	64%
65+	15%
ETHNICITY	
White	79%
Black	2%
Asian	13%
Spanish speaking	5%
Family households	39%
College educated	17%
HOUSEHOLD INCOME	
Below $25,000	46%
$25-40,000	21%
$40-60,000	18%
$60,000+	15%

Zanys.com user comments: Bensonhurst is a "nice neighborhood," usually "very safe."

Noise: Neighbors are considerate of one another and traffic is confined to the daytime, so at night you should be able to hear a pin drop.

Parking: Private garages are common and the street side parking is adequate.

Kids & Families: Though the population is growing older, this is still a family neighborhood. Kids tend to stick together and can often be seen roaming the streets looking for mischief.

Safety: Make friends with your neighbors and you'll have no problems; outsiders are advised against causing too much trouble.

THE NEIGHBORHOOD

AVERAGE MONTHLY RENT

Studio	$500-800
1 br	$600-1,000
2 br	$700-1,300
3 br	$800-1,500

AVERAGE SALE PRICE

Studio	$40,000-80,000
1 br	$40,000-150,000
2 br	$50,000-200,000
3 br	$100,000-300,000

COMMUTING

The B and M train stops at Bay Pkwy. The N train stops at 63rd Street and 18th Avenue.

DISTANCE

Time to midtown	70-90 min
Time to downtown	55-65 min

Entertainment: Step back in time to the 1950's. Maple Lanes Bowling Alley will have you looking to score big. There is also Nellie Bly Amusement Park, which is open Easter through Halloween. The Regina Opera Company at Regina Hall offers the real thing at a fraction of the price you'd pay for the National Opera House. Those looking to wet their whistle can stop by one of the many charming bars—rest assured, they'll always have old blue eyes on the juke box.

Restaurants: Well, it's obvious, really. You'll swiftly become a connoisseur of the various Italian cuisine and

WWW.ZANYS.COM
Find a NYC apartment now!

their regional definitions. If you're sick of spaghetti and linguine, there are a smattering of Greek, Korean, Arab and Israeli establishments to choose from.

Parks & Gardens: The nearby public beach provides residents with a place to relax in summer and some blustery walks in winter. There are few public parks, though, so residents with children have to make do with asphalt playgrounds.

Shopping: All the essentials are available, as well as delicious pastries from local bakeries. Traditionalists will be in raptures over the old-world style butchers and fishmongers.

Final Words: Though the times are a changin', Bensonhurst remains an old-fashioned Italian community. If you can fit into their ways of tradition, family and religion, you'll do fine. If conformity and continuity aren't your kind of thing, then you should really look elsewhere.

BOROUGH PARK
➤ BROOKLYN ➤

orough Park is Jerusalem revisited, replete with a full cross-section of synagogues and lots of good matzo. If you want to live where you can take your religion home with you, or relax in words of the Torah at the end of a 9-5 grind, Borough Park beckons.

Like much of Brooklyn, Borough Park used to be a rural and rustic locale. With the development of more accessible transportation to and from Manhattan, people swiftly began to settle in this neighborhood. Russian Jews were among the first to move, abandoning the overcrowded Lower East Side around 1910. By 1930, half the population of Borough Park was Jewish.

Borough Park became predominantly an Orthodox Jewish community after World War II. Many less

> "A natural New Yorker is a native of the present tense."
>
> **V.S. PRITCHETT**

devout Jewish families joined the middle-class masses fleeing the city for suburbia. The 1940s and 50s saw an influx of Hasidic Jews to the area, most of whom were either escapees of World War II or part of the 1956 uprising in Hungary. Today, the population here is mostly Hasidic.

Bounded by Fort Hamilton Parkway, 18th Avenue, 18th street and New Utretcht Avenue, this neighborhood is a striking contrast to much of modern New York. The residents here dress in traditional clothing: bearded men wear long black coats, and women sport long skirts and shirts with high necklines. There are over thirty sects and 300 synagogues ranging form the lavish and newly built temples to modest storefronts. Family is important in this community. Having more than four children is the norm, as is apparent from the number of children who can be spotted playing out on the streets.

Borough Park is an enclave unto itself. Home to the largest concentration of Orthodox Jews outside of Israel, the area has the distinct feel of being from another time. On Fridays, before the Sabbath and several hours before sundown, the streets hum with activity and commotion as people scramble to get their last-minute tasks in order. On Saturday the neighborhood becomes a ghost town.

Of course, stores selling kosher foods are plentiful, but Borough Park is also known for its discount shopping. Almost anything you can dream up, from high-quality items to laundry detergent, can be snapped up at often 50% less than normal department store prices. Though the restaurants are not fancy, they provide wholesome kosher food. However, residents are more prone to take-out than they are to dining out. This neighborhood has an ambiance all its own.

Even the architecture of their houses is indicative of the neighborhood's religious convictions. Each building has staggered balconies to provide for the holiday of Succoth: at that time, families must dine in a four-sided

Find a NYC apartment now!

enclosure open to the sky. Hasidic Jews do not use electricity during the Sabbath. Thus, all the houses here are low rise. Tall buildings would be disastrous since residents would have to climb story after story every Saturday, when the electronically powered elevator is off limits.

Only those who are prepared to live with the rhythms and culture of this highly devout and exclusive community should consider moving to Borough Park. Those just visiting should remember to dress appropriately: scantily clad visitors, beware.

THE PEOPLE

POPULATION	140,000
AGE	
0-18	35%
18-64	48%
65+	17%
ETHNICITY	
White	82%
Black	7%
Asian	11%
Spanish speaking	7%
Family households	30%
College educated	17%
HOUSEHOLD INCOME	
Below $25,000	52%
$25-40,000	17%
$40-60,000	14%
$60,000+	17%

Noise: The hustle and bustle on pre-Sabbath days is quite hectic, especially on Fridays. But come Sabbath, there is hardly any noise.

THE NEIGHBORHOOD

AVERAGE MONTHLY RENT

Studio	$500-800
1 br	$600-1,200
2 br	$800-1,800
3 br	$1,000-1,500

AVERAGE SALE PRICE

Studio	$50,000-85,000
1 br	$70,000-230,000
2 br	$90,000-250,000
3 br	$100,000-300,000

COMMUTING

The B and M trains stop at Fort Hamilton Pkwy, 50th and 55th street. The F train stops at Bay Pkwy. The N train stops at 63rd Street and 18th Avenue.

DISTANCE

Time to midtown	70-90 min
Time to downtown	55-60 min

Parking: Come here on the Sabbath, and you'll have no trouble finding parking, though you may have trouble finding a person to talk to or a store to carouse through.

Kids & Families: Education is an integral factor in the Hasidic community. On non-Sabbath days, the neighborhood is littered with yellow school buses, since the families here are quite large, and the children are not sent to public school. Families are understandably religious, and typically the younger ones are raised to study Judaism.

Safety: This is not an intrusive neighborhood, and it doesn't feel particularly foreboding. The residents here seem to keep more or less to themselves, their business and their families.

Entertainment: Just visit this neighborhood and you will be entertained by scenes, experiences, foods and smells that are probably new to you.

Parks & Gardens: There are no major parks in the area.

Restaurants: Restaurants that serve kosher food are available, though this neighborhood's claim to fame is not its fine cuisine. Most of the residents tend to cook at home or take out food.

Shopping: The majority of the shopping lies on 13th Avenue between about 40th and 54th streets. There are other smaller stores scattered throughout.

Final Words: Just visit Borough Park once, even if you have no intention of moving here. It is a great cultural experience, and you can really see the effects of years of tradition and religion. Living in a time when most New Yorkers don't really adhere to tradition or ritualistic lifestyles, Borough Park represents a return to older, religious customs.

BRIGHTON BEACH
BROOKLYN

righton Beach is Coney Island's slightly more respectable and definitely more religious younger brother. Back in its glory days, Brighton Beach was a sight to behold. From the 1920s through to the 60s, the area was a Jewish social Mecca. The beach and the boardwalk thronged with people, and world-renowned entertainers would amuse the populace with songs, dances and jokes well into the early hours.

Today, all this has gone and only a few of the older residents remember those good times. But, recent Russian immigrants have adopted and renovated Brighton Beach, and it is once again a neighborhood on the rise with a character all of its own.

The area did not start to develop until the 1880s when it was named after the garish seaside resort in England. It was intended as a posh contender to Coney Island, complete with a casino, racetrack and major hotels. In 1907, Brighton Beach Baths, a salubrious establishment boasting multiple pools, tennis, mini-golf and live entertainment, was opened. Unfortunately, all of this was short-lived. With an anti-gambling sentiment sweeping the country, the casinos and racetracks vanished, and by the 1920s, the hotels were replaced by apartment complexes. By the 1930's, the beach was a booming residential district with a considerable Jewish presence.

When the Soviet Union relaxed its emigration policies in the late 1980s, Soviet Jews began to flock to New York. Many came to Brighton Beach where rents were low, and there was plenty of room to house them. For many immigrants coming from Odessa in Ukraine, Brighton Beach was a nostalgic reminder of their homeland by the Black Sea. Soon enough, the Russian-Jewish culture flourished, and Russian stores, restaurants and nightclubs began popping up throughout this area.

Bordered by Neptune Avenue to the north, Brighton Beach lies in between Coney Island and Manhattan Beach on the southern shore of Brooklyn. Aside from a noisy main thoroughfare, the neighborhood is generally tranquil, and perfect for retirees who want to enjoy some R&R by the soothing waves of the sea. Due to the aging population, finding a place to live is not overly difficult, though it helps to be Russian. There are some great views from the boardwalk, but that's a far cry from the what you'll see inside most apartment buildings in Brighton Beach: buildings here tend to be eyesores. Though some more attractive housing can be found to the north of the district, property value and personal security are both better closer to the ocean.

Brighton Beach Avenue, the main street running parallel to the boardwalk, is laden with Russian delis, restaurants, clothes stores and Cyrillic shop signs. The streets are bustling with activity everywhere, from old men playing dominos to cyclists and strollers cruising along the walkway. Everyone here seems to smoke cigarettes constantly, although chances are they've made the transition to the Marlboro man. More people in Brighton Beach speak Russian than English, and the residents, like any newcomers to America, exist in their own old world cultures and traditions. You won't feel especially welcome here, especially if you can't speak some simple Russian, but everyone is tolerated. Although Brighton Beach is at present predominantly Russian and Jewish, successful Russian immigrants have slowly but steadily been moving

Find a NYC apartment now!

to more prosperous neighborhoods, while their vacant slots are being filled by newcomers from Asia and the Middle East.

An evening trip to Brighton Beach can be a lot of fun, even if you don't plan to stay very long. The club scene is active, and where better to find long-legged dancers, good Russian peasant food and the best borscht? Whether you decide to pitch your tent here or keep on looking, take a walk along the ocean, breath in the Atlantic air and enjoy Brighton Beach for what it is: a slice of old world on the edge of the new.

THE PEOPLE

POPULATION	33,000
AGE	
0-17	15%
18-44	24%
45-64	36%
65+	25%
ETHNICITY	
White	71%
Black	25%
Asian	4%
Spanish speaking	18%
Family households	27%
College educated	24%
HOUSEHOLD INCOME	
Below $25,000	24%
$25-75,000	58%
75-150,000	16%
150,000+	2%

Noise: Listening to the lapping of ocean waves will put you to sleep at night. There is little traffic, and aside from the elevated train, the neighborhood is almost disarmingly quiet.

Parking: Many of the high-rise housing communities have underground parking spaces. Permits can be obtained for parking on the street, and meters are generally available for short-term stays. If you plain to travel into the city much, a car is advisable, since the subway service is limited.

THE NEIGHBORHOOD

AVERAGE MONTHLY RENT

Studio	$500-700
1 br	$600-900
2 br	$700-1,300
3 br	$800-1,500

AVERAGE SALE PRICE

Studio	$50,000-85,000
1 br	$40,000-120,000
2 br	$45,000-150,000
3 br	$50,000-180,000

COMMUTING

The F train stops at Neptune Avenue, the D train stops at Ocean Parkway and Brighton Beach and the Q train stops at Brighton Beach.

DISTANCE

Time to midtown	50-65 min
Time to downtown	45-55 min

Kids & Families: This is mainly an older community. Though many first generation New Yorkers grew up here and will reminisce about their great childhood experiences, kids are going to make a run for Coney Island when they discover what's next door.

Safety: Rumors fly that the Russian mafia performs a variety of dirty deeds here, but little evidence of such behavior is apparent to the average resident. If you mind your own back and avoid wandering around alone late at night, you should be fine. Crime tends to be limited to petty theft, purse snatching, and burglary.

Entertainment: Russian techno clubs are clustered along Brighton Beach Avenue. You can also find a variety of old world beers and good drink at assorted pubs nearby.

Restaurants: Eating along the boardwalk in summer is a unique and enjoyable experience. The food is excellent, but unless you speak Russian expect the service to be abysmal.

Parks & Gardens: In keeping with the aesthetic bias of the neighborhood, the beach is your best bet for outdoor recreation. Green spaces are hard to find and most apartment complexes offer some sort of asphalt playground.

Shopping: A good shopper can get stocked up at a good price. Stores along Brighton Beach Avenue offer good deals on fresh produce, meat and fish. You will also find a plentiful supply of Russian delicacies including lox, smoked herring and caviar.

> "The last time anybody made a list of the top hundred character attributes of New Yorkers, common sense snuck in at number 79...."
>
> **DOUGLAS ADAMS**

Final Words: Brighton Beach is a great place to visit, but unless you're thinking about retirement or want free Russian language lessons, you probably won't want to live here.

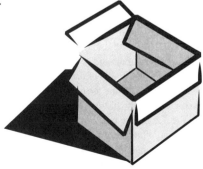

BROOKLYN HEIGHTS
◆ BROOKLYN ◆

Brooklyn Heights has been one of New York's premier neighborhoods for the past two centuries. The magnificent views of the Manhattan skyline have changed drastically since Walt Whitman's day, but they still inspire the same poetic impulses in residents and visitors alike.

Brooklyn Heights was New York's first historic district, and it is easy to see why preservationists were eager to keep the neighborhood's grand old mansions and street fronts intact. Indeed, this is one of the oldest neighborhoods in the city. The Canarsie Indians were the first people known to have lived in the area, which they called Ihpetonga, meaning "high sandy bank" The Heights is actually one of the highest points on the Brooklyn side of the East River, and the first Dutch settlers found it an attractive place to reside, as well.

> "New York is the meeting place of the peoples, the only city where you hardly find a typical American."
>
> **DJUNA BARNES**

The Dutch first established Brooklyn Heights as the terminus for their ferries to and from Manhattan, and the neighborhood came to prominence in 1814 when Robert Fulton developed steam powered ferries. Thus began a ritual still familiar to many Brooklynites: the daily commute to Manhattan. Brooklyn Heights became an upper-class neighborhood, and the grand residences built in the 19th century remain today.

However, the construction of the Brooklyn Bridge and the subway system made the ferries obsolete and ushered in a new era of Heights history. The area was no longer exclusive; the rich moved out, and quite a few writers and artists, such as Whitman and Hart Crane, moved in. Brooklyn Heights remained a literary hotspot well into the 20th century, with Truman Capote, Arthur Miller,

WWW.ZANYS.COM
Find a NYC apartment now!

Tennessee Williams and W.H. Auden all calling the neighborhood home.

Brooklyn Heights is bordered by Fulton Street, Atlantic Avenue and Court Street. The majority of the homes in the area are brownstones and row houses, many of which remain fully intact as they were built in the 19th century. Though the residences are lovely, the Heights also features Brooklyn's largest business district. Services and stores of all kinds are located on the neighborhood's main thoroughfare, Montague Street, though most businesses close early in the evenings. Brooklyn Heights features some excellent restaurants, ranging from fast food to first-class.

The neighborhood has a stunning collection of large homes in various 19th century architectural styles. On a walk through Brooklyn Heights, you will see Federal, Greek Revival, Gothic Revival and Queen Anne style buildings. The homes on Columbia Heights have extraordinary views looking out across the river and are near the Promenade, where you can take in the vista at one of the many cafes or restaurants.

Rent here is high, but you are paying to live in one of the country's most charming urban historic centers. Brooklyn's prominence is on the rise, and thus, the Heights is as popular as ever. The charm that drew New York's wealthiest to this spot one-hundred and fifty years ago, is still attracting new residents today.

Zanys.com user comments: Brooklyn Heights is a "nice area." Though a "little busy during the daytime," otherwise it's "perfect."

Noise: The neighborhood is very quiet, and you can expect to get scolded by the neighbors if you make too much noise.

Parking: Difficult on metered streets, but not impossible. You can also pay to park your car at a number of garages in the neighborhood.

Kids & Families: Brooklyn Heights is a wonderful place to raise a family. Although the population is growing old, it remains ideal to settle down if you can afford it. Packer and St. Anne's are two terrific local private schools.

Safety: Brooklyn Heights is exceptionally safe.
Entertainment: The bulk of entertainment pleasures
are found on Montague Street and the Promenade, where
locals take lazy strolls or dine at outdoor restaurants.

Restaurants: Almost everything is concentrated on
Montague Street, where summer meals are served on outdoor patios. Under the Brooklyn Bridge is the renowned
River Cafe, with four-star food and a majestic view of
Lower Manhattan. For casual meals try Patsy Grimaldi's,
which is without question one of the finest and oldest
pizza joints in the city.

Parks & Gardens: Although there isn't a major park in

THE PEOPLE

POPULATION	43,000
AGE	
0-17	17%
18-44	50%
45-64	27%
65+	6%
ETHNICITY	
White	63%
Black	30%
Asian 7%	
Spanish speaking	20%
Family households	42%
College educated	53%
HOUSEHOLD INCOME	
Below $25,000	29%
$25-75,000	47%
75-150,000	18%
150,000+	6%

the neighborhood, everything about Brooklyn Heights seems green. You'll fall in love with the promenade and the casual air of sophistication that permeates the whole community.

Shopping: Most of the shopping options, from women's clothing to gourmet foods, can be found on Montague Street. A green market is held on the weekends at the public courthouses.

Final Words: Brooklyn Heights is the best place in New York to find 19th century charm and grace. This is a great neighborhood in which to settle down and raise a family. The surroundings are beautiful, there's a quiet, comfortable neighborhood feel and ten subway lines and two bridges makes it an ideal place for any commute.

THE NEIGHBORHOOD

AVERAGE MONTHLY RENT

Studio	$1,000-1,500
1 br	$1,200-2,700
2 br	$1,500-4,000
3 br	$3,000+

AVERAGE SALE PRICE

Studio	$100,000-175,000
1 br	$150,000-350,000
2 br	$200,000-700,000
3 br	$300,000-1,000,000

COMMUTING

The N and R trains stop at Court Street, the 2 and 3 trains stop at Clark Street, and the 4 and 5 trains stop at Borrough Hall. The F, G, A and C trains are only a brief walk away. Due to the convenience of trains, buses are rarely needed.

DISTANCE

Time to midtown	15-20 min
Time to downtown	10-15 min

Cambria Heights is a middle-class neighborhood near the outer edge of Queens County. Residents enjoy living in this quiet, suburban community, full of tree-lined streets and modest homes. However, for anyone planning to commute into Manhattan, it can be quite a trek to this neighborhood all the way on the eastern outskirts of the city.

Until the 20th century, the area which now makes up Cambria Heights consisted mainly of forests and farms. The region was known for the vegetables it produced, which supplied New Yorkers all over the city with their daily doses of vitamins. Where the neighborhood got its name is unclear; however, the "heights" part is quite accurate. Cambria Heights is one of the highest spots in the city.

In the 1920s, developer Oliver B. LaFreniere began creating suburbia out of this rural community. Houses went up and soon businesses moved into the area, as well. When the Belt Parkway was completed in the 1940s, development increased and Cambria Heights became a popular new neighborhood.

Cambria Heights is bounded by Springfield Boulevard to the west and the Cross Island Parkway to the east. The neighborhood lies between 114th and 121st Avenues. It is made up of a middle-class suburban mix of mostly brick houses on attractive, well-kept streets. The homes suffer a bit from a case of mid-twentieth century overly-homogenous building—they tend to all look the same. However, at least their "look" is attractive. The neighborhood shows some signs of wear and tear around the edges but has held up fairly well through the years.

Cambria Heights is almost completely dominated by African-American families, and there is a strong sense of community. Neighbors know each other and are usually ready to lend a helping hand whenever it's needed. The neighborhood has a small town feel and is full of families whose children play together on the sidewalks.

Though Cambria Heights is dominated by residential streets, there are commercial shopping areas, as well. Stores and businesses of all kinds are available on Hillside Avenue. The major drawback to living in this neighborhood is the fact that no subways reach this far out into Queens. Residents have to take the bus to Jamaica Center for subway access. On the bright side, this inaccessibility has kept Cambria Heights on a small-scale. The community-minded residents have thus far held on to the peace and quiet of this suburban neighborhood and will no doubt continue to fight to preserve Cambria Heights' small town feel.

THE PEOPLE

POPULATION	169,000
AGE	
0-18	26%
18-64	61%
65+	13%
ETHNICITY	
White	32%
Black	56%
Asian	12%
Spanish speaking	2%
Family households	32%
College educated	21%
HOUSEHOLD INCOME	
Below $25,000	23%
$25-40,000	14%
$40-60,000	25%
$60,000+	38%

Noise: The neighborhood stays pretty quiet, except when ice cream trucks roll by.

Parking: You should find plenty of spots on the street, and most folks have houses with driveways.

Kids & Families: Cambria Heights is a very family-friendly neighborhood and is dominated by homeowners with children.

Entertainment: You won't find much to do in this suburban part of town.

Restaurants: There's a selection of fast food and sit-down establishment on the commercial edges of the neighborhood.

Parks & Gardens: Unfortunately, there aren't any large parks near Cambria Heights, but kids usually have small yards to play in.

THE NEIGHBORHOOD

AVERAGE MONTHLY RENT

Studio		$500-800
1 br		$600-900
2 br		$700-1,000
3 br		$800-1,200

AVERAGE SALE PRICE

Studio		$55,000-90,000
1 br		$55,000-100,000
2 br		$60,000-120,000
3 br		$65,000-150,000

COMMUTING

The E and F trains end at Jamaica. LIRR leave from Penn station to Flatbush Avenue and Jamaica every hour M-F.

DISTANCE

Time to midtown	45-70 min
Time to downtown	60+ min

WWW.ZANYS.COM
Find a NYC apartment now!

Shopping: You can find pretty much anything you need on Hillside Avenue.

Final Words: Cambria Heights is a nice suburban community. However, for people planning to commute to Manhattan, it's mighty inconvenient.

CANARSIE
• BROOKLYN •

anarsie seems to be transformed with the passing of each generation. In just over one hundred years, the neighborhood has gone from fishing village to beach resort to suburban town and seen countless waves of immigrants come and go. Today, Canarsie offers residents the unique opportunity to simultaneously live in the city and enjoy a laidback beachfront atmosphere.

Canarsie was nothing more than a sleepy fishing village until the late 19th century. German immigrants were the first group to make a large impact on the neighborhood when they began moving in to fish what were once oyster-rich waters in Jamaica Bay. As Canarsie's population grew, so did its blossoming tourism industry. The Golden City Amusement Park opened in 1907, and day-trippers from all around the New York area began making their way to this smaller, less chaotic alternative to Coney Island. Speakeasies and vaudevilles proliferated in the 1920s, and Canarsie's economy boomed. However, the Great Depression hit this neighborhood especially hard. Pollution drove the oysters out of Jamaica Bay, and the amusement park burned down in 1939, marking

> "Living in New York is like being at some terrible late-night party. You're tired, you've had a headache since you arrived, but you can't leave because then you'd miss the party."
>
> **SIMON HOGGART**

the end of an era.

But it was not long before Canarsie sprang back to life in an entirely new form. Developers recognized the potential of this neighborhood and began building split-levels and row houses to attract the young baby-booming families of the 1950s. Canarsie became a tight-knit neighborhood, consisting of mostly Jewish and Italian families, who were replaced in later decades by African-Americans and Caribbean immigrants. At first, these newcomers were met with hostility, but today Canarsie has achieved a smooth blending of different cultures into a unique community.

Bordered to the north by Ditmas Avenue and to the south by the Belt Parkway, Canarsie sits next to Jamaica Bay and runs from Ralph Avenue around the Glenwood Public Houses to East 108th Street. Canarsie is infused with a beach atmosphere unlike anywhere else in the city. Many of the locals, particularly retired residents, take a relaxed attitude towards life. The neighborhood is truly suburban—most residents live in houses and own cars. The brick homes sit back from the street, usually allowing for an attached garage and tiny front yard. Canarsie is too spread out to be comfortably navigated on foot, and the L train is the only way out on public transportation.

Since the vast bulk of the neighborhood's housing was constructed in a brief period during the 1950s, the brick row houses tend to all look the same in the suburban style of that era. Trees line the streets, where children play and ice cream trucks roll merrily along. Many residents own their homes, although renting is also common. The public housing here resembles most other projects in the city, except for the high and wide views over the ocean. Units in the Jamaican Bay Housing Complex, originally built for veterans returning from WW II, were designed after the huts of the Quonset Indians who once lived in the area.

The Canarsie Pier and Canarsie Beach Park are both great recreational areas, where residents enjoy outdoor activities of all types. Both are lovely places to catch an ocean breeze, enjoy a picnic or even go fishing. This access to the beach and the neighborhood's family-friendly feel continue attracting young couples on the lookout for a laidback place to raise their kids. The front yards are small, but the warm, conscientious community has helped to raise generations of contented kids.

THE PEOPLE

POPULATION	59,000
AGE	
0-17	19%
18-44	44%
45-64	27%
65+	10%
ETHNICITY	
White	64%
Black	30%
Asian	6%
Spanish speaking	11%
Family households	73%
College educated	18%
HOUSEHOLD INCOME	
Below $25,000	33%
$25-75,000	53%
$75-150,000	13%
$150,000+	1%

Noise: Canarsie is fairly quiet and dead still at night.

Parking: Most homes have their own parking spaces, but you shouldn't have a problem finding a curbside spot.

Kids & Families: Canarsie is a great place to raise children. Local schools are good, and extra-curricular activities are plentiful. This could easily qualify as the Little League capital of New York.

Safety: Canarsie is a very safe place to live, and major crimes are rare.

Entertainment: Summer fun is concentrated in Canarsie Beach Park, where the water from Jamaican Bay stays warm from late May to early September. Sailing and motorboating are both popular, as are more simple pleasures like sunbathing and people-watching. The beach has a real family atmosphere.

Restaurants: At the Abbracciamento on the Pier, diners can order and eat on their own boats at the dock. You had better like seafood if you plan to move to Canarsie.

Parks & Gardens: Canarsie Beach Park, now a part of the Gateway National Recreation Park, was renovated in the late 1990s. The Canarsie Yacht and Canarsie Canoe clubs are private organizations.

THE NEIGHBORHOOD

AVERAGE MONTHLY RENT

Studio	$600-800
1 br	$700-1,000
2 br	$800-1,200
3 br	$1,000-1,800

AVERAGE SALE PRICE

Studio	$50,000-80,000
1 br	$50,000-100,000
2 br	$55,000-150,000
3 br	$60,000-200,000

COMMUTING

The L train stops at E 105th Street and Rockaway Parkway

DISTANCE

Time to midtown	50-60 min
Time to downtown	45-55 min

Shopping: Most of the shops in the area are found along Rockaway Parkway, Flatlands Avenue and Avenue L.

Started in 1942, the Brooklyn Terminal Market survives as a successful shopping center for fresh produce.

Final Words: Canarsie is an affordable, family-focused neighborhood suitable for many types of suburban-minded people. The beach atmosphere is surprisingly relaxed, so if you thrive on the over-caffeinated energy for which New York is famous, Canarsie may not be for you.

CARROLL GARDENS
◆ BROOKLYN ◆

Brooklyn's community of Carroll Gardens is one New York neighborhood that lives up to its name. The area is chock full of bounteous front-yard gardens and lovely streetside trees. Old time residents know they have a good thing in this tight-knit neighborhood, and more and more transplanted yuppies are beginning to find out about it for themselves.

Carroll Gardens was originally part of Red Hook, but with the construction of the BQE subway line, the neighborhood was cut off from the waterfront. Its name is derived from the only Roman Catholic Irishman to sign the Declaration of Independence, Charles Carroll. His Maryland regiment protected the Old Stone House at Gowanus, now a local landmark, from the redcoats during the Revolutionary War.

This neighborhood used to be an Italian stronghold, known as much for its rowdy machismo as its nicely maintained houses. Neighbors always kept an eye out for each other, and everything that occurred in this community was a personal matter. The Italian influence here is still strong, as deliciously evidenced by the many

> "Babies here seem to be as rare as panda cubs."
> **TREVOR FISHLOCK**

bakeshops selling fresh made tiramisu and cannoli. The area also has quite a few family-style Italian restaurants that provide ample quantities pasta and sauce.

THE PEOPLE

POPULATION	36,000
AGE	
0-17	13%
18-44	40%
45-64	27%
65+	20%
ETHNICITY	
White	54%
Black	42%
Asian	4%
Spanish speaking	35%
Family households	41%
College educated	45%
HOUSEHOLD INCOME	
Below $25,000	37%
$25-75,000	47%
$75-150,000	15%
$150,000+	1%

In the 1980s and 1990s, a flock of entrepreneurs, professionals, artists and writers began moving in and changing the area's old-fashioned feel. Young couples seeking to raise their kids in a safe locale near the city have found that Carroll Garden mixes the right blend of great public schools, diverse people and enough open space for developing the pliable minds of their youngsters.

The tree-lined streets with hardly any traffic or noise add to the serenity and the sense of solace. The residents also have access to gardens and parks that are perfect escapes for weekend picnics and excursions. The people living here have a tendency to consider their neighbors as more or less like family. Some people find such folks to be

WWW.ZANYS.COM
Find a NYC apartment now!

nosey pests, while others appreciate having someone around to watch their backs. The glass is either half full or half empty. Take your pick.

Though they may be wary of their surroundings, the people here are by no means xenophobic. Characteristic of Brooklyn, this neighborhood welcomes fresh faces from all around the globe, and newcomers need not fear ever feeling out of place here. Everyone belongs. And once you belong, you'll always belong.

THE NEIGHBORHOOD

AVERAGE MONTHLY RENT

Studio		$1,200-1,500
1	br	$1,400-1,900
2	br	$1,800-2,700
3	br	$2,100-3,000

AVERAGE SALE PRICE

Studio		$90,000-150,000
1	br	$120,000-300,000
2	br	$150,000-500,000
3	br	$200,000-800,000

COMMUTING

The F and G trains stop at Carroll Gardens and Smith/9th Street

DISTANCE

Time to midtown	25 min
Time to downtown	20 min

Noise: The neighborhood stays fairly quiet. Trucks are not allowed on Carroll Gardens' side streets, and there are no major thruways.

Parking: Ample metered parking is available along most streets, but long-term parking is hard to find. A few of the newer houses have private garages.

Kids & Families: Carroll Gardens is an ideal place to

raise children. A lot of new parents have moved into the neighborhood, joining Italian-American families who have lived here for generations.

Safety: The streets here are quiet and safe, and neighbors are attentive to unfamiliar traffic. Avoid walking around the Gowanus Canal area at night.

Entertainment: As younger residents have begun moving into Carroll Gardens some new restaurants and bars have popped up. Walk along Smith Street for a taste.

Restaurants: Carroll Gardens is home to many classic Italian markets, delis and bakeries. Newer French and fusion restaurants along Smith Street are also noteworthy.

Shopping: in the past few years, a number of unique fashion accessory boutiques have opened up shop in the area. Retail is modest, but all the creature comforts are available.

Final Words: Carroll Gardens is definitely on the upswing. Renters love its charm and close proximity to Manhattan. Expect more and more restaurants, bars and, yes, correspondingly high rents in the years to come.

CENTRAL PARK WEST AND SOUTH, AND FIFTH AVENUE
─ MANHATTAN ─

t's payday! Pass Go, collect $200 and move to the Upper West Side. Or make that $20,000,000. Perhaps the most desirable address in New York, only the extremely well-heeled can afford this swanky neighborhood. Central Park is the Beverly Hills of the East Coast and one of the most expensive areas in the world to make your home.

Be prepared to spend what amounts to most people's annual pay on one of the few available pads that overlook magnificent Central Park—and that's just for the security

Find a NYC apartment now!

deposit. These apartments and condominiums are in such demand that people are willing to wait for years and pay disproportionately high broker fees to live in them. The lengths that some New Yorkers go in order to buy a prestigious address alongside Central Park may seem laughable, until you see the view.

The astronomical rents and exclusive nature of these high-status addresses result in an unusual community of residents. Cabs and limousines pick up stars on their doorstep and deliver them to their destination quicker than you can say "Hey, isn't that…?" Many are so wealthy or famous that they are extremely protective of their privacy. Reclusive superstars rub shoulders with foreign diplomats and the latest dot com billionaires. The reclusive feel of this moneyed environment can make for a cold atmosphere.

As if the locale was not enough, the real beauty of these apartments is found in the architectural detail and craftsmanship that went into their construction. Central Park features some of New York's earliest luxury apartment complexes, built by the city's most renowned architects. The area started to develop in the 1880s, with the majority of apartments being built between the turn of the century and the 1930s. Most buildings consist of luxurious, multi-bedroom apartments with doormen and elegant fixtures like working fireplaces and penthouse patios. Central Park South is distinguished by its more modern residential high-rises and is home to many of New York's best hotels.

> "New York is a city of conversations overheard, of people at the next restaurant table (micrometers away) checking your watch, of people reading the stories in your newspaper on the subway train."
>
> **WILLIAM E. GEIST**

If real estate is all about location, then these buildings have it in spades. Being next to Central Park is like having an 843-acre backyard in the middle of Manhattan. The benefits of this location are almost endless—from ice-skating in the winter to Frisbee in the summer. With outdoor public concerts and Shakespeare in the Park, Central Park offers a full year's worth of free entertainment, not to mention a little welcome fresh air. If you ever get bored of the Park, Museum Mile has more cultural stimuli then even Leonardo Da Vinci could handle. You can explore everything from ancient art at the Met to the cosmos at the Rose Center for Earth and Space on the Upper East Side. Such a wealth of resources is great for kids, and with all of these attractions on your doorstep you'll never have to worry about how to entertain out of town visitors again.

On the other hand, do not expect to be knocking on Donald Trump's door to borrow a cup of sugar. Residents don't really interact with their neighbors. Then again, when you're paying the kind of cash these residents are, you should be able to do just about anything you like—including disappear.

If you're not struck blind by the price, you'll be instantly awestruck at the beauty of a Central Park vista. Although not technically a neighborhood, Central Park West, Central Park South and Fifth Avenue share a character that sets them apart from all other communities in New York.

Noise: Although street traffic is steady, you won't even notice it from your top-floor penthouse.

Parking: Central Park offers street-side parking (with regular street-sweeping rules in effect during the early morning). Meters make it extra difficult to leave your car for long, but most residents don't mind since they have a chauffeur to handle that kind of thing.

Kids & Families: Growing up here would be a child's dream come true—where else would they get to live in the best city in the world and have a sprawling park complete with a zoo, dozens of playgrounds and an ice skating rink right across the street?

Safety: Central Park is safer than it was two decades ago, but it's still advisable to use caution when crossing at night. Cabs are easy to come by on all sides of the park, except for the northern border.

Entertainment: Almost endless—Fifth Avenue is home

to such terrific institutions as the Guggenheim Museum, the Frick Collection, the Museum of the City of New York, the Museo Del Barrio and the Jewish Museum. Lincoln Center gives the Central Park West community something to discuss over hors d'oeuvres.

Restaurants: Barely a restaurant exists on Fifth Avenue or Central Park West, adding in part to the residential appeal of the neighborhood. Central Park South has a few tourist traps and a wealth of hotel bars. In general, you're better off going elsewhere to eat.

THE PEOPLE

POPULATION	32,000
AGE	
0-17	15%
18-44	24%
45-64	33%
65+	28%
ETHNICITY	
White	94%
Black	1%
Asian	5%
Spanish speaking	4%
Family households	29%
College educated	54%
HOUSEHOLD INCOME	
Below $25,000	3%
$25-75,000	10%
$75-150,000	38%
$150,000+	49%

Parks & Gardens: Two words: Central Park.

Shopping: With 24-hour doormen and hired help in most every apartment along these streets, it's smart to assume the shopping is left to someone else. For do-it-yourselfers, most services are only a few blocks in any direction, but be ready to pay inflated prices.

THE NEIGHBORHOOD

AVERAGE MONTHLY RENT

Studio	$1,800-2,200
1 br	$2,000-2,800
2 br	$2,600-3,800
3 br	$4,000+

AVERAGE SALE PRICE

Studio	$250,000-400,000
1 br	$300,000-600,000
2 br	$550,000-200,000
3 br	$1,000,000+

COMMUTING

The B and C trains stop at 59th, 72nd, 81st, 86th, 96th, 103rd and 110th Streets, the 1, 9, B and D trains stop at 59th Street/Columbus Circle, and the N and R trains stop at 5th Avenue and 59th Street.

DISTANCE

Time to midtown	5-10 min
Time to downtown	20-30 min

Final Words: If you can afford the address, Central Park West, South and Fifth Avenue provide the most prestigious and glamorous digs in all of Manhattan. The rest of the world could only dream of living somewhere this good.

CHELSEA
MANHATTAN

I f Chelsea continues to develop in such a rapid fashion, it might soon become the Cultural Capital of New York City. Galleries, fashion havens, modeling agencies, restaurants, clubs, theaters, film production offices and sports complexes can all be found here in mass quantity. In the late 1980s what was once an old residential area with brownstones and townhouses metamorphosed into a neighborhood of art and commerce.

Chelsea was little more than a city suburb prior to the 1870s. But when the elevated railroads were built, theaters, music halls and department stores moved into the neighborhood. Fashionable folk began flocking here to shop or take in a show. Eventually, however, New Yorkers found newer and better places to take their business, and for many years Chelsea was neglected. All that has changed in past decades, though, and today the neighborhood has reached new heights.

If you want to feel the pulse of New York at its fastest, living in the area between 14th and 23rd streets west of 5th Avenue is sure to keep you on your toes at all times. No other neighborhood has undergone as many changes as Chelsea has in such a short time, and it is definitely at its peak right now. As the cardinal West Side address, it embodies everything from funkiness to creativity to some of the city's most successful entrepreneurs. Compared to the small square footage of the neighborhood, vivacity here is unbelievable.

Chelsea is home to New York's second largest gay population, but you would never know it just from walking down most of the streets. The only thing that might give it away are the rows and rows of gay restaurants and bars on 8th Avenue. In general, the neighborhood is extremely diverse in both its inhabitants and living spaces. The brownstones, townhouses, apartment buildings and lofts all form an extremely neat and geometric area, in other words a perfect grid decorated with flowers, trees, and unique street lamps. If there is one thing that residents care most about, it is maintaining the high aesthetic value and cleanliness of their neighborhood. The west end is

noticeably more deteriorated than the eastern side, but is a prime location nevertheless. Given the popularity of this hot-to-trot spot, gentrification has become part of the local vocabulary, and real estate seems to get more costly by the minute.

If history is of interest to you, the district between 20th and 23rd Streets from 8th to 10th Avenues will astound you with attractions like the Joyce Theater, the Dia Center for the Arts, and incredible architecture in general. If you're more of a party person, travel further west between Seventh Avenue and the West Side Piers for some of the city's most famed clubs and bars.

Residents are well aware that Chelsea is a precious treasure of accessibility and sophistication and can actually be quite snotty about it. The stereotype of New Yorkers dressed in head to toe black always on their cell phones is definitely reinforced here. If you are lucky enough to land a Chelsea location, you'd be a fool to ever give it up.

Noise: Since it is bounded by 14th and 23rd Streets, two of the busiest byways in New York, you'd better get used to the sounds of ambulances, stereos and drunks lulling you to sleep every night.

Parking: There are lots of garages but hardly any street parking.

Kids & Families: Since mostly singles live here, many of whom are gay, there aren't too many kids romping around.

Safety: Stay away from the river at night, and you'll be fine, though it's still best not to travel solo given the high quantity of clubs.

THE PEOPLE

POPULATION	20,000
AGE	
0-17	15%
18-44	53%
45-64	12%
65+	20%
ETHNICITY	
White	74%
Black	12%
Asian	7%
Spanish speaking	23%
Family households	33%
College educated	42%
HOUSEHOLD INCOME	
Below $25,000	20%
$25-75,000	42%
$75-150,000	36%
$150,000+	02%

Entertainment: So many nightspots to choose from you won't know what to do with yourself!

Restaurants: If people watching is your favorite pasttime, the swank Chelsea eateries are the places to go. Many are known for their intimacy and are some of the few places that you can schmooze for hours and not be asked to leave.

Parks & Gardens: Chelsea is home to the garden of the General Theological Center on Ninth Avenue, an extremely peaceful place to meditate or commune with nature.

Shopping: Chelsea has shopping options, which are unique even by New York standards, including some of

THE NEIGHBORHOOD

AVERAGE MONTHLY RENT

Studio	$1,400-2,300
1 br	$1,600-3,500
2 br	$2,600-3,700
3 br	$2,800-4,000

AVERAGE SALE PRICE

Studio	$150,000-300,000
1 br	$200,000-450,000
2 br	$500,000-700,000
3 br	$700,000-1,000,000

COMMUTING

The N and R trains stop in the area, from 14th Street on up. Buses are helpful, especially for cross-town commutes.

DISTANCE

Time to midtown	10-15 min
Time to downtown	25-30 min

the world's most unusual and cutting-edge fetish-wear shops. If latex and leather are on your list, you don't have far to go. There are also many boutiques, gourmand food shops and distinctive home decorating shops.

Final Words: It doesn't get more New York than this. Being chic and á la mode is the code of life here. Though not as snooty as nearby Soho and Tribeca, you still need to be super confident to fit in. Don't take lip from anyone. As residents of an ever-changing neighborhood, the creative minds that live here take pains to contribute to the area's growth. Think of Chelsea as Manhattan's Land of Opportunities.

CHINATOWN
• MANHATTAN •

Dragons, and monkeys, and snakes—oh my! New York City has its fair share of pigeons and rats alright, but in Chinatown, you will be met by some more beautiful and foreign animals—stuffed ones that is, which you can find at many of Chinatown's street vendors. Sure, Chinatown has an exotic exterior, but underneath its chaotic façade is a remarkably functional and well-organized community. Yet if you aren't familiar with any Chinese tongues, this might be a little difficult for you to understand.

The history of Chinatown could fill volumes; for the complete treatment, visit the Chinatown History Museum at 70 Mulberry Street and Bayard. Chinatown was the first major settling point for Chinese immigrants on the East Coast, and today it's still one of the largest and most active enclaves of Asian immigrants in the country. It all got started in the late 1870s, when a group of Chinese immigrants were illegally smuggled into New Jersey to work in a hand laundry. Many soon made the move to New York, sparking an explosion of Chinese hand laundries, which still dominate the neighborhood today.

> "New York is my Lourdes, where I go for spiritual refreshment.... A place where you're least likely to be bitten by a wild goat."
>
> **BRENDAN BEHAN**

Chinatown's official boundaries are Canal Street to the north, Worth Street to the south, the Bowery to the east and Church Street to the west. However, the local population in Chinatown continues to spread outward past its formal boundaries, since unlike other ethnic neighborhoods, Chinatown remains a thriving destination for newly arrived immigrants. In recent years, the neighborhood has become home to Dominicans, Puerto Ricans, Burmese, Vietnamese, Thai and Filipinos among others, who also inhabit apartments south of Chinatown. Residents enjoy the area for many reasons, one being its convenient location next to several major subway lines and another being its proximity to the downtown financial district.

Another admirable quality of Chinatown is its self-sufficiency. Most locals have no reason to venture outside of the neighborhood. A large percentage of Chinatown residents live within walking distance of work. On the way home they can buy fresh produce, fish or livestock from one of many sidewalk markets. If they don't have time to cook at home, one of the hundreds of local restaurants will suffice. Nightly entertainment is limited to a couple of Chinese movie houses, dance clubs and billiard halls. Most of the retail shops in Chinatown close early, and restaurants rarely stay open past 11 p.m.

If you don't speak Chinese or have someone to interpret for you, it will certainly be harder to find a space. Most of Chinatown's Asian residents got their apartment from a friend, business colleague or Chinese-speaking landlord or broker. Only on rare occasions will you see a public listing for a Chinatown apartment in English newspapers. Many newcomers to the area complain that they are forced to pay higher prices than their Chinese counterparts, and these assumptions are often more than just xenophobic paranoia. Chinatown landlords are notorious for breaking the legal occupancy levels in their buildings and violating other health codes to make an extra buck. Crazy numbers, such as 5 to 15 people in a subdivided two-room apartment, are typical Chinatown figures. Such landlords are understandably hesitant about giving outsiders access. When communicating with Chinatown landlords, it's best not to appear too overbearing or overly inquisitive. Gentle persistence is the best approach when scouring the neighborhood for an apartment.

Chinatown continues to be a highly residential neighborhood, but it is also beginning to become more commercial.

Many smaller internet companies have taken advantage of the petite yet comfortable office spaces that Chinatown has to offer in its numerous warehouse facilities. The neighborhood is also quite unique in its refusal to gentrify in the manner of other nearby areas, like Tribeca, Nolita and Soho. This is partly because of the difficulty of finding places to live here, due to the tremendous demand for habitable spaces from the continuing influx of immigrants. Chinatown is one spot where ethnic culture is holding its own against the demands of the Manhattan real estate market.

THE PEOPLE

POPULATION	86,000
AGE	
0-17	23%
18-44	39%
45-64	23%
65+	15%
ETHNICITY	
White	29%
Black	17%
Asian	54%
Spanish speaking	40%
Family households	65%
College educated	15%
HOUSEHOLD INCOME	
Below $25,000	55%
$25-75,000	38%
$75-150,000	6%
$150,000+	1%

Zanys.com user comments: "Amazing, and definitely up and coming." The area is "being cleaned up and is now almost posh." I "fell in love" with the neighborhood.

THE NEIGHBORHOOD

AVERAGE MONTHLY RENT

Studio	$1,000-1,600
1 br	$1,400-2,500
2 br	$1,600-2,700
3 br	$2,100-3,300

AVERAGE SALE PRICE

Studio	$150,000-175,000
1 br	$200,000-250,000
2 br	$250,000-400,000
3 br	$300,000-600,000

COMMUTING

Chinatown has an ideal centralized location allowing residents to walk to most any train line. The A, C, E, J, M, N, R, Z and 6 trains stop at Canal Street.

DISTANCE

Time to midtown	15-20 min
Time to downtown	5-10 min

Noise: Chinatown's street-side cacophony is a fact of life. Canal Street to the north is congested with trucks making daily deliveries. Sidewalks are narrow and must be shared with noisy food vendors, fruit markets and souvenir peddlers. In addition to the street traffic, apartments tend to be overcrowded and noisy. Thankfully, things quiet down a bit at night.

Parking: It's next to impossible to park along the streets in Chinatown. Near the courthouse buildings to the south are several municipal lots. One-way streets and constant traffic make cars the worst way to get around.

Kids & Families: The tight confines of Chinatown apartments don't allow for particularly large families. Most of the area's families are of Asian descent, though second and third-generation children often move elsewhere when they grow up.

WWW.ZANYS.COM
Find a NYC apartment now!

Safety: Chinatown is generally safe, especially in the central tourist area, but as you venture off into the periphery, you'll feel less secure. Obviously, it helps to speak Chinese and to look like a New Yorker when walking around. Large numbers of cops around the courts and the nearby police headquarters tend to make criminals think twice.

Entertainment: Chinatown has terrific all-Chinese clubs for anything from Mahjong to techno dancing and, best of all, you don't have to be Chinese to go to them. Several movie theaters play films imported from mainland China, Hong Kong and Taiwan.

Restaurants: The quality and number of small but delicious restaurants in Chinatown is astronomical—there are over 300 in all. Every type of Asian fare can be had here: Vietnamese, Thai, Korean, Japanese, even Tibetan. A good strategy is to find out where the locals eat, and avoid the overpriced meals just south of Canal Street.

Parks & Gardens: In Chinatown, true green space only exists in a cup of tea, although Confucius Park offers a mild respite from the bustle of the neighborhood's main drag.

Shopping: Trinkets galore! Chinatown has whole blocks of stores full of American knock-offs and cheap Asian imports. Pearl River at Broadway and Canal Street is well known for its complete range of Chinese must-haves. You'll see stuff for sale here that you've never seen before, from grass jelly beverages to foot-washing powders.

> "As one comes down the Henry Hudson Parkway along the river in the dusk, New York is never real; it is always fabulous."
>
> **ANTHONY BAILEY**

Final Words: Chinatown is great for several exciting visits but a tough place to find an apartment. Without local connections, you're liable to strike out entirely or get robbed blind trying. Truly good finds require a significant amount of investigation.

CLINTON
MANHATTAN

C linton is one of the least well-known neighborhoods in Manhattan, at least by name. That could be because Clinton is much better known by its old nickname—Hell's Kitchen. Once upon a time, this was one of the most impoverished and dangerous neighborhoods in the country, and although the days of gangsters and tenements are long gone, Clinton's shady reputation is hard to shake.

The first Dutch settlers named the area Bloemendael, which means "Vale of Flowers." In the late 18th century, a rich New Yorker, DeWitt Clinton, owned the farmland in the area, and his name stuck as the neighborhood's official moniker. So when did New Yorkers start referring to this valley of flowers in satanic terms? It started when railroads moved into the neighborhood in the mid 1800s, kicking off an era of lickety-split expansion. Irish and German immigrants began pouring in to work in Clinton's new railroad yards, factories, slaughterhouses and breweries. Soon, miserable tenements had sprung up to house the workers in notoriously awful living conditions.

Clinton witnessed three days of extraordinarily bloody riots during the Civil War, when protesters reacted violently to a new law instituting the draft. Violence was to become commonplace in the neighborhood, as the poor living conditions led to an outbreak in both organized and disorganized crime. This was New York's original gangland, where homeless children wandered the streets, committing random acts of violence. Just who first dubbed the wretched neighborhood "Hell's Kitchen" is unclear, although it's first known appearance was in an 1881 New York Times article describing the area around as the filthiest and most crime-ridden district in the city. Although the twentieth century saw vast improvements in the neighborhood's living conditions and crime rates,

Find a NYC apartment now!

only in recent decades has respectable Clinton slowly begun to replace the image of sordid Hell's Kitchen in New Yorker's minds.

Modern Clinton spreads from West 34th to West 59th Streets and between the Hudson River and 8th Avenue. The once repulsive tenements have been converted into attractive brick row houses. Side streets are lined with beautiful trees and well-planted flower boxes. Wealthier residents tend to live closer to Central Park and further away from the once seedy atmosphere of Times Square and the Port Authority bus terminal.

Clinton row houses are predominantly five or six-story walkups, so top floor residents must contend with many flights of stairs. On the other hand, since street noise is a real concern, upper floors tend to be much quieter than those closer to street level. Before settling on an apartment in Clinton, you should be sure to consider the relative size of your utility spaces such as the bathroom, kitchen and closets. Newly renovated Clinton apartments will have much more space for these purposes.

> "A hundred times I have thought: New York is a catastrophe, and 50 times: It is a beautiful catastrophe."
>
> **LE CORBUSIER**

Clinton is home to a diverse mix of residents, ranging from the descendants of European immigrants of previous centuries to a more recent influx from Latin America and various parts of Asia. You'll find an exceptional range of incomes that makes for an unusual and lively variety of ideas and agendas. Residents tend to be very vocal when it comes to politics and are adamant about preserving Clinton's charm; you'll find lots of volunteer associations and community boards are active. So far, the Special District Clinton Coalition has been remarkably successful in lobbying against large-scale developers ruining the quaint appeal of the neighborhood.

One thing almost all Clinton residents have in common—a fierce loyalty to their neighborhood. Most tend to remain here for a lifetime, knowing that despite its tumultuous history, Clinton is a real gem. With the real estate market continuing to boom, Clinton is sure to be ransacked one way or another by interested parties looking to build high-rises. New Yorkers are likely to become much more familiar with this neighborhood in the future, and Clinton is bound to change dramatically in coming years.

THE PEOPLE

POPULATION	44,000
AGE	
0-17	20%
18-44	38%
45-64	36%
65+	6%
ETHNICITY	
White	47%
Black	40%
Asian 13%	
Spanish speaking	28%
Family households	37%
College educated	29%
HOUSEHOLD INCOME	
Below $25,000	25%
$25-75,000	34%
$75-150,000	37%
$150,000+	4%

Noise: Avenues are very noisy thoroughfares for taxis, trucks and commuter traffic. When looking for apartments, look for upper-level flats.

Parking: Streetside parking is available in Clinton, but be ready to feed the bottomless meters. Chances are you'll rake in enough parking tickets to pay for the cabs and subways you could have taken in the first place.

Kids & Families: Clinton is a great place to bring up a small family. Apartments are small but still rather affordable. Also, kids will find a good number of playmates in the area at the many outdoor playgrounds and community gardens. With most trains only a short walk away, children can easily get to both private and public schools in the city.

Safety: It took much more than a change of name to remove the stigma attached to this area in the past. A concerted community-wide effort to better police the area, arrest drug offenders and push out prostitutes has saved the neighborhood. It's still Midtown, though, so watch your back.

Entertainment: In Clinton, you're truly in the middle of it all. Everything from Broadway theaters to strip clubs are nearby. Unfortunately, this also means you must contend with a constant flow of tourists.

THE NEIGHBORHOOD

AVERAGE MONTHLY RENT

Studio	$1,200-1,600
1 br	$1,500-2,600
2 br	$1,900-3,300
3 br	$2,800-3,700

AVERAGE SALE PRICE

Studio	$130,000-330,000
1 br	$150,000-400,000
2 br	$300,000-800,000
3 br	$550,000-900,000

COMMUTING

The C and E trains stop at 42nd and 50th Street, the 1 and 9 trains stop at 50th Street, and the N and R trains stop at 49th and 57th Streets, and at 7th Avenue.

DISTANCE

Time to midtown	5-10 min
Time to downtown	10-15 min

Restaurants: Restaurant Row is acceptable, though mainly frequented by tourists. Your best choices for chow are up and down Eighth and Ninth Avenues, where you'll find exceptional yet affordable eats from all over the globe. For moderately priced evenings out, Clinton is one of the best neighborhoods in all of Manhattan.

Parks & Gardens: Everyone knows about Central Park, but locals keep DeWitt Clinton Park on West End Avenue as their own private hideaway. Clinton is also famous for its well-kept community gardens and public playgrounds. Despite the amount of asphalt in these parts, residents keep it looking green, and tree-lined streets don't hurt.

Shopping: Clinton is not known for its retail shopping, but most every essential item you'll ever need is never more than a block away. For used fashions you'll find the Salvation Army on West 42nd Street a real gem. For first-run merchandise you're better off on 5th Avenue.

Final Words: Clinton remains an affordable option for middle-income New Yorkers who value convenience over apartment size. If you work in Midtown, it's an ideal place to look.

COBBLE HILL
◆ BROOKLYN ◆

Cobble Hill is a pleasant neighborhood bound by Atlantic Avenue, Court, DeGraw and Hicks streets. With its abundance of trees, gardens, and other foliage, many of the residents here casually forget that they are in Brooklyn. They might as well be living in Westchester as far as they're concerned.

This neighborhood's name actually derives from a 1766 map that marked a long-gone hill near the present-day intersection between Court Street and Atlantic Avenue. The neighborhood remained a rather sleepy community until the mid 1800s when many well-to-do residents began moving in. The upscale townhouses that were built to accommodate these upper-class Brooklynites still remain today.

A notable number of Middle Eastern immigrants flocked to this little cove in Brooklyn during the early 1900s. After a period of economic difficulty, Cobble Hill was rejuvenated and revived by young professionals, community activism and the brownstone revival movement. Residents also managed to secure landmark status and block public housing, causing the real estate values to rise rather abruptly during the 1970s.

Today, this neighborhood houses one of Brooklyn's largest concentration of Arabs from all over the Middle East. Many of the residents here are descendants of the families that were relocated during the excavation of the Holland Tunnel from Battery Park City. There is definitely a sense of community and pride that pervades this locale, and the people work hard to keep their little hamlet trimmed and presentable.

This neighborhood is one-of-a-kind; you won't really find any other like it. The people here tend to have occupations that are rather flighty and fast-paced, and they revel in the serenity and suburban feel of this neighborhood after a hectic day at work. Gardens seem to be a requisite in every household, even in the lowlier residences. People take pride in their homes, no matter how dingy or small, and they maintain their yards and grounds quite regularly.

In some ways, Cobble Hill has the feel of a small Southern town, where everyone knows about everything that goes on in each other's lives. Those who value their privacy and have adopted the get-out-of-my-way, no-eye-contact vibe of Manhattan may feel a bit suffocated here by the somewhat nosey residents. These people are proud of their neighborhood and feel that if you live here, you are part of a family. As Manhattanites continue crossing the East River in search of lower rents, Cobble Hill is bound to become more popular and more expensive.

Noise: Not much, unless you live right next to Long Island College Hospital, where the ambulances can be a bit noisy.

Parking: Parking is good in Cobble Hill, but some streets are more crowded than others, particularly if you live next to one of the many churches or a hospital.

Kids & Families: This is a great family area. Neighbors are neighborly, and the entire area is a throwback to an earlier era when people kept watch over each other's safety and lives.

Safety: There isn't much crime here thanks to an effective neighborhood watch.

THE PEOPLE

POPULATION	32,000
AGE	
0-17	20%
18-44	52%
45-64	17%
65+	11%
ETHNICITY	
White	65%
Black	22%
Asian	2%
Other	11%
Spanish speaking	26%
Family households	59%
College educated	33%
HOUSEHOLD INCOME	
Below $25,000	41%
$25-75,000	51%
$75-150,000	6%
$150,000+	2%

WWW.ZANYS.COM
Find a NYC apartment now!

Entertainment: You'd best go to the city to find what you're looking for. This is a place where people come to relax, not wind up. On the third Sunday in September, the community hosts the Atlantic Antic, a street fair encompassing everything from belly dancing to camel rides.

Restaurants: There aren't a lot of restaurants around here, although you will find plenty of tasty Middle Eastern eateries.

Parks & Gardens: People here like to tend their own gardens. You'd have to venture out of the area to find a park of note.

Shopping: Atlantic Avenue is chock full of food merchants selling Middle Eastern delicacies like fruits, nuts, Arabian coffee, dates and olives. Other import companies offer brass water pipes, backgammon sets and an assortment of ethnic music.

Final Words: Cobble Hill has a more peaceful feel to it

THE NEIGHBORHOOD

AVERAGE MONTHLY RENT

Studio	$1,200-1,500
1 br	$1,300-1,600
2 br	$1,600-2,000
3 br	$1,900-2,800

AVERAGE SALE PRICE

Studio	$90,000-160,000
1 br	$180,000-325,000
2 br	$200,000-500,000
3 br	$250,000-800,000

COMMUTING

The N and R trains run to Court Street, and the 2, 3, 4 and 5 trains run to Borough Hall.

DISTANCE

Time to midtown	25-30	min
Time to downtown	20-25	min

than most of the rougher-edged neighborhoods in the outer boroughs. You'll either love it or hate it, depending on what type of living experience you're looking for.

CONEY ISLAND
• BROOKLYN •

Though the resort's heyday has long since past, Coney Island's old-fashioned amusement parks and boardwalk endure as a symbol of supreme pleasure and indulgence in a bygone era. The memories of what Coney Island once was endure as an important aspect of New York's cultural history. Unfortunately, little of the resort's turn-of-the-century grandeur remains today and has been replaced by a run-down, crime-infested atmosphere.

Coney Island's first beach resort was built in 1824 on what had hitherto been primarily grazing land. By 1840, the neighborhood had become a thriving summer destination for wealthier city residents. However, the resort really took off when trains made it possible for even New Yorkers of modest means to take an inexpensive daytrip to the beach. Coney Island was a unique resort where Americans from all social classes mingled together in their various pursuits of happiness.

The famous Coney Island amusement parks didn't arrive until political boss John Y. McKane lent his support to the project in the late 1880s. In the early days, all sorts of entertainment could be found at Coney Island—including brothels, boxing matches, race tracks and freak shows. Roller coasters were new inventions that thrilled vacationers of the era, and around the turn-of-the-century amusement parks began competing for tourists' attentions with such attractions as parachute jumps, human roulette wheels, and 'Trips to the Moon.' For inhibited Victorian visitors, Coney Island offered the most titillating amusements imaginable.

By 1904, close to a hundred thousand people were descending on Coney Island daily in search of fun.

Though most were daytripping New Yorkers, the resort's fame attracted visitors from around the world. At night the new electric lights beamed out for miles at sea, beckoning visitors with the promise of all things modern, exciting and fun. Throughout the early decades of the 20th century, visitors continued flocking to Coney Island, but by the time of World War II, the resorts' golden era had come to an end. Fires plagued the amusement parks, and the advent of air travel and the interstate system gave New Yorkers more vacationing options.

Modern Coney Island, which runs from West 37th Street to Ocean Parkway on the east, and from Coney Island Creek and the Belt Parkway on the north to the boardwalk and ocean, is only a shadow of what it once was. People still visit to learn a little New York history and delight in what's left of the area's amusements, including Nathan's, the birthplace of the hot dog. Coney Island is still an easy trip from Manhattan, Queens, Brooklyn and Staten Island via the B, D, N and F trains.

Architecturally beautiful (though not well-maintained) row houses still stand between West 15th and West 22nd Streets. Today, Coney Island is home to an aging population, some of whom can still remember the resort's glory days. The neighborhood has a struggling local economy and seedy reputation—particularly the area close to the beach. Crime is worse here than in most parts of the city, with everything from pickpockets to drug pushers. Of course, if you find anything inhabitable, a Coney Island apartment can be yours for next to nothing. Long-time residents and many New Yorkers still hope that a developer will some day pour millions into the beachfront to restore it to the tourist destination it once was, but nobody's holding his breath.

Noise: Coney Island is all about bells and whistles, but there's also the soothing sounds of the ocean to lull you to sleep.

Parking: Plenty of spaces, but many reports of theft.

Kids & Families: A great place to bring the children, but not to bring them up.

THE PEOPLE

POPULATION	53,000
AGE	
0-17	26%
18-44	33%
45-64	20%
65+	21%
ETHNICITY	
White	60%
Black	37%
Asian	3%
Spanish speaking	22%
Family households	38%
College educated	14%
HOUSEHOLD INCOME	
Below $25,000	59%
$25-75,000	35%
$75-150,000	5%
$150,000+	1%

Entertainment: Coney Island is the home of sleazy entertainment, from boardwalk freak shows to illegal games of three-card monty. You'll find everything from batting cages to go-karts to pinball machines tempting your wallet towards tilt.

Restaurants: A few seafood restaurants remain from the glory days, including Carolina on Mermaid Avenue and Garigiulo's on West 15th Street.

Parks & Gardens: Let the rides take you back to your childhood when you went on the Cyclone a dozen times

WWW.ZANYS.COM
Find a NYC apartment now!

in a row. And don't forget the beach!

Shopping: Limited to the random collection of street merchants on Surf Avenue.

Final Words: Take a brief vacation in Coney Island to enjoy its history and its oddities, but leave by subway or car before the sun sets.

THE NEIGHBORHOOD

AVERAGE MONTHLY RENT
Studio	$200-400
1 br	$300-600
2 br	$400-700
3 br	$600-1,000

AVERAGE SALE PRICE
Studio	$25,000-40,000
1 br	$35,000-65,000
2 br	$40,000-80,000
3 br	$50,000-100,000

COMMUTING
The B and D trains stop at Stillwell Avenue.
The F train stops at West 8th, NY Aquarium
and Stillwell Avenue.

DISTANCE
Time to midtown	60	min
Time to downtown	50	min

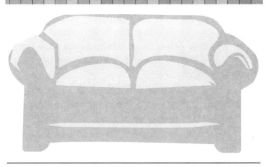

CORONA
QUEENS

Literature students may not realize that F. Scott Fitzgerald's descriptions of a bleak "Valley of Ashes" between Long Island and Manhattan in *The Great Gatsby* actually refer to the neighborhood around Corona, Queens. Luckily for residents, the ash dump is gone and has been replaced by scenic Flushing Meadows-Corona Park. Today, Corona is a strictly working-class neighborhood with cheap rents and a neighborhood-feel. However, modern outbreaks of crime may make Fitzgerald's take on the neighborhood seem once again appropriate.

Originally the home of Matinecocks Indians, Dutch and English settlers quickly discovered the area's abundant fruit trees and created large orchards. As New York sprawled eastward, the neighborhood became a commuter's suburb for Manhattan workers who wanted to live in a countrified atmosphere. In the 1850's, an extravagant race track was built in the community, attracting developers, such as Benjamin W. Hitchcock who gave the neighborhood the name Corona, meaning "Crown of the Hill." Hitchcock began promoting his new development as an attractive alternative to the Lower East Side for Italian immigrants. When rapid transit came to New York, Corona's fate was sealed as a working-class commuter neighborhood.

> "New York is notoriously inhospitable to the past, disowning it whenever it can."
>
> **JOHN D. ROSENBERG**

Corona is in central Queens on the west side of Flushing Meadows-Corona Park. The neighborhood is bisected by Roosevelt Avenue and 108th Street and rimmed on three sides by the Grand Central Parkway and the Long Island Expressway. Louis Comfort Tiffany made his glass creations from a studio in Corona, and the World's Fair has made two stops in the area, in 1939 and 1964. Louis Armstrong lived here off and on for his entire life, and today his house on 107th Street is a museum. Old-timers still tell tales of Armstrong sitting on his front stoop with his trumpet and enchanting the neighborhood kids.

The neighborhood is home to an ethnically diverse mix of people. Corona has a large Asian population with many Indian, Greek, Middle Eastern and Hispanic residents. Families love the area because of nearby Corona Park, which hosts families playing frisbee, riding bikes or just lazing in the grass.

The neighborhood features one large middle-income apartment complex, Lefrak City. Otherwise, most homes are two to four family cookie-cutter red brick row houses. In general, most of the houses in Corona aren't in the best condition, but you may run into a landlord willing to cut you a deal if you're willing to put some work into the place. Everyone in this close neighborhood knows everyone else and keeps an eye out for suspicious interlopers. On the downside, if you live in a more questionable part of Corona, you'll get to see and hear it all in your backyard.

The nearby garden and park attract people with kids, who generally come to stay in this low-rent neighborhood. The police presence is fairly high, so single women should do all right as long as they know where not to venture late at night. However, crime has been a serious problem here in the past, so always be careful and watch your back.

Noise: Noise can be a problem here, with Latin tunes drifting through the air at all hours.

Parking: You should be able to find plenty.

Kids & Families: Corona is a poor neighborhood, where people stay because they can't afford to leave. This makes for a less-than-ideal environment in which to raise kids.

Safety: Corona can be dicey in parts, even with lots of cops on the street.

Entertainment: There are lots of video stores and a

couple of movie theaters, but not much in the way of entertainment here.

Restaurants: Plenty of Latin food, but with a sizable portion of Asian eateries as well.

Parks & Gardens: Flushing Meadows-Corona Park is huge and easily accessible.

Shopping: Look for stores along the busy streets, such as Corona Avenue and 108th Street. The chic Madison Avenue experience this is not, but it's affordable, serviceable and kid-proof.

Final Words: Corona is a working class neighborhood with many typical urban problems. The close-knit community looks after their own, but it can take a while to feel

THE PEOPLE

POPULATION	76,000
AGE	
0-17	25%
18-44	47%
45-64	17%
65+	8%
ETHNICITY	
White	30%
Black	30%
Asian	11%
Other	29%
Spanish speaking	52%
Family households	74%
College educated	17%
HOUSEHOLD INCOME	
Below $25,000	46%
$25-75,000	47%
75-150,000	6%
150,000+	1%

Find a NYC apartment now!

comfortable and accepted. Once you're in, though, you're in for life.

THE NEIGHBORHOOD

AVERAGE MONTHLY RENT

Studio	$600-900
1 br	$700-1,100
2 br	$800-1,300
3 br	$900-1,600

AVERAGE SALE PRICE

Studio	$50,000-80,000
1 br	$55,000-200,000
2 br	$60,000-250,000
3 br	$80,000-350,000

COMMUTING

The 7 stops at Junction Boulevard and 103 Street. There are several good bus routes into Manhattan.

DISTANCE

Time to midtown	30-45 min
Time to downtown	45-60 min

DOWNTOWN
MANHATTAN

I t's hard to believe that the downtown financial district is actually the oldest part of Manhattan. With post-modern skyscrapers dwarfing the few remaining historic relics of New York's colonial days, the downtown area feels as if it must have sprung to existence, sometime after World War II, fully formed. But in actuality, this is where the first Dutch settlers lived, and though it has become dominated by office buildings in the past century, many modern New Yorkers are once again residing here as the desperate search for housing forces residents to the geographically lowest part of Manhattan.

Once a long time ago, all of New York City was located in a small cluster down here at the tip of the island. Bowling Green, the original pastureland in the middle of the Dutch settlement, is still a small green space today in the midst of steel skyscrapers. George Washington was sworn in as president at Federal Hall, which is near Trinity Church, Manhattan's oldest place of worship. And, of course, across Wall Street stands the New York Stock Exchange, where many of the nation's economic highs and lows have been predetermined.

The vast majority of buildings here are financial offices of one kind or another. The area is busiest during the working day, as important-looking business-folk crowd the streets around the World Trade Center and other huge office highrises. This part of the city does sleep and in fact, goes to bed rather early. There are a couple twenty-four hour delis, but for the most part stores and restaurants close before eight p.m. Many businesses are closed on Sundays, and the streets are generally deserted at night, especially on the weekends. This means lots of peace and quiet but also no midnight pizza runs.

During the day, however, there are many different restaurant and shopping options. It is hard to be more than four blocks from a Duane Reade drug store, and the streets are lined with small delis and cafes catering to the business lunch crowds. As this is the financial capital of the world, banks are everywhere, and though they close early, the ATM's are, of course, always available. Perhaps the most convenient part of living downtown, though, is the proximity of so many different subway lines. You are never far from a subway and have an array of options as to which one to take. And if you don't feel like going too far and want to relax in the area, there are a few local options, like Battery Park, City Hall Park, and the South Street Seaport (for those who don't mind hobnobbing with tourists).

As for the actual apartments in the area, they are, like most everything else down here, generally quite modern and tall. This is not the place for quaint walk-ups; downtown is dominated by skyscrapers. Most are rather spacious on a Manhattan scale, and there are quite a few lofts. More residential space has become available in the past years, and though in the daytime the area is dominated by business people, all different sorts of Manhattanites are living here these days.

If you get a place up high enough in these super-tall buildings, you can score fabulous views of Manhattan and Brooklyn. But you also run the risk of looking out into one of the claustrophobically tall and skinny "caverns" of skyscrapers the area is known for. With so many tall buildings in such close proximity, sunlight can sometimes seem scarce even on a crystal clear day. Then again, there is something breathtaking about looking up to see the sun peeking out from behind the towering twins of the World Trade Center. Though it lacks the charm of more traditional residential neighborhoods, downtown has a glitzy, skyscraping romance all its own.

> "When the Dodgers left, it was not only a loss of a team, it was the disruption of a social pattern…. A total destruction of a culture."
>
> **JOE FLAHERTY**

THE PEOPLE

POPULATION	3,900
AGE	
0-17	2%
18-44	70%
45-64	22%
65+	6%
ETHNICITY	
White	59%
Black	33%
Asian	8%
Spanish speaking	1%
Family households	1%
College educated	74%
HOUSEHOLD INCOME	
Below $25,000	25%
$25-75,000	44%
75-150,000	15%
150,000+	16%

Noise: During the daytime, you may be distracted by some hustle and bustle, but at night, the area is very quiet.

Parking: You had better not count on parking down here, because there is hardly any place to do so.

Kids & Families: Because it is not a particularly residential neighborhood, downtown is not ideal for families. However, there are nearby parks, and it is nice and quiet.

Safety: The streets become isolated at night, but safety is not a problem.

Entertainment: You have to go uptown to get your

WWW.ZANYS.COM
Find a NYC apartment now!

kicks. There is a new movie theater nearby and a few random bars and pubs, but otherwise, everything is closed in the evening.

Restaurants: At lunchtime, the streets are covered with fast food options. However, at night, you will have trouble finding anything that's open, except at the South Street Seaport.

Parks & Gardens: Battery Park is nearby, as well as City Hall Park.

Shopping: You will find dozens of drug stores but hardly any supermarkets. Grocery shopping can be a problem depending on where you live.

Final Words: Downtown lacks many of the conveniences of more residential neighborhoods, but may be just the place to find a slightly roomier Manhattan apartment than your budget will allow in trendier neighborhoods.

THE NEIGHBORHOOD

AVERAGE MONTHLY RENT

Studio	$1,600-2,300
1 br	$2,000-2,800
2 br	$2,400-3,800
3 br	$3,000-6,500

AVERAGE SALE PRICE

Studio	$150,000-300,000
1 br	$220,000-400,000
2 br	$500,000-750,000
3 br	$700,000-1,000,000

COMMUTING

The 1, 9, N, R, 4, 5, 6, A, C and E trains all stop here at the southernmost tip of Manhattan.

DISTANCE

Time to midtown	15-25 min
Time to downtown	You are here!

DUMBO
• BROOKLYN •

Yes, Dumbo is the name of an adorable little elephant, but it is also what folks are calling a quirky "new" Brooklyn neighborhood. Dumbo is actually an acronym for "down under the Manhattan Bridge overpass," and the quirky name befits this neighborhood's character. Many consider this to be the new East Village, with cobblestone streets, loads of warehouses that are rapidly being converted into living quarters and spectacular views of the Manhattan skyline.

The area was once the landing place for the ferries that carried New Yorkers from Manhattan to Brooklyn before the completion of the Brooklyn Bridge in 1883. Odds and ends of old neighborhoods are been lumped together to create the community of Dumbo, since its inception about thirty years ago. Vinegar Hill lies to the northeast and was one of the city's first Irish enclaves. Dumbo has also grown to include the a housing project built in the 1950s called the Farragut Houses and the Brooklyn Navy Yard.

The neighborhood has been officially residential since the 1970s, when a group of artists discovered this waterfront jewel. The task of converting the buildings into private apartments was not an easy one, and it was initially illegal. But the new community was extremely forceful and successfully lobbied against the government to revoke these regulations. Since then, Dumbo has gained approximately 600 full time residents, not including Farragut, which itself has 3,000 residents. This is amazingly underpopulated compared to most other New York neighborhoods.

Dumbo's boundaries are a little hard to map out, but they are mainly formed by Main Street and Jay Street, with the East River cutting it off to the north and the Brooklyn-Queens Expressway bordering it to the south. It

WWW.ZANYS.COM
Find a NYC apartment now!

is easiest to think of Dumbo "Between the Bridges," or the expanse between the Brooklyn and Manhattan Bridges.

Until recently, it was relatively easy to find a place to live in Dumbo. At first it was considered to be too cold, shady and inconvenient because of its direct adjacency to the river. Without question, Dumbo is a little out of the way, especially due to its lack of neighborhood subways. But nonetheless, younger individuals and artists see past this to its incomparable allure and relatively cheap studio and loft accommodations.

New York is surrounded by water on all sides, right? Then why is it so difficult to find riverside real estate? If it's beautiful views that you're after, Dumbo is the perfect place. Residents agree that its frontier feel is due largely to its shipyard past and public-service-free streets.

> "Vehement silhouettes of Manhattan—that vertical city with unimaginable diamonds."
>
> **LE CORBUSIER**

Dumbo's sequestered location is one of its biggest draws, as any area with privacy in New York is a gold mine. Its buildings are primarily deserted warehouses and factories, many of which have been converted into generously proportioned lofts by avant-garde types. In Vinegar Hill, 19th century row houses also line the streets. Recently, the old Fulton Street Eagle Warehouse and Storage Company of Brooklyn, a huge brick building with a glass clock in the penthouse, has been transformed into condominiums.

Real estate mogul David Walentas has been the leading man in Dumbo for a decade, and his plans for the neighborhood are almost complete. With Fulton Ferry State Park and the unbelievable amount of convertible space, Walentas forcasts a new, dynamic growth of Dumbo, with shopping, living and recreation along the East River. But until then, residents revel in the seclusion they have created for themselves in the middle of the world's busiest city.

Noise: Dumbo is too quiet for the average New Yorker in the evening hours. Residents are usually hidden away in their studios, and the streets see little car or pedestrian traffic. During the day, expect to hear delivery trucks passing by. The occasional barge foghorn adds to the atmosphere.

Parking: Plenty of opportunities for parking along the meter-less streets are available. Many residents consider a car or truck an absolute necessity.

Kids & Families: Dumbo is not a good place for kids. There is nothing for them to do here, as most residents are in their 20s and 30s.

THE PEOPLE

POPULATION	12,000
AGE	
0-17	9%
18-44	48%
45-64	35%
65+	8%
ETHNICITY	
White	85%
Black	12%
Asian 3%	
Spanish speaking	7%
Family households	13%
College educated	31%
HOUSEHOLD INCOME	
Below $25,000	38%
$25-75,000	47%
75-150,000	14%
150,000+	1%

Safety: As a fairly deserted neighborhood, you might be a little spooked-out walking down the street at night alone, so be sure you meet your neighbors!

Entertainment: The Anchorage Bar is probably your

best and only bet. Otherwise private parties are a great source of entertainment.

Restaurants: While there are few, the ones that are here like Between the Bridges and Le Gamin Café are excellent. Residents wish there were more like them.

Parks & Gardens: Shrubbery is not to be found in Dumbo, but the Brooklyn Bridge definitely makes up for it.

Shopping: Dumbo has absolutely no shopping. Grocery stores, laundromats and other necessities are even hard to find.

Final Words: Dumbo is a uniquely situated neighborhood, perfect for the right type of person. You should have tough skin, an artistic bent and a love of walking if you plan to move in. If you can afford to buy, you're likely to see your property value double when new developments transform the area.

THE NEIGHBORHOOD

AVERAGE MONTHLY RENT

Studio	$700-1,100
1 br	$900-1,400
2 br	$1,100-1,900
3 br	$1,500-2,400

AVERAGE SALE PRICE

Studio	$80,000-200,000
1 br	$150,000-250,000
2 br	$180,000-400,000
3 br	$200,000-600,000

COMMUTING

Walk up the hill to the F train at Jay Street. Nearby Brooklyn Heights has plenty of trains available. A bicycle over the Brooklyn Bridge is sometimes your best choice.

DISTANCE

Time to midtown	15-20	min
Time to downtown	10-15	min

DYKER HEIGHTS

• BROOKLYN •

While Dyker Heights is one of the farthest neighbor-hoods from Manhattan, its tight-knit community and beautiful landscape make it an ideal place to live for self-sufficient people who don't mind commuting. The neighborhood was conceived way back in 1719, when the Dutch Van Dyke brothers helped to divide the land from the surrounding marshes and make it livable. Dyker Heights is named after them and coincidentally for the dykes that originally permeated the area.

In between Bay Ridge and Bensonhurst, the neighbor-hood encompasses Dyker Beach Park on Gravesend Bay and the public Dyker Beach Golf Course. Dyker Heights officially extends from Seventh to 14th Avenues, and from 65th Street to the beach.

Most of the residents are blue-collar workers, giving the area a more suburban feel than other Brooklyn neighborhoods closer to Manhattan. Italian-Americans dominate the neighborhood, although Russians, Chinese and Middle Easterners have recently found their way here. Most locals have remained in the neighborhood for subsequent generations, in part because of the community's shared social and religious core.

It is one hell of a commute to the city from here, but a manageable hour or so via public transportation. Most people rely on their cars, especially since necessities like laundromats and grocery stores are not within walking distance.

Smallish two-story family houses are the most popular real estate in Dyker Heights. Most are equipped with private garages, lush green lawns and grand entrances. The neighborhood is rather hilly, so if you are up in the actual "Heights" you'll have amazing views of the bay. Monstrous new homes are popping up in between the middle class dwellings, which aren't so pretty to look at, but offer invaluable space. Tacky Greek columns that dwarf the small homes they're attached to, oversized bay windows and marble walkways leading to brick houses are just a few of the design touches you'll spot on a walk through the area. Such exuberance for excessive decoration continues into the holiday season. Dyker Heights is a sight to behold at Christmas time, when the area glitters with hundreds of outdoor displays.

Moving this far out of the city is a great decision if you are ready to settle down and raise a family. Given the distance from Manhattan, real estate is fairly reasonable, and its suburban atmosphere makes it ideal for kids. Renting is ok, but buying a home will save you a lot of money.

> "What else can you expect from a town that's shut off from the world by the ocean on one side and New Jersey on the other?"
>
> **O. HENRY**

Dyker Heights residents take a lot of pride in their community and their work ethic, but along with this comes a group of stubborn old men who enforce the mentality and the community's rules. Dyker Heights is an old-world part of town that is not going anywhere fast. The consistency of their lifestyles is what the residents most enjoy about their neighborhood.

Noise: Dyker Heights truly sounds like a suburb — any unusual noise catches the entire neighborhood's attention.

Parking: Since cars are the residents' main transportation, a surplus of parking spaces is guaranteed, especially since most locals rely on their private garages.

Kids & Families: Suburbia should be synonymous with kids, enough said.

Safety: Many residents are either current or former police officers. It's still rare to see people walking alone at night, especially women.

Entertainment: Good ol' fashioned eating and drinking are the most popular pastimes in Dyker Heights. During lunch hours, expect to see large groups of work-

THE PEOPLE

POPULATION	38,000
AGE	
0-17	19%
18-44	39%
45-64	23%
65+	19%
ETHNICITY	
White	92%
Black	2%
Asian	6%
Spanish speaking	7%
Family households	38%
College educated	19%
HOUSEHOLD INCOME	
Below $25,000	35%
$25-75,000	50%
$75-150,000	14%
$150,000+	1%

ers sitting on the curb devouring enormous Italian-style sandwiches from local delis.

Restaurants: Seemingly home-cooked Italian food is the best thing to indulge in here. Plus the portions of pasta and seafood are family style at most of the local joints. In other words, expect a lot of leftovers.

Parks & Gardens: Dyker Beach Park shelters 242 acres of public grounds complete with large athletic fields, a golf course and a terrific beach.

Shopping: Food is really the only specialty here, so look for retail shopping somewhere else.

THE NEIGHBORHOOD

AVERAGE MONTHLY RENT

Studio	$400-600
1 br	$500-800
2 br	$600-1,000
3 br	$700-1,100

AVERAGE SALE PRICE

Studio	$50,000-65,000
1 br	$50,000-80,000
2 br	$55,000-100,000
3 br	$60,000-150,000

COMMUTING

For subway service you're out of luck. The 7 bus line services the community, linking you up with the N and R trains. Most residents rely on cars.

DISTANCE

Time to midtown	55-60 min
Time to downtown	50-55 min

Final Words: If you don't mind travelling, Dyker Heights is a fine choice for small families who want their own house.

EAST HARLEM
• MANHATTAN •

Viva Espagne! Also called Spanish Harlem and El Barrio, this neighborhood is one of the most flavorful in New York. Even if you are not of Latin American descent, do not overlook this area. Although the population is mostly Puerto Rican and Dominican, there are also many African-American, white, and Asian residents. It is one of the few places where people are always casually sitting on the street talking or playing music. There is a real sense of community here.

Since the 1830s, immigrants have found East Harlem to be a good place to begin life in America—a refuge of cheap property and housing. In the 1870s, East Harlem was the site of a massive wave of speculative development that resulted in the construction of numerous new single-family row houses, tenements, luxury apartment houses and cultural institutions. The deterioration of East Harlem housing, which began in the 1920s, can be attributed in large part to the high cost of living in the community and the increased demands on the neighborhood brought by the rising population. Both white and black landlords are responsible for the distressing scenario in which rents continued to increase while maintenance and services were neglected. Unfortunately, East Harlem remains an economically distressed neighborhood, but it seems to be getting better gradually, as the government is finally paying more attention to it.

East Harlem covers the expanse from 96th to 125th Streets, from First to Fifth Avenues. It is unconscionable that such a large neighborhood has been neglected for so long. Most of the buildings are rundown brownstones, but for true go-getters it is a great place to buy a dirt cheap building or floor of a building and completely fix it up. The government will even provide a tax break for people with such ambitious intentions in this neighborhood. If this seems a little too ruthless, the neighborhood projects are always an option but not a desirable one. They are ridden with crime, violence, and drugs, but for some people it is New York's only affordable option.

All of this sounds extremely distressing, but East Harlem is on the road to recovery. Finally, bigger establishments have been built here, like a Pathmark store and a cinema multiplex, to help improve the local economy. Where there were once vacant stores, now there are new green awnings inviting customers into the Make My Cake bakery, Elizabeth Hair Styling and Salon, and Bianca's on the Park banquet hall.

Long-time residents know that their neighborhood has far more to offer than it may at first appear and are making grand efforts to improve East Harlem. One particularly ambitious woman started the Harlem Renaissance Local Development Corporation, which is aimed at assessing the needs of the eighty businesses from 110th to 113th Street and from Fifth Avenue to Frederick Douglass Boulevard. As real estate on the Upper East Side is increasingly more difficult to find, people are looking a little further north and realizing that this area ain't so bad—it's actually quite beautiful. Within a few years, East Harlem is sure to undergo a total change.

> "Man has made a sewer of the river—and spanned it with a poem."
>
> **ANDY ROONEY ON THE COMPLETION OF THE VERRAZANO-NARROWS BRIDGE**

Noise: Since many locals enjoy hanging out on the streets, noise pollution is a major problem in East Harlem. But don't think of it as offensive, as it is representative of the vivacity here. Ambulances and police car sirens however are real nuisances.

Parking: There is a lot of available parking, but don't leave your car on the street unless you are equipped with a Club to protect it against a break-in. Private garages might be a better option.

Kids & Families: Services for raising children are varied in quality but tend to be less than ideal. East Harlem is populated by a large group of working-class poor and

THE PEOPLE

POPULATION	46,000
AGE	
0-17	33%
18-44	36%
45-64	21%
65+	10%
ETHNICITY	
White	32%
Black	67%
Asian	1%
Spanish speaking	58%
Family households	64%
College educated	6%
HOUSEHOLD INCOME	
Below $25,000	66%
$25-75,000	32%
$75-150,000	1%
$150,000+	1%

low-income families whose children are often lacking in basic housing, health care and food.

Safety: The area has not enjoyed the phenomenal growth found in other parts of Manhattan.

It is best not to travel alone at night.

Entertainment: There is a little something for everyone here, but it is mostly homemade. Residents have fun just chilling together on the street. There are some bars, but they are guaranteed to be uncomfortably packed. Hanging out on apartment stoops is where the real good times are had. The annual El Barrio Three Kings Day Parade is a special treat.

Find a NYC apartment now!

Restaurants: Inexpensive ethnic dishes are everywhere. Staples like soul food and rice and beans are supplemented by the occasional terrific Jamaican or Spanish restaurant. El Fogons Café and Restaurant has the best Puerto Rican food in the city. Pizza doesn't get much better than the $10 pies at Patsy's Pizza on First Avenue between 117th and 118th Streets.

Parks & Gardens: Central Park is only a short walk from all parts of East Harlem.

Shopping: Consumer selection has been dismal in these parts for decades, but it is finally getting better. Although the city encourages businesses to move into East Harlem, many retail merchants remain hesitant.

Final Words: East Harlem should have a sign on it that says "Enter at your own risk." For those who can handle a rough neighborhood, you can make a great home for yourself surrounded by lots of interesting people. In

THE NEIGHBORHOOD

AVERAGE MONTHLY RENT

Studio	$400-800
1 br	$600-1,300
2 br	$700-1,500
3 br	$1,100-1,700

AVERAGE SALE PRICE

Studio	$55,000-100,000
1 br	$60,000-180,000
2 br	$80,000-270,000
3 br	$100,000-350,000

COMMUTING

The 6 train stops at 103rd, 110th, 116th and 125th Streets, and the 4, and 5 trains stop at 125th Street.

DISTANCE

Time to midtown	25-35 min
Time to downtown	30-40 min

upcoming years, even less daring types should be able to find comfort here.

EAST VILLAGE
• MANHATTAN •

One of the trendiest and most up and coming spots in lower Manhattan, the East Village is part hype and part reality. Located near New York University and Cooper Union, the area is populated by a motley mix of starving students, mainstream rejects, punks, tattooed Goths, pierced artists and your basic New York homeless person, with a token few normal types tossed in for diversity.

During the `80s, the area was far more rough and ready then it is today. The neighborhood was overrun with drugs and crime, and that caused unemployment and lingering poverty. Tensions came to a head in the early `90s when police in riot gear arrived in helicopters to evict a ragtag assortment of squatters from Tompkins Square Park, one of the East Village's two major parks.

In its seedier days, the East Village was home to such artistic types as Jean Michel Basquiat and Madonna, who traces at least some of her pizzazz back to her urban beginnings in the Village. Back in the day, the low rents in what was then a mainly working class ethnic neighborhood attracted a bohemian crowd. More recently, scads of not-so-welcome yuppies have arrived to sightsee, party and move in. This new crowd has blunted the area's cutting-edge appeal, and today, the East Village's fashionable status and increasingly high rental prices have caused longtime residents to complain that the area has been taken over by yuppies in search of some borrowed color.

One thing you don't have to worry about here is being appropriate in any way whatsoever. People come to the East Village to let their hair down and forget that they have a job they hate, or that their parents made them go to college or even that they have parents. Indeed, visiting older relatives will probably hate the neighborhood, but if you moved to the big city to indulge in some lingering adolescent angst and live the life of the urban rebel, then you'll be proud to call the east village home.

There is still a considerable homeless presence in the East Village, especially along the less populated streets and in the area known as "Alphabet City" between Avenues A and C. Don't go alone there at night, especially after a drink in a short skirt. Although Mayor Giuliani has continued to make the neighborhood a major police beat, especially along super-trendy St. Marks Place, remember that it is still up-and-coming and has not actually "arrived" just yet.

> "In Manhattan, every flat surface surface is a potential stage and every inattentive waiter an unemployed, possibly unemployable, actor."
>
> **QUENTIN CRISP**

Nighthawks love the East Village, and locals don't seem to like daylight very much. Gotham residents descend here after dark looking for a bit of R & R at some of the neighborhood's plentiful watering holes.

With wealthier residents setting up home, rents have been steadily increasing. Although it is still possible to find a deal, your chances increase as you get closer to the East River. Apartments here tend to be on a teeny-tiny scale and are often laid out in odd, all but unlivable designs. Still, trendy folks shell out cash to live in closet-sized dwellings in this funky Manhattan zip code. East Village apartments move fast, and it is advisable to show up waiving a checkbook. But, with everything from people to rents to apartment availability moving at the speed and sound of a bolt of lightning, don't expect to find anything or anyone, for the long term in East Village.

Noise: Loud on Eighth Street and Avenue A, particularly at night and just slightly less so on side streets. The streets further into Alphabet City tend to be quieter, but sirens and shouting matches are still likely to disrupt your slumber.

Parking: Better than average for New York. If you have trouble, there are some nearby parking lots, too.

Kids & Families: There are lots of kids and parks around here, which is good news for young families. School quality is spotty, though. The area used to boast a lot of so-called "alternative" schools, many of which have relocated. Both residents and schools are very ethnically diverse.

Safety: Even cops sport Mohawks in the East Village, and they definitely make their presence known on weekends on all of the major streets. This type of vigilance has made the East Village a generally safe neighborhood. However, the less populated areas, such as Avenue B and C, can feel dangerous late at night, and there are occasionally reports of roaming gangs of kids harassing people.

THE PEOPLE

POPULATION	52,000
AGE	
0-17	12%
18-44	54%
45-64	18%
65+	16%
ETHNICITY	
White	72%
Black	9%
Asian	8%
Oher	11%
Spanish speaking	22%
Family households	53%
College educated	52%
HOUSEHOLD INCOME	
Below $25,000	40%
$25-75,000	50%
$75-150,000	5%
$150,000+	5%

WWW.ZANYS.COM
Find a NYC apartment now!

THE NEIGHBORHOOD

AVERAGE MONTHLY RENT

Studio	$1,200-1,700
1 br	$1,300-2,400
2 br	$1,700-3,000
3 br	$2,800-3,700

AVERAGE SALE PRICE

Studio	$130,000-200,000
1 br	$175,000-350,000
2 br	$200,000-600,000
3 br	$300,000-1,000,000

COMMUTING

The 6 train runs to Astor Place, the 4 and 5 to 14th Street, the N and R to 8th Street and the F to 2nd Avenue. Buses are plentiful.

DISTANCE

Time to midtown	15-20 min
Time to downtown	5-10 min

Entertainment: The East Village probably has the highest percentage of clubs and bars of any neighborhood in the city. It seems like every block has a bar and every other one has a club, from pubs and dives to trance dens and lounges. It is almost impossible to walk a block without stumbling across at least one drinking hole. People who love the grungier side of life will love it here. Most establishments are dimly lit and divey, ideal for various forms of conversing, playing pool or just tying one on.

Restaurants: The East Village boasts a virtual United Nations of cuisines, from Indian, Ukrainian and Russian to Middle Eastern, Mexican and Italian. East 6th Street between 1st and 2nd Avenues is called "Little India" for its dozens of dirt-cheap subcontinental eateries. With the recent gentrification, more expensive choices spring up daily all around Avenue A that vary in quality and longevity. If your wallet can stretch that far, though, you'll certainly have fun trying them out.

Parks & Gardens: Though not very green, Tompkins Square Park is the main open area in the East Village. Though it is constantly populated by a smattering of homeless residents drinking out of brown paper bags, Tompkins Square is definitely cleaner than it was back in the `80s. East River Park along the river isn't well maintained, but the view and air are great, and on weekends it's full of families and young lovers smooching along the waterfront.

Shopping: Clothing is one thing the East Village excels at. Choose your new outfit from one of the fashionable designer boutiques, or check out the trendy thrift stores but don't expect to pay bargain prices. With the recent addition of the Gap, yupsters are getting their day, too. Once you're dressed to impress, the East Village stores will also provide you with a range in eccentric accessories and makeup, and there are plenty of hair salons to complete your oh-so-fashionable new look.

Final Words: If you're young, hip and want to live in the big bad city, this part of town has the exciting edge you're after. The atmosphere might seem a little shallow at times, but you can cross your fingers and hope that a lot of upscale types will move out soon after the novelty wears off. If you're a sucker for personal hygiene and cleanliness, the grime of the East Village will have you running scared.

FLATBUSH
◆ BROOKLYN ◆

F latbush is located in the heart of Brooklyn and roughly includes areas Midwood, East Flatbush and areas in the vicinity of Prospect Park. The name derives from the area's Dutch heritage, although a visit today shows no remnants of the farmland and pastures that once covered

WWW.ZANYS.COM
Find a NYC apartment now!

Brooklyn and was populated by Dutch immigrants. The Dutch first settled Flatbush in the 17th century, and the area remained rural and relatively secluded from the rest of the world until the Coney Island Railroads were built in the late 19th century. The new ease of transportation caused the growing upper middle class from Manhattan to flock to this area, and the development boom began soon thereafter.

By 1920, the subway lines were extended to Flatbush, and the new business for the nearby amusement parks pushed people and development further inland.

What began as a predominantly Jewish immigration prior to World War II soon expanded to include immigrants from other areas and backgrounds. First among those were immigrants from the Caribbean, and now the area is home to people, customs and food from Asia, Central America and Russia, as well as just about everywhere else. Flatbush is a melting pot of New York's many melting pots. It is filled with ethnic delis and restaurants and plenty of shopping that offers a better selection than whatever was available in the old country. Visit Caribbean East Flatbush to taste the exotic collection of fruits and vegetables vividly displayed.

The types of houses are as varied as the religions, foods and faces of the residents of Flatbush. Victorian mansions stand side by side with terrazzo palazzos, art-deco buildings, Dutch farmhouses, brick bungalows and all-American one-family homes. Victorian Flatbush, south of Prospect Park, is home to particularly posh residences, no two alike: developers in the early 1900s wanted to make their mark on the area, and the houses are their legacies, definitely worth a trip even if you don't play to stay.

Flatbush is mostly middle class and home to tolerant, generally hard working and open-minded people. Expect new folks to continue coming to settle here. As Brooklyn fills up with yuppies eager for apartment deals, Flatbush is likely to see a surge in its popularity.

Noise: This is definitely not a sedate locale. But there is not an overbearing or overriding din that prevents one from putting up his feet after a long and drawn-out day at work.

Parking: Streetside parking is available, and it is not a too stressful trying to find a parking spot.

Kids & Families: This neighborhood is a nice place to raise children, with just enough laxity to keep the parents off their twenty-four hour surveillance of every minute aspect of their kids' lives.

THE PEOPLE

POPULATION	163,000
AGE	
0-18	31%
18-64	58%
65+	11%
ETHNICITY	
White	54%
Black	38%
Asian	8%
Spanish speaking	10%
Family households	34%
College educated	30%
HOUSEHOLD INCOME	
Below $25,000	50%
$25-40,000	19%
$40-60,000	14%
$60,000+	17%

Safety: This neighborhood is not particularly dangerous, but being cautious never hurts.

Entertainment: Aside for a couple of movie theatres in town, your best bet is to go out to shop.

Restaurants: You will not have the best of luck trying to find that perfect restaurant that combines ambiance with great food and a great time, though there are a

WWW.ZANYS.COM
Find a NYC apartment now!

bunch of places to try and buy ethnic foods.

Shopping: Discount. Discount. Discount. Looking for clothing and accessories for affordable and very affordable prices? You've come to the right place.

THE NEIGHBORHOOD

AVERAGE MONTHLY RENT

Studio	$400-700
1 br	$600-800
2 br	$700-1,000
3 br	$1,100-1,300

AVERAGE SALE PRICE

Studio	$55,000-75,000
1 br	$60,000-95,000
2 br	$70,000-120,000
3 br	$80,000-200,000

COMMUTING

The 2 and 5 trains stop at Church Avenue through Flatbush Avenue.

DISTANCE

Time to midtown	45-60 min
Time to downtown	30-55 min

Final Words: It is endearing to see a neighborhood filled with so much of everything; it is definitely one-of-a-kind. Though it may seem overwhelming at times to get hit with so much at once, it is also rather enticing and keeps you looking around that bend for more surprises.

FLATIRON DISTRICT
• MANHATTAN •

latiron District? Literally, this neighborhood does seem to be a "metal district" because of its modern and unique buildings made mostly of pewter, brass and bronze metals. The individuality of the neighborhood attracts an appropriately innovative group of people who are looking to literally concoct their own living space, as opposed to buying something that is pre-designed.

The Flatiron District encircles the immediate vicinity of Madison Square Park from 14th to 32nd streets between Union Square/Park Avenue and the Hudson River. The area has its own distinct landmark, which is an oddly shaped triangular old skyscraper called the Flatiron Building. Located at the sliver of a corner formed by Broadway and Fifth Avenue at 23rd Street, the Flatiron Building was the world's tallest skyscraper when it was built in 1903.

The community is one of New York's trendiest, comprised of resident's who are generally artists by nature; many are recording artists and web page designers. Along the same lines, the businesses found here are hip and modern, such as contemporary coffee houses, leather goods shops, music studios and commercial internet establishments. No neighborhood in New York is as diverse in its economy as the Flatiron District, with residents ranging from older blue-collar workers to younger, wealthy singles and couples.

> "The visitors, they question you—they like to know what's that building, where's Brooklyn, which way's New Jersey. They observe the view. That's why it's called an observatory."
>
> **FRANK FUSARO, OBSERVATORY STAFF, EMPIRE STATE BUILDING**

WWW.ZANYS.COM
Find a NYC apartment now!

Most buildings in the neighborhood have recently been blessed with multi-million dollar renovations, making it extremely cutting-edge. Many of the older buildings continue to be remodeled into condominiums and high rises, which does not rest well among some older residents. If you're just passing through, the area might seem a bit run down, but this is only on the exterior. Once you get inside, you will be pleasantly surprised by the huge and modernized spaces.

As is true with so many neighborhoods in New York, the Flatiron District is up-and-coming, and rents have skyrocketed in the past few years. But among such newly hip areas, it is the unknown sibling, making it one of the best trendy places to invest. Residences further west towards the river are also significantly cheaper.

Along with real estate costs, the quantity of businesses and cultural establishments are rising, mainly art galleries and boutiques. The Flatiron District is also home to many unique clubs and bars. While most of the newer residents have a passion for partying, shopping, and dining, community elders complain that the area is not physically equipped to service it all.

Flatiron's younger residents are extremely extroverted and want to make their lives and lifestyles successful here. Since the prices are more affordable than nearby Chelsea, Soho and Tribeca, it is a great place to feel the hippness of the city without going bankrupt. During the day, the neighborhood is bumping with professionals, but at night, it is a bit quieter as people tend to travel further up or downtown to party, making it an ideal place if you wish to keep a low-profile while being in the middle of grooviness. If you have always dreamed of designing your own apartment completely from stage one, the Flatiron District is the most affordable place in town to make all of your real estate fantasies come true.

Noise: Busy on the main thoroughfares.

Parking: Given the commercial establishments of the neighborhood, parking is actually not that hard to find. That's a rarity in New York. Just be sure to use the Club.

Kids & Families: As a fairly low cost neighborhood, it's a good place to start a family, although there aren't many kids in the neighborhood.

Safety: This is a fairly safe neighborhood because so many people are always walking around.

Entertainment: Several high-profile clubs are in the neighborhood, and there is every type of salon and shop.

Restaurants: For lunch and dinner, there is a cross sections of every type of cruisine, and the choice is growing.

Parks & Gardens: Madison Square is something of a green space in the midst of the urban jungle.

THE PEOPLE

POPULATION	32,000
AGE	
0-17	7%
18-44	59%
45-64	22%
65+	12%
ETHNICITY	
White	91%
Black	4%
Asian	4%
Other	1%
Spanish speaking	7%
Family households	25%
College educated	68%
HOUSEHOLD INCOME	
Below $25,000	27%
$25-75,000	49%
$75-150,000	12%
$150,000+	12%

WWW.ZANYS.COM
Find a NYC apartment now!

Shopping: You may have to do some traveling to find groceries and other necessities.

Final Words: Flatiron is perfect for your first Manhattan home, given its relatively low costs compared to Park Avenue. Despite the fact that typical conveniences aren't right at your doorstep, it is a great location for versatility, and a step up to the plate for the young professional.

THE NEIGHBORHOOD

AVERAGE MONTHLY RENT
Studio	$1,600-2,300
1 br	$1,700-2,600
2 br	$1,900-3,500
3 br	$2,800-4,000

AVERAGE SALE PRICE
Studio	$150,000-250,000
1 br	$200,000-350,000
2 br	$500,000-1,000,000
3 br	$700,000-1,000,000+

COMMUTING

The 1, 2, 3, 9, A, C, E, N and R trains run through Flatiron.

DISTANCE
Time to midtown	10-20	min
Time to downtown	15-25	min

FLUSHING
QUEENS

Flushing is a huge neighborhood, known for its large Asian community and generally diverse ethnic make-up. Many New Yorkers don't know that the community has a long history of diversity and in fact was the site of one of Colonial America's landmark debates on religious freedom. This has been a vital neighborhood for centuries and continues to host scores of eager immigrants recently arrived in New York.

English settlers, mostly Quakers fleeing religious persecution in New England, founded Flushing. When Dutch governor Peter Stuyvesant banned the practice of their faith in his colony as well, the Quakers protested by declaring their religious freedom in the Flushing Remonstrance. This was the first time in the colonies that a group of citizens had demanded religious tolerance, and the incident caused Stuyvesant and many others to take notice.

For centuries, Flushing remained a cozy town, noted for its nurseries and orchards. All that changed in 1909 with the construction of the Queensboro Bridge. Flushing quickly became a commuter town, and throughout the 20th century waves of immigrants brought more and more residents to what used to be a simple farming community. Many families moved here in the 1960s because of the perception of Manhattan and Brooklyn as areas with crumbling infrastructures and failing school systems. Queens, by contrast, was relatively new and full of hope.

Flushing is situated to the east of Flushing Meadows-Corona Park and is bounded by Cross Island Parkway to the north, the Long Island Expressway to the south and Utopia Parkway to the east. Most residents of Flushing wouldn't live anywhere else, and some even have a slightly dismissive attitude towards Manhattan and Brooklyn.

WWW.ZANYS.COM
Find a NYC apartment now!

Many have strong ties to their ethnic communities and find that Flushing has the best of both worlds—New World convenience and Old World goods and services.

The neighborhood's Asian-American community continues to grow. Lately, many of Chinatown's newer residents have moved here to work in the sweatshops built nearby. The area's demographics have gradually shifted as older Korean residents and their children turn to white-collar work and sell their retail businesses to more recent arrivals.

Flushing is known for its pleasant landscape of white houses. Meanwhile, the downtown area around Main Street and Roosevelt Avenue is a busy, commercial dis-

THE PEOPLE

POPULATION	240,000
AGE	
0-17	21%
18-44	51%
45-64	17%
65+	11%
ETHNICITY	
White	37%
Black	20%
Asian	24%
Other	20%
Spanish speaking	37%
Family households	73%
College educated	25%
HOUSEHOLD INCOME	
Below $25,000	41%
$25-75,000	52%
$75-150,000	6%
$150,000+	1%

trict. Perhaps the neighborhood's biggest claim to fame is Shea Stadium, home of the New York Mets. Flushing Meadows-Corona Park also hosts the U.S. Open, and has been the site of two World Fairs. The Queens Botanical Gardens are a lovely escape from the urban jungle and house 38 acres of gardens, including six acres of roses. In Colonial times, Flushing was home to world-famous nurseries, which have left a legacy of over 70 varieties of trees scattered throughout the neighborhood.

Some old-timers complain that the neighborhood has become overcrowded. However, most still see it as a lovely, low-cost alternative to Manhattan, with a distinctive quality all its own.

Noise: This area can be very noisy right off the main drags and next to the expressways.

Parking: There is generally plenty of parking.

THE NEIGHBORHOOD

AVERAGE MONTHLY RENT

Studio	$600-1,000
1 br	$800-1,200
2 br	$1,300-1,500
3 br	$1,800-2,400

AVERAGE SALE PRICE

Studio	$50,000-100,000
1 br	$75,000-150,000
2 br	$80,000-200,000
3 br	$80,000-250,000

COMMUTING

The 7 train, the only commuter line running through both Times Square and Grand Central Station, stops at 111th Street, Willets Point and Main Street.

DISTANCE

Time to midtown	15-20 min
Time to downtown	25-30 min

WWW.ZANYS.COM

Find a NYC apartment now!

Kids & Families: Flushing is a good place to buy or rent a starter house if you're planning to raise a family.

Safety: Overall, this is not a scary place, but check out your prospective neighborhood after dark.

Entertainment: Not much in the way of entertainment, unless you count drag racing.

Restaurants: Get out your chopsticks, because Flushing boasts some of the city's best Asian dining.

Parks & Gardens: With Flushing Meadows-Corona Park and the Queens Botanical Gardens at your fingertips, you'd be hard-pressed to find a greener neighborhood.

Shopping: This is a great area for regular manicures or pedicures. Otherwise, shopping is largely confined to small bodegas or large chains stores.

Final Words: Flushing is a great place to get a flavor for New York's ethnic mix.

FOREST HILLS
• QUEENS •

You could live forever in Forest Hills and never feel the need to leave the neighborhood. Houses in this ritzy section of Queens are plenty big enough to give you lots of space to roam around, and they all come equipped with big back and front yards. There are neighborhood cinemas, restaurants, stores of all kinds and plenty of coffee shops to satisfy all of a resident's earthly desires. With all this, you'll never even need to take the train to Manhattan.

Forest Hills remained an area of undeveloped farmland until the 20th century. Developer Cord Meyer bought 600 acres between Elmhurst and Jamaica but became nervous about his investment afterwards. He sold off a chunk of the land to the Sage Foundation Homes Co., headed by Margaret Olivia Slocum Sage, and together they began creating the community of Forest Hills. Sage envisioned an upper-class development and quickly set about creating strict regulations for the neighborhood. She hired the man who designed Central Park, Frederick Law Olmstead, to plan a quiet, attractive development of winding, tree-lined streets.

The plan was a success, and today, Forest Hills remains an exclusive, high-class suburban neighborhood. Located in central Queens, Forest Hills is bounded by Flushing Meadows Park to the east and Forest Park to the south. The community is easily accessible by a number of subways and the Long Island Railroad. The neighborhood's developers chipped in to help build the gorgeous railway station, complete with cobblestones and stone steps and arches. Of course, most everyone here owns a car, but be forewarned, that parking is only available with a permit on Forest Hills' pristine residential streets.

> "If the United States is a melting pot, then New York makes it bubble."
>
> **ANONYMOUS**

Forest Hills is chock full of grand houses set back from quiet, winding streets. Luxury cars line the streets, and a general air of affluence wafts through the area. Even the street signs look classy. Houses here are a mix of 20th century styles, with a lot of neo-Tudor and Colonial designs. Everyone seems to have well-kept gardens in their front yards and backyards, alike.

Along the commercial thoroughfare of Austin Street, amenities of every kind are available. You will find all sorts of restaurants, from chains and fast food, to unique ethnic establishments. There are three movie theaters, sports clubs, huge bookstores and shopping of all kinds. The area is well-maintained and exudes the same sense of class as the residential neighborhood.

The Forest Hills Gardens Corporation is an active group of property owners who oversee the development and maintenance of the neighborhood. They keep Forest Hills up to the standards set by the original developers. Though the neighborhood is dominated by large houses, there are a few tasteful apartment buildings on the outer edges.

WWW.ZANYS.COM
Find a NYC apartment now!

Forest Hills is a lovely place to live if you've got the dough and are looking for a suburban hideaway. The area is home to a diverse mix of residents, but everyone has money in common. This is not the kind of place that is given to sudden changes, so expect Forest Hills to stay as is for quite some time to come.

THE PEOPLE

POPULATION	63,000
AGE	
0-18	17%
18-64	63%
65+	20%
ETHNICITY	
White	75%
Black	14%
Asian	11%
Spanish speaking	8%
Family households	44%
College educated	43%
HOUSEHOLD INCOME	
Below $25,000	39%
$25-40,000	19%
$40-60,000	19%
$60,000+	23%

Noise: People can throw wild parties in their huge houses here, and their neighbors would never know the difference. The only noise you're likely to hear is neighborhood birds, tweeting in the morning.

Parking: You've got to live here and have a parking permit to leave your car on the neighborhood streets. Of course if you do live here, you'll probably have your own driveway and garage, so it shouldn't be that much of a concern.

Kids & Families: This is a very family-friendly atmosphere, where kids have gorgeous yards in which to play and lots of fellow rich kids with whom to play there.

Entertainment: There are cinemas, bars and an assortment of other amusements on Austin Street. If all else fails, there's always Blockbuster.

Restaurants: You can satisfy pretty much any craving on Austin Street from fast food to swanky candlelit date spots.

THE NEIGHBORHOOD

AVERAGE MONTHLY RENT

Studio	$700-1,200
1 br	$900-1,400
2 br	$1,300-2,500
3 br	$1,900-2,700

AVERAGE SALE PRICE

Studio	$55,000-80,000
1 br	$80,000-250,000
2 br	$100,000-400,000
3 br	$120,000-600,000

COMMUTING

The E, F, G and R trains stop at Forest Hills and 71st Avenue.

DISTANCE

Time to midtown	30-45	min
Time to downtown	45-60	min

Parks & Gardens: Forest Hills has easy access to Flushing Meadows Corona Park and Forest Park, both great places to have a picnic, play sports or just commune with trees.

Shopping: Again, Austin Street's the place to go, with supermarkets, specialty stores, bookstores, boutiques and plenty of drugstores.

Final Words: If you want the feeling of living further out in a ritzy Long Island subdivision, while staying close to the heart of the city in Queens, Forest Hills could be just the place for you. Once you've settled here, you're likely to stay put for years to come.

FORT GREENE
◄ BROOKLYN ►

ort Greene has long held a reputation as a diverse neighborhood. The architecture represents many different styles, people of various ethnic backgrounds live happily as neighbors and an exciting array of artists and musicians create unique cultural opportunities for residents. Above all, Fort Greene is home to a uniquely harmonious blending of races.

In fact, the neighborhood is one of the oldest African-American communities in Brooklyn. In the mid 1800s, a large population of black workers settled here, and their ranks grew throughout the century. When it was first built in 1860, the Hanson Place Baptist Church became a stop on the Underground Railroad. In the twentieth century, many outstanding African-Americans have hailed from Fort Greene including Richard Wright, Wesley Snipes, Branford and Wynton Marsalis and, most famously in recent years, Spike Lee.

South of Brooklyn Heights and east of the Bedford-Stuyvesant neighborhood, Fort Greene is home to some of New York's happiest commuters. A short way from Manhattan, the neighborhood is filled with some of the city's finest brownstones, many of which have been fully renovated in recent years. Fort Greene features a wonderful park and two historic districts.

A number of artists and creative types who can't afford to live in the East Village have settled instead for the delightful diversity of Fort Greene. Quite a few jazz musicians, including Cassandra Wilson and Terence Blanchard, call this neighborhood home. Many musicians move here to attend the Brooklyn Academy of Music, or BAM as it's commonly known.

Spike Lee's production company, 40 Acres and a Mule, has its headquarters here on DeKalb Avenue. Lee's store, Spike's Joint, shares space with a variety of fashion outlets that cater to a very chic or up-and-coming clientele. Junior's and Gage & Tollner are two of Brooklyn's best-known eateries, famous for their unique decor and distinctive dishes.

Fort Greene Park is a glorious 30-acre expanse of green, dotted with delicate Asian trees and some of the area's largest elms. Walt Whitman is credited with the idea of turning this land into a public space. Today, visitors can tour a rebuilt fort modeled on one used against the British during the Battle of Brooklyn. The remains of some of the 11,000 former prisoners are buried in the park, which is now home to nature and history exhibits and a new junior ranger program for kids.

Overall, Fort Greene is a very diverse place and home to many intersecting slices of life. The neighborhood's history of racial tolerance is rare, even by the standards of multicultural New York. Artists and up-and-comers continue to flock here, but the demand for housing has quickly raised the once reasonable rents.

Noise: Depending on where you live, the noise level is reasonable in most parts of Fort Greene. There's a lot of traffic around BAM, however, so expect more noise near DeKalb Avenue.

Parking: Finding a space can be challenging in this neighborhood.

Kids & Families: There are increasing numbers of families with children here (even Spike Lee chose to take the parenthood plunge). Families tend to be

WWW.ZANYS.COM
Find a NYC apartment now!

younger, but this is changing as the neighborhood grows up.

Safety: The area is generally safe and well-populated at night.

Entertainment: BAM offers an exciting line-up of unconventional productions, ranging from music and dance to theater and cinema.

Restaurants: Check out the great soul food and Caribbean restaurants.

Parks & Gardens: This neighborhood has excellent parks, including its namesake. People from nearby neighborhoods come to enjoy the greenery here.

Shopping: Eclectic and not for all tastes, but definitely colorful and distinctive.

THE PEOPLE

POPULATION	44,000
AGE	
0-17	23%
18-44	50%
45-64	19%
65+	9%
ETHNICITY	
White	15%
Black	79%
Asian	2%
Other	4%
Spanish speaking	11%
Family households	78%
College educated	31%
HOUSEHOLD INCOME	
Below $25,000	43%
$25-75,000	50%
$75-150,000	6%
$150,000+	1%

Final Words: Fort Greene is undergoing a latter-day renaissance, with many well-known artists of all backgrounds moving in. People here are aware of their heritage and not shy about expressing themselves. Expect rents to continue their upwards spiral as the neighborhood's popularity grows.

THE NEIGHBORHOOD

AVERAGE MONTHLY RENT

Studio	$900-1,300
1 br	$1,200-1,500
2 br	$1,700-2,800
3 br	$1,900-2,900

AVERAGE SALE PRICE

Studio	$65,000-100,000
1 br	$110,000-250,000
2 br	$150,000-350,000
3 br	$180,000-500,000

COMMUTING

The G train runs to Classon Avenue.

DISTANCE

Time to midtown	15-20	min
Time to downtown	5-10	min

WWW.ZANYS.COM
Find a NYC apartment now!

FRESH MEADOWS
• QUEENS •

Fresh Meadows was supposed to be a model community when it was built in the 1950s. Though most residents probably don't feel like they're living in a utopian paradise, the neighborhood does offer many carefully planned conveniences. For the most part, Fresh Meadows lives up to its developers' promise of suburban bliss within a well-constructed housing project.

For centuries, Fresh Meadows was a rural suburb to the south of Flushing. During the Revolutionary War, Benedict Arnold led British troops through the neighborhood, stopping at local farms along the way. That was about all the excitement the neighborhood saw for the next couple of hundred years, until development came in the 1930s.

In 1923, the Fresh Meadows Country Club opened and was the site of a major golf course. However, in the 1940s, the country club relocated and sold their land to the New York Life Insurance Company. Real estate was booming along with babies in this post-war era, and the company planned to create a housing development for veterans and their young families. Hailed as an ideal example of community planning, the neighborhood included stores and amenities of all sorts and began attracting residents as soon as it was completed.

Fresh Meadows is bounded by the Long Island Expressway, Union Turnpike and Cunningham Park. Today, the housing project makes up a sizeable chunk of the community, along with other suburban developments. The development itself is made up of mostly low and high-rise apartment buildings, with some row houses thrown in, as well.

The housing complex features three shopping centers, and residents will be able to find everything they need in the many stores. There are plenty of restaurants and forms of entertainment in the area as well. Unfortunately, public transportation in the neighborhood is lacking, so commutes may be difficult, and most residents will find that owning a car is a necessity.

When Fresh Meadows was still a farming community, Parsons Nurseries was a commercial garden. Today, the old nurseries have been turned into Kissena Park, a huge green space with everything from a golf course and tennis courts to boating facilities on the park's own lake. This is a wonderful place to spend a Sunday afternoon in any sort of outdoor activity.

Fresh Meadows was developed as an answer to the problems found in so many other communities on the outskirts of large cities. In many ways, it has remained a model

THE PEOPLE

POPULATION	690,000
AGE	
0-18	22%
18-64	65%
65+	13%
ETHNICITY	
White	60%
Black	20%
Asian	20%
Spanish speaking	18%
Family households	38%
College educated	30%
HOUSEHOLD INCOME	
Below $25,000	34%
$25-40,000	21%
$40-60,000	20%
$60,000+	25%

WWW.ZANYS.COM
Find a NYC apartment now!

community through the years and residents have a strong sense of community, whether they live within the original housing complex or in the more suburban neighborhoods.

Noise: The neighborhood stays calm and quiet most all the time.

Parking: You shouldn't have any problems finding a place for your car in this automobile-friendly neighborhood.

Kids & Families: Lots of kids call Fresh Meadows home, and it's a nice, suburban place to raise a family.

Entertainment: There's a movie theater in the housing complex, but that's about as exciting as the neighborhood gets at night.

Restaurants: You'll find all sorts of restaurants to suit your particular tastes.

Parks & Gardens: Kissena Park is a gorgeous park with

THE NEIGHBORHOOD

AVERAGE MONTHLY RENT

Studio	$600-900
1 br	$700-1,000
2 br	$800-1,200
3 br	$900-1,500

AVERAGE SALE PRICE

Studio	$55,000-70,000
1 br	$65,000-100,000
2 br	$75,000-160,000
3 br	$90,000-200,000

COMMUTING

The F train only stops at Jamaica, but there are many buses available from there.

DISTANCE

Time to midtown	45-60	min
Time to downtown	50-90	min

plenty of room for everyone to enjoy themselves.

Shopping: You can find whatever you need within and without the housing development.

Final Words: Fresh Meadows is a nice, suburban neighborhood in which to raise a family. However, for anyone who finds the idea of a model community a little creepy or needs a convenient commute to Manhattan, Fresh Meadows may not be so ideal after all.

GRAMERCY PARK
MANHATTAN

Enter the gates of Gramercy Park (if you are lucky enough to have access), and you will feel like you have stepped into an old-world Dickens village. It is the only downtown area of its kind, serene and entirely tree-lined, and Gramercy Park feels more like it belongs on the calm Upper East Side.

The charms of 19th century New York come alive in this quiet residential neighborhood. Back in 1831, architect Samuel B. Ruggles built the park after which the neighborhood is named. All of the astounding townhouses around the park were built before the Civil War and are still some of the most magnificent buildings in the city. On East 17th Street stands the oldest apartment building in all of New York, which was built in 1879. As you meander from 20th to 34th streets between the East River and Park Avenue, you will feel like a tourist even if you are a native New Yorker. This place just has that much history!

Gramercy Park has the many charms of a wealthy community. It's rare to see litter on the streets or even a cluttered window. All of the larger apartment buildings in the area have doormen and many of the stone row houses are single-family dwellings. Residents in the area can afford such posh homes because they are typically older, successful professionals.

Commercial businesses dominate the western parts of

Gramercy, but the more eastern blocks are a lot quieter and strictly residential. Despite the extravagant buildings and seeming wealth of the neighborhood, Gramercy isn't for millionaires only. Yes, homes in the area tend to sell for huge amounts, but there are some cheaper apartments, too. The most inexpensive buildings are those closest to the East River and furthest from the subway, though they are also quite lovely.

The beautiful park itself is the center of the neighborhood, but only wealthy folks living in the adjoining apartments have keys to it, in the old-fashioned European style. This is New York's only private park, and passers by will have to be content with peering through the wrought-iron fence. Gramercy outcasts will find equal pleasure though by visiting nearby public Stuyvesant Park from 15th to 17th streets on Second Avenue.

If you travel further west in Gramercy, you will be met by Silicon Alley, an area dominated by new internet businesses. They tend to keep to themselves, though, and do nothing to disturb the hush and the pristine state of the neighborhood. Some of New York's top restaurants have also relocated in the western area, such as the famous Gramercy Tavern.

Gramercy Park really has a bit of everything. It is both quiet and busy, historic and trendy. Neighborhoods like this are hard to find. Gramercy residents know that they have the best of both worlds and will do everything in their power to preserve their precious home. Some of the toughest landlords operate in these buildings. Noise will not be tolerated after a certain hour. This ancient neighborhood will probably remain exactly the same way until the apocalypse. No one who lives here desires change. A key to Gramercy Park is a true New York status symbol, shared by only a few.

> "In New York... not an inch of free space is spared except that of advertisements."
>
> **GILBERT ADAIR**

Noise: One of the most peaceful neighborhoods in New York. Any violators of noise regulations will be politely asked to leave.

Parking: It's very difficult to find adequate parking around here.

Kids & Families: If you know how to discipline your children, it is a great place to raise a family. The exclusiveness of the neighborhood will let kids get away from the hustle and bustle of surrounding areas.

Safety: Residents enjoy the neighborhood for its relative safety.

Entertainment: Perfect for intimate gatherings and a fireside reading with your sweetheart.

Restaurants: Ooh-la-la, deciding where to eat here is a true challenge as there are so many good choices. Union Pacific, Gramercy Tavern and Bolo are among the top, top picks.

THE PEOPLE

POPULATION	26,000
AGE	
0-17	9%
18-44	36%
45-64	38%
65+	17%
ETHNICITY	
White	88%
Black	4%
Asian	8%
Spanish speaking	12%
Family households	34%
College educated	42%
HOUSEHOLD INCOME	
Below $25,000	12%
$25-75,000	28%
$75-150,000	37%
$150,000+	23%

WWW.ZANYS.COM
Find a NYC apartment now!

Parks & Gardens: It's named after a park. Enough said.
Shopping: Gramercy Park is well-outfitted for older residents' needs, with plenty of pharmacies and dry cleaners. Younger residents will need to walk a little bit to find stores to suit their trendiness.

THE NEIGHBORHOOD

AVERAGE MONTHLY RENT

Studio	$1,500-2,000
1 br	$1,600-2,800
2 br	$2,500-4,500
3 br	$5,000-7,000

AVERAGE SALE PRICE

Studio	$150,000-250,000
1 br	$210,000-400,000
2 br	$550,000-1,000,000
3 br	$800,000-1,000,000+

COMMUTING

The 6 train stops at 23rd Street, and the N and R trains stop at 23rd Street.

DISTANCE

Time to midtown	10-15	min
Time to downtown	10-15	min

Final Words: For people who need peace and quiet, but still want to live in the big city it doesn't get better than this.

GREENPOINT
• BROOKLYN •

reenpoint, Brooklyn is one of the few spots in New York that has remained an ethnic enclave for over one hundred years. Today, it is estimated that almost 80% of the neighborhood's population is Polish—a fact which is obvious to any visitor who hears the area's many Polish-speakers or looks at one of the many local Polish restaurant's menus. Whether you speak Polish or not, though, Greenpoint offers a rich mix of industrial, commercial and residential spaces, along with a terrific quality of life.

In the 19th century, industry flourished in Greenpoint. The waterfront was one of America's shipbuilding centers, particularly noted for producing the famous Civil War warship the Monitor. Greenpoint was an important center for shipping, as well, and coffee and spices from around the world found their way to the busy docks. In 1867, the Standard Oil refineries were built on nearby Newton Creek and were responsible for providing kerosene, which fueled America's lamps and stoves.

Though the last century saw the shipbuilding industry decline and the oil refineries literally go up in flames, many new businesses have found their way to Greenpoint. The neighborhood has long been home to a significant Polish population but also includes some Italian, Russian and Hispanic residents. Notable twentieth century residents have included Mae West and Pat Benatar.

Greenpoint makes up the northwest corner of Brooklyn and shares a border with Queens along Newtown Creek to the north. The south side is demarcated conveniently by the Brooklyn Queens Expressway. Greenpoint also borders the East River and looks across into Manhattan. Since it has no subway service beyond the barely useful G line, a higher percentage of Greenpoint's population walks to work than almost any-

WWW.ZANYS.COM
Find a NYC apartment now!

where else in the country. It's no surprise, then, that this remains an insular community. Strong bonds within the various immigrant populations mean that daughters and sons rarely leave the neighborhood to start their own families. Much of this tradition is credited to the overwhelming devotion shown to the Catholic Church. The largest Polish congregation in Brooklyn crowds services in at the St. Stanislaus Kostka Vincentian Fathers Church every Sunday, and the entire neighborhood shuts down on major holidays like Easter.

Housing generally consists of inexpensive row houses covered in aluminum siding. Inside the quaint Greenpoint Historic District you will find much nicer pre-war brownstones that are exceptionally large and well-kept. Although residential spaces are dispersed throughout the neighborhood, prime housing can be found near the East River from Greenpoint Avenue to Green Street. These streets are still one of the best places to see traces of 19th-century Brooklyn-style cast-iron filigree. A steady turnover of unused warehouses into habitable loft spaces continues along the East River. Since most of the surrounding buildings are six stories high or less, the views of Manhattan from rooftops can be spectacular. Nearby Monsignor McGolrick Park is a lovely place to enjoy romantic walks, with great views across the East River. McCarren Park, meanwhile, is perfect for outdoor activities, and you can observe the melting pot in action as a host of different ethnic groups play sports side by side. A large Latin American contingent plays organized soccer on the weekends, and Dominican and Puerto Rican teams regularly square off on the baseball diamond. Italian-Americans prefer bocce ball and pavement softball, while others run on the all-purpose track, use the tennis courts or play basketball.

This is one neighborhood that has certainly not lost its individuality to gentrification. With Polish papers on the newsstands and bars where you may not hear anyone speaking English, Greenpoint remains a tight-knit immigrant community. However, its proximity to ultra-trendy Williamsburg is causing some logical spill-over of young artist-types into this Old World neighborhood.

THE PEOPLE

POPULATION	150,000
AGE	
0-17	18%
18-44	45%
45-64	24%
65+	13%
ETHNICITY	
White	86%
Black	7%
Asian	7%
Spanish speaking	44%
Family households	59%
College educated	15%
HOUSEHOLD INCOME	
Below $25,000	38%
$25-75,000	53%
$75-150,000	8%
$150,000+	1%

Noise: Street traffic is contained on busy Manhattan and McGuiness Avenues, both of which are filled with commuter traffic and loud trucks making deliveries. Side streets, where most of the residences are found, are extremely quiet.

Parking: It's very easy to find street parking without meters. Parking on residential streets is safe.

Kids & Families: Many families, mostly first or second-generation immigrants, call Greenpoint home. Local kids tend to be bilingual, and many residents and parents still speak poor English. There are several parochial schools in the neighborhood, as well as decent public schools.

Safety: The residential sector is generally very safe and cops regularly patrol the main avenues.

Entertainment: Almost every block has a neighborhood pub with great European beer on tap. For the youngsters, there's the techno club Europa and the bohemian ambiance of Enids at Manhattan and Driggs Avenue.

Restaurants: Low prices for sensational food like latkas, pierogies, blintzes and kielbasas are the norm in an enormous number of Polish eateries. Food tends toward the hearty, not necessarily the healthy.

Parks & Gardens: McCarren Park is a gift from heaven. Residents co-exist beautifully in Greenpoint, and the park's decidedly small-town European feel helps everyone's peace of mind.

Shopping: Greenpoint is home to a tremendous

THE NEIGHBORHOOD

AVERAGE MONTHLY RENT

Studio	$700-1,500
1 br	$1,000-1,400
2 br	$1,300-2,000
3 br	$1,300-2,500

AVERAGE SALE PRICE

Studio	$65,000-100,000
1 br	$160,000-180,000
2 br	$180,000-250,000
3 br	$200,000-300,000

COMMUTING

The G train stops at Nassau and Greenpoint Avenues. Taking this to Queens and transferring is your quickest route to midtown. Many residents also walk or take a bus to the L train to get to Manhattan

DISTANCE

Time to midtown	20-25	min
Time to downtown	25-35	min

amount of discount stores standing next to mom and pop businesses. Retail outlets are located along Manhattan Avenue and McGuiness Boulevard. All types of services, from laundromats to a gourmet supermarket, are a short walk away. On Saturday mornings, a market in McCarren park offers farm-fresh produce and baked goods.

Final Words: Greenpoint is a quaint, peaceful neighborhood full of hardworking blue-collar residents. Most newcomers choose Greenpoint for its cheap rents and generously sized apartments, but be forewarned that the lack of trains makes daily commutes to Manhattan difficult.

GREENWICH VILLAGE
• MANHATTAN •

When trying to define New York City, the word "eclecticism" should come to mind. Greenwich Village is the neighborhood that most aptly embraces this definition, as its inhabitants are everyone from celebrities, to starving artists, to homosexuals, to conservative politicians.

What was once considered as the "Paris of New York" in the 1960s and `70s is still a breeding ground for culture and counter-culture in the new millennium. Most famously, the Village is known for the cultural, artistic and sexual revolution that occurred here only thirty years ago, among star residents like Allen Ginsburg, Andy Warhol and Gloria Steinem. Current residents most definitely maintain the alternative lifestyle of years past. Yet they are not as concerned with being rebellious as they are with being cutting-edge.

Residents have always been drawn here because it is one of few places where outcasts feel that they can be accepted. At the turn-of-the-century, it was mostly populated by lower-class Italian, Irish and German immigrants, but as time went on, the Village became overrun by liberal artists and intellectuals seeking a territory where they could rule. And indeed, here they found their promised land.

In New York, nothing should surprise you, but in the Village strangeness is taken to new levels. The area is a sanctuary for the likes of transvestites, drag queens, avant-garde fashionistas and everyone in between. Sexuality is one of the main distinguishing characteristics here. Basically, anything goes. Even under Giuliani, the lasciviousness continues, though some things have become a little harder to find. The center of most of the action lies on Christopher Street, which is gay dominated, but nevertheless fun for everyone. You will find some of the best restaurants in the city here, as well as upscale boutiques and quirky little stores.

On a physical level, the Village is home to some of the city's most beautiful townhouses, antique shops, gardens and landmarks. But with this high aesthetic value comes equally hefty rents. Buying a place here could clear out your life savings, no joke. Washington Square Park and the famous Arch are central to Village life, and also the center of the NYU campus. Other gardens and parks are equally as nice, but the city's largest population of homeless people seem to have autonomy over them.

"A New Yorker is a person with an almost inordinate interest in mental health, which is only natural considering how much it takes to live here."

NEW YORK TIMES

Finding real estate in the Village is one of the hardest things a New Yorker can ever attempt to do. It is one of the most in-demand neighborhoods, and consequently, rents are up to ten times more than most other neighborhoods. But if money flows like water for you, the apartments here are well worth the investment. Most are equipped with huge windows, fireplaces, courtyards or gardens and old brick walls (and lots of them).

What it comes down to is that the Village is possibly the most exciting place in the city. Even if you can't afford to live here, it is still a great place to hang out, people watch and learn what being a true New Yorker really means. The neighborhood is all about fun, which means lots of noise and commotion. So forget all the hype for a minute and seriously consider if you really want to live in a neighborhood where flamboyant drag queens are as common as babies in strollers.

THE PEOPLE

POPULATION	78,000
AGE	
0-17	7%
18-44	60%
45-64	20%
65+	13%
ETHNICITY	
White	90%
Black	4%
Asian	3%
Other	3%
Spanish speaking	7%
Family households	39%
College educated	68%
HOUSEHOLD INCOME	
Below $25,000	27%
$25-75,000	49%
$75-150,000	11%
$150,000+	13%

Noise: Busy streets like West 4th and 6th Avenue can be noisy; however, the peaceful residential sections are nice and quiet.

Parking: Virtually impossible to find, and garages are sparse.

WWW.ZANYS.COM
Find a NYC apartment now!

Kids & Families: If you have money, it is a desirable place to live with kids given its quaintness and many parks. There are also numerous wonderful private schools in the area.

Safety: Since the neighborhood is predominantly gay, it's a safer place for women than the rest of New York. But even so, you should exercise caution. Some blocks are dicier than others, but you should always watch your back.

Entertainment: There are at least two dozen gay and unusually-themed clubs in the area, most open until all hours of the morning. Clubs usually have plenty of gay nights with straight thrown in, so check local listings.

Restaurants: Many of all types, from nouvelle cuisine to ethnic eateries galore.

Parks & Gardens: There are a few extremely cute and

THE NEIGHBORHOOD

AVERAGE MONTHLY RENT

Studio	$1,600-2,500
1 br	$1,800-3,600
2 br	$2,000-4,000
3 br	$3,300-4,600

AVERAGE SALE PRICE

Studio	$150,000-300,000
1 br	$250,000-400,000
2 br	$300,000-100,000,000
3 br	$400,000-100,000,000+

COMMUTING

The PATH train and the 1 and 9 lines stop at Christopher Street, and the F, A, C and E trains stop at West 4th Street.

DISTANCE

Time to midtown	15-20 min
Time to downtown	5-10 min

quaint little parks in the neighborhood. And you're always sure to see something interesting in Washington Square Park.

Shopping: The Village is awash with oodles of fun, quirky, avant-garde, artistic, retro, kitschy, sophisticated shops. You'll find everything from club gear and fetish-wear to antique dealers.

Final Words: As the most accepting neighborhood in the city, there is something for everyone and everything. Anyone can be made to feel at home here.

HARLEM
MANHATTAN

arlem is more than a neighborhood. For many, the history and culture of this area of northern Manhattan is a significant part of the ethnic identity of African-Americans everywhere. Though Harlem's glorious renaissance may have come and gone, the community remains an exciting reminder of the past and holds promise for the future, as well.

Harlem is bounded by 5th Avenue to the east, 110th Street to the south, and Morningside Heights, St. Nicholas Avenues to the west, and the Harlem River to the north. Development came to the neighborhood in the 1880s with the extension of the elevated railroads. Immigrants began pouring into the newly built tenements and brownstones, and in the early days of the 20th century, the neighborhood was home to the city's second-largest Jewish population. Soon, the population began shifting, and Harlem became dominated by African-Americans. Many were fleeing the racism and violence that had become commonplace in lower Manhattan, and soon black men and women from around the country began making their way to this haven of African-American community and culture.

What happened next was one of history's perfect coincidences of time, place and talent. Black artists of all different kinds made their way to Harlem, finding that they could express themselves in entirely new ways in this safe, self-segregated environment. Jazz music poured out of such institutions as the Cotton Club and Apollo Theater, played by the likes of Duke Ellington and Fletcher Henderson. Artists like Romane Bearden and William H. Johnson developed their unique visual styles here using collage and pastiche. The poets Countee Cullen and Langston Hughes coined the title by which history still remembers this era—the Harlem Renaissance.

The seeds of the Civil Rights movement were sown during this era, with such notable activists as Marcus Garvey and W.E.B. Du Bois fighting for change of the racist status quo. Garvey called for African-American nationalism, and Du Bois joined hands with the Communist Party, which adamantly opposed segregation from its headquarters in Harlem. Sadly, the Great Depression brought the Harlem Renaissance to an abrupt conclusion, but did not crush the cultural scene altogether. A source

> "The sensual mysticism of entire vertical being."
>
> **E.E. CUMMINGS ON NEW YORK CITY**

of great pride at the time was the boxer Joe Louis, who became the first African-American heavyweight champion.

Only vestiges of the neighborhood's glory days remain today. Following the political gains and tumult of the 1960s, Harlem experienced almost two decades of structural and spiritual decay. As an epidemic of drugs and crime swept the area, residents began to flee and real estate values plummeted. The once vital neighborhood became known as just another dilapidated, crime-ridden urban wasteland. However, hard times and neglect have failed to crush the area's spirit entirely. Many institutions, like the Baptist churches, the Dance Theater of Harlem, the Schomburg Center for African-American Research and the Studio Museum have continued to thrive. Today, the streets are lined with dilapidated but graceful brownstones. Recently, a period of economic growth has stimulated parts of Harlem with new businesses, jobs and much-needed services.

Real estate pros agree that it's only a matter of time before Harlem experiences a complete overhaul. A new Starbucks has recently opened up in the neighborhood, so who knows what will be next. Right now, however, individuals (especially whites folks) continue to fear a legacy of danger and decay, even though tax incentives make the move more appealing. Nearly every block has an abandoned brownstone or two that needs renovation. Apartments are yours for the picking, but be prepared to devote yourself to a fixer-upper.

THE PEOPLE

POPULATION	52,000
AGE	
0-17	24%
18-44	46%
45-64	18%
65+	12%
ETHNICITY	
White	1%
Black	98%
Asian	1%
Spanish speaking	19%
Family households	57%
College educated	12%
HOUSEHOLD INCOME	
Below $25,000	46%
$25-75,000	42%
$75-150,000	11%
$150,000+	1%

Noise: Car alarms, loud stereos and frequent sidewalk parties can make sleeping impossible. Side streets are usually much quieter than the busy avenues, and most of the traffic can be found on 125th Street. On the bright side, old buildings are surprisingly well-insulated against neighbor noise.

Parking: Very good parking is available on the streets. There are a few modestly priced private garages if protecting your vehicle is a concern. Due to the desolate streets at night, vehicle theft is more common in Harlem than in other parts of the city.

Kids & Families: Harlem is an affordable place to bring up children, if not the safest. School issues are a concern, though, and suffer from continuing drug and crime problems.

THE NEIGHBORHOOD

AVERAGE MONTHLY RENT

Studio	$400-1,000
1 br	$700-1,500
2 br	$900-1,700
3 br	$1,300-1,900

AVERAGE SALE PRICE

Studio	$70,000-90,000
1 br	$80,000-200,000
2 br	$85,000-350,000
3 br	$100,000-400,000

COMMUTING

The B and C trains stop at 110th, 116th, 125th, 135th and 145th Streets, the D train stops at 125th and 145th Streets, and the 2 and 3 trains stop at 110th, 116th, 125th, 135th and 145th Streets. Regular buses along 125th Street provide easy access to LaGuardia Airport.

DISTANCE

Time to midtown	25-35	min
Time to downtown	35-45	min

Safety: This is not the place to count your money on the street or leave your keys in your car. Although Harlem's reputation as a combat zone is overrated, it still remains one of the dicier neighborhoods in the city.

Entertainment: You can get a glimpse of jazz history at the long-standing Lenox Lounge and other such landmark establishments.

Restaurants: Sublime soul food like fried chicken and collard greens can be had most anywhere. Many people prefer the classic tastes of standbys like Sylvia's.

Parks & Gardens: Other than Central Park on Harlem's southern border, greenery here is hard to find, so many residents rely on the area's concrete basketball courts and playgrounds. The YMCA is one of the best-equipped of its kind in the country.

Shopping: Retail has been suffering for some time. The main thoroughfare, 125th Street, is full of stores selling sneakers and urban wear.

Final Words: Harlem is a historic neighborhood full of brownstones and turn-of-the-century tenements in various states of disrepair. Incredible fixer-uppers exist for the brave at heart, and one of these days the neighborhood is bound to go through a real estate renaissance.

HOBOKEN
◆ NEW JERSEY ◆

Hoboken is a funny town with a funny name. There it sits, doomed forever to stare across the river at its much bigger sister city, Manhattan. Though this New Jersey town has seen its share of ups and downs, it has recently become a popular low-cost alternative for would-be city dwellers looking for a place to live.

The city was actually the creation of a single developer and inventor, Colonel John Stevens, who bought the land that makes up Hoboken in 1784. Stevens marketed his young development as a resort, and important New Yorkers of all sorts began ferrying over to mingle at the town's posh yacht club. The Stevens family remained in control of Hoboken well into the 19th century, but eventually, they sold their lands to the new industrial businesses setting up shop in the area.

Hoboken became a major manufacturing center around the end of the 19th century, known mostly for shipbuilding. Immigrants began poured in, mostly from Germany, and this small New Jersey town became an important hub of transportation—not only connecting Manhattan to mainland America via train but also as a port for European steamships. The waterfront was booming with industry, travelers, restaurants and organized crime.

World War I put a major dent in this development. Anti-German sentiment led to the city's piers being shut down by the government and the city was put under martial law for a brief spell. The German families got the message and began giving up their stronghold on Hoboken. Italians quickly moved in to replace them, and it was during this era that Hoboken's favorite son, Frank Sinatra, was born.

Hoboken is one of the few spots on the Jersey side of the Hudson where the land is flat enough to support buildings all the way down to the water. Today, though, the waterfront is dead, and Hoboken has become a quiet commuter's town. Old guard residents have pulled up stakes and moved on to buy their dream homes, opening up the area to the next generation.

> "Everywhere outside New York City is Bridgeport, Connecticut."
>
> **FRED ALLEN**

Hoboken is a pleasant blend of not-quite-suburban but definitely-not-Manhattan, with a main strip full of shops, eateries, video stores and grocery stores. The neighborhoods are mostly Italian in origin, but with the recent influx of younger people from other parts of New Jersey and New York City, Hoboken's ethnic mix is diversifying. Hoboken dwellings most nearly resemble those in parts of Boston or Philadelphia, with each floor split into two good-sized one-bedroom apartments.

Residents have access to the best New York has to offer, but don't have to put up with the hassle, crowds and noise of Manhattan. Stores tend to cater to those with ample budgets, staying open late enough for commuters to get their errands done. This neighborhood is probably the best near New York if you have a car and wish to use it regularly, since free parking is plentiful.

Most locals are friendly, fairly trusting and relaxed. The singles and couples who live here, mostly in their 20s and 30s, like to go out and have fun, but aren't prepared to pay the rents that most Manhattan landlords demand. Most of Hoboken's inhabitants work hard and want to return to a relaxing and stress-free home. Everything is extremely quiet after about eight p.m., and even on the weekends it only gets busy on the main drag. Most residents own cars, and most have kids in the yard or on the way.

One common complaint that Hoboken residents have

THE PEOPLE

POPULATION	34,000
AGE	
0-17	15%
18-44	49%
45-64	15%
65+	12%
ETHNICITY	
White	79%
Black	6%
Asian	4%
Other	11%
Spanish speaking	30%
Family households	48%
College educated	44%
HOUSEHOLD INCOME	
Below $25,000	37%
$25-75,000	48%
$75-150,000	10%
$150,000+	5%

WWW.ZANYS.COM
Find a NYC apartment now!

THE NEIGHBORHOOD

AVERAGE MONTHLY RENT

Studio	$700-1,400
1 br	$900-1,800
2 br	$1,200-2,400
3 br	$1,500-3,000

AVERAGE SALE PRICE

Studio	$130,000-150,000
1 br	$150,000-350,000
2 br	$180,000-450,000
3 br	$200,000-600,000

COMMUTING

The PATH train runs to Hoboken from the World Trade Center or West 33rd Street.

DISTANCE

Time to midtown	35-40	min
Time to downtown	15-20	min

is that their Manhattan friends don't want to come out to Jersey to see them. Many New Yorkers definitely have some kind of aversion to New Jersey, but with a little persuading they can be coaxed into leaving their cramped, noisy, expensive joints for a more relaxed neighborhood, if only for a day or so. For all the jokes that people crack about New Jersey, Hoboken is a good blend of New York and the suburbs. The streets are very well-maintained, and older, recently renovated brownstones are common. Hoboken is proud of what it is and tends to attract tenants who are likewise happy to live here.

Noise: Practically none. Sirens are rare.

Parking: Excellent. You'll probably find something within a block of your house, especially before eight p.m. and in the morning, and it's usually for free.

Kids & Families: Hoboken is very safe and kid-friendly. This isn't a prime family area, however, and there really aren't that many kids around yet. This is likely to change in the next few years as newcomers start breeding.

Safety: Hoboken is very safe. About the only uniformed officers you're likely to see are those checking meters and giving out parking tickets.

Entertainment: There are a few bars and nightclubs in the area with Top-40 DJs or live bands. There's usually something going on throughout the week.

Restaurants: Mainly Italian or American—great if you love burgers and wings, but if you're looking for something more adventurous on a regular basis, you'll have to go further afield or (gasp!) into New York. Hoboken has an unusual mixture of Italian bakeries, nouveau diners and gourmet health-food shops.

Parks & Gardens: There aren't many parks around here, but the streets are fairly wide open, and with lots of trees.

Shopping: Hoboken caters to people with cash to spend on the more upscale things in life like health food and expensive knickknacks. Shopping for the necessities is easy, with lots of grocers, video stores and drugstores to choose from.

Final Words: Hoboken is for people looking to slow down, not speed up. As the population ages, the neighborhood's dynamics may change. As it is, Hoboken is a blend of urban and small town—some would say combining the best of both.

INWOOD
MANHATTAN

When it comes to neighborhoods, Inwood is quite possibly Manhattan's best-kept secret. Of course, the community is so far north that it hardly even seems like it's part of the island, and getting downtown to Manhattan's core can take a while. However, many New Yorkers are finding it worth the commute to live in lovely surroundings at such reasonable prices.

It was in Inwood that the infamous transaction between Native Americans and the Dutch took place, wherein the Indians sold Manhattan Island for approximately $24. At that time, this area was a lovely wilderness of cliffs perched over the Harlem and Hudson Rivers. Soon, the natives were forced out by Dutch and English settlers, eager to turn the fertile area into farmland. Inwood retained its rural atmosphere for the next couple of centuries; it was not until the IRT subway was extended into the neighborhood that major development took place. European immigrants quickly moved into newly built housing in an effort to escape Downtown's congestion. Throughout the 20th century, new waves of immigrants came to Inwood from all over the world. Today the area is home to a large Latin American population—mostly Dominicans, with a healthy splash of Cubans and Puerto Ricans. Inwood also has populations of Koreans, Soviet Jews and a few remnants of the earlier German Jewish settlers.

> "The skyline of New York is a monument of a splendor that no pyramids or palaces will ever equal or approach."
>
> **AYN RAND**

Inwood takes up the northernmost end of Manhattan Island, beginning at Dyckman Street (a.k.a. 200th Street). The streets here don't follow the strict grid found elsewhere in Manhattan, since they are based on early Indian trails. Most of the apartments were built in the early 20th century and are in reasonable condition. Some high-rises fill this mostly residential neighborhood, where developers were allowed to have their own way more than in the southerly regions of Manhattan. The area tends to be rather loud and boisterous at night, especially around busy streets.

Perhaps the best part of living in this neighborhood is the spectacular Inwood Hill Park. The park extends for 196 acres of natural wonders and is the only park in the city which features original forest lands. You can spend countless hours here and may forget completely that you're in New York City.

This up-and-coming area is changing as more Manhattanites hear raves about the cultural diversity, cheap rents and amazing views from the high-rises. Prices are still low, though, and those on a budget will love the convenience and the opportunity to live cheaply in Manhattan. Be forewarned that if you stay here for long, you may fall in love with Inwood's unique charms.

THE PEOPLE

POPULATION	42,000
AGE	
0-17	21%
18-44	50%
45-64	18%
65+	11%
ETHNICITY	
White	44%
Black	21%
Asian	3%
Other	32%
Spanish speaking	64%
Family households	64%
College educated	22%
HOUSEHOLD INCOME	
Below $25,000	51%
$25-75,000	42%
$75-150,000	6%
$150,000+	1%

Zanys.com user comments: Inwood Hill Park is "wonderful" and "one of the city's largest."

Noise: Unless you live right next to a park and away from other buildings, you'd better be prepared to buy earplugs or develop insomnia.

Parking: Finding a space can be tricky.

Kids & Families: The neighborhood isn't the safest in which to raise a family, but there are those gorgeous parks….

Safety: Safety can be an issue, especially in the outer corners of Inwood. Women in particular need to be cautious, especially at night. Break-ins are fairly common, but as long as you have bars on your windows, you should be fine.

Entertainment: None whatsoever, except for a few tame watering holes.

Restaurants: Local eateries serve mostly Latin and Jewish food.

Parks & gardens: Inwood Hill Park is one of New York's loveliest green spaces.

Shopping: You shouldn't have a problem finding groceries but will have to go downtown for anything fancy.

Final Words: Overall, Inwood offers great bang for your buck. Just remember that the bulk of Manhattan is quite far away, both in terms of geography and spirit.

THE NEIGHBORHOOD

AVERAGE MONTHLY RENT

Studio	$500-900
1 br	$700-1,200
2 br	$1,000-2,000
3 br	$1,500-2,200

AVERAGE SALE PRICE

Studio	$50,000-100,000
1 br	$65,000-150,000
2 br	$85,000-300,000
3 br	$120,000-500,000

COMMUTING

The A, 1 and 9 trains go to Inwood.

DISTANCE

Time to midtown	35-45	min
Time to downtown	45-50	min

JACKSON HEIGHTS
• QUEENS •

Most New Yorkers only catch brief glimpses of Jackson Heights on their ways in and out town via nearby LaGuardia Airport. Those who take the time to get to know the neighborhood, however, usually find themselves in for a pleasant surprise. Jackson Heights houses an ethnically diverse population in lovely garden apartments. Though the area has been through its share of ups and downs, it is currently undergoing a renaissance of sorts.

Bordered by Roosevelt Avenue to the east and 74th Street to the north, the neighborhood consists of many pre-war structures in an imposing Elizabethan architectural style concealing off-kilter apartments with landscaped courtyards, fireplaces and cathedral ceilings. It may come as a surprise that until the 20th century, Jackson Heights was known as the "Cornfield of Queens." Developer Edward A. MacDougall envisioned a way to turn corn into gold and began buying area farms in order to create a new community. In 1916, he created the Queensboro Development Corporation to begin building apartments in this new neighborhood. MacDougall favored garden apartments, which enclose a centralized courtyard area for residents to enjoy. When the IRT line arrived along Roosevelt Avenue, the area took off.

> "New York is an exciting town where something is happening all the time, most unsolved."
>
> **JOHNNY CARSON**

At one time or another, such luminaries as Charlie Chaplin and Carroll O'Connor called this neighborhood home, and Alfred Butts invented the game of Scrabble here with some help from his Jackson Heights neighbors at the Community Methodist Church. The area has been a refuge for asylum-seekers for decades, with many residents who fled sticky political situations in their home countries. Immigrants from Argentina and Cuba arrived in the 1960s, to be joined in the '80s by Colombians, Peruvians, Mexicans, Salvadorans and Ecuadorians.

Most recently, an influx of immigrants from India has moved into the neighborhood, and the street scene around 74th Street in Jackson Heights resembles an Indian bazaar. Ladies stroll about in gorgeous saris, and large families shop together for rice and ghee. Indian, Pakistani and Bangladeshi shoppers from up and down the East coast are drawn by hundreds of Indian retail businesses, including restaurants, grocery, jewelry and clothing shops.

Jackson Heights is known for its great, tacky, overcrowded shops. Bargains are plentiful, and you'll never cease to be surprised by what you find. Restaurants of all sorts are available to feed the most diverse of cravings. One of the neighborhood's best-known landmarks is The Jackson Heights Diner on 74th Street, which isn't a diner at all, but an extravaganza of cheap, yummy eateries from southern Indian that attracts gourmands from all over the city.

If you choose to live near the airport, the noise level is astounding and frequent, although many residents put up with it in exchange for cheap rents. Residents are very proud of their new community, and in many ways, Jackson Heights represents an opportunity to start afresh, while retaining a strong sense of the culture they left behind. The flow of people from around the world into the neighborhood is likely to continue adding excitement to this once quiet farming community.

Noise: Try to live out of the flight path of LaGuardia airport if you can.

Parking: Parking is good here, although it's not recommended that you keep your sports car visible.

Kids & Families: There are a lot of children here, and most are bilingual. If you have children and want them to learn Spanish, this is a good place to raise them.

Safety: The cops have a somewhat standoffish attitude with the neighborhood, given that many of the residents view men in uniform with extreme suspicion. In general, residents feel safe, although women probably shouldn't walk around alone after ten pm, and the neighborhood has had some problems with drugs.

Entertainment: Jackson Heights has some lovely local pubs and bars, but formal entertainment is lacking here.

Restaurants: This area boasts many notable restaurants, including La Pequena Colombia and The Jackson Diner. You can find whatever suits your fancy—including Thai, Filipino, Peruvian and Uruguayan eateries.

THE PEOPLE

POPULATION	58,000
AGE	
0-17	16%
18-44	45%
45-64	23%
65+	16%
ETHNICITY	
White	64%
Black	4%
Asian	17%
Other	15%
Spanish speaking	43%
Family households	59%
College educated	28%
HOUSEHOLD INCOME	
Below $25,000	39%
$25-75,000	52%
$75-150,000	5%
$150,000+	4%

WWW.ZANYS.COM
Find a NYC apartment now!

THE NEIGHBORHOOD

Studio	$700-1,000
1 br	$900-1,200
2 br	$1,000-1,800
3 br	$1,300-2,400

AVERAGE SALE PRICE

Studio	$55,000-65,000
1 br	$75,000-100,000
2 br	$80,000-150,000
3 br	$90,000-300,000

COMMUTING

The 7 train local goes to 82nd Street.
The E, F, G, N and R stop at Roosevelt
Avenue station.

DISTANCE

Time to midtown	25-40	min
Time to downtown	40-60	min

Parks & Gardens: Jackson Heights has so many gardens that parks are superfluous, but Travers Park is nearby and colorful.

Shopping: Shopping is plentiful here, consisting mainly of ethnic clothing, perfume, clothing and ties. For food shopping, the ethnic shops and bodegas can't be beat.

Final Words: Jackson Heights is a trip down memory lane, to a time when greenery abounded and you could actually have a view out your window. It's a community committed to revitalizing itself, so be prepared to lend a helping hand if you should decide to call Jackson Heights home.

JAMAICA
QUEENS

Jamaica, Queens is a city in its own right, and in fact, officially was its own city until the consolidation of New York's five boroughs in 1898. In fact, Jamaica was at one time the British capital of the entire colony of New York. Unfortunately, the area has not fared particularly well in the second half of the twentieth century, and Jamaica has become a rather depressing example of gradual urban decay. However, the neighborhood remains a vital community with a large, constantly fluctuating immigrant population.

Jamaica has been an important crossroads for centuries. What is today Jamaica Avenue, began as a Canarsie Indian trail, has always been an important link between Long Island and Manhattan. British settlers founded the town and named it Jamaica, apparently mispronouncing the Indian word "Ahmeco," which means "beaver."

When Queens was established as a colonial county, Jamaica became the county seat and was indeed the capital of New York for a short time. The area was a prosperous farming and cattle-raising community, and one of the founding fathers, Constitution-signer Rufus King, had a grand country estate in Jamaica, which still stands as a museum today. It wasn't until the late 19th century that shops began popping up along the busy thoroughfares of Jamaica; however, it didn't take long for the town to become the commercial center for all of Queens. The completion of the Sutphin Boulevad "El" in 1913 brought in even more business. Jamaica boasted grand moviehouses and premiere shopping centers that were the state-of-the-art in their day. However, this heyday did not last long. The underground subways replaced the "El" and the introduction of shopping malls meant the beginning of the end for Jamaica's commercial preeminence.

WWW.ZANYS.COM
Find a NYC apartment now!

Jamaica comprises a large area, though the downtown area is centered around Jamaica Avenue. Jamaica is located south of Union Turnpike and east of the Van Wyck Expressway. The fringes of the Jamaica area are largely suburban and more well-kept than downtown. The area around Jamaica Avenue still bustles, but today hardly any of the area's 1920s grandeur remains. Past the discount shops and restaurants of the downtown area are seemingly endless rows of rather dirty, dismal-looking apartment buildings. Jamaica has become a sprawling urban landscape of mostly grim strip malls and low-cost housing. All the businesses appear to be run-down and covered in a veil of dirt.

However, many residents of the community are trying to improve Jamaica. The Jamaica Center for Arts and Learning and CUNY's York College are just two of a number of academic and cultural institutions in the area. An attractive, multi-ethnic Farmer's Market has been established downtown in part to sell food and in part as a community center. Likewise, some care has been taken to preserve the historic landmarks along Jamaica Avenue, including some beautiful 19th century churches.

Jamaica may never return to its economic and political glory days, but there is some hope that the neighborhood may be revitalized in years to come. The neighborhood may still pull through, but Jamaica has a long way to go.

Noise: The commercial streets can be quite loud and noisy, but in the residential areas, noise should not be a problem.

Parking: You will find plenty of places to park on the street, in lots or in large garages.

Kids & Families: Unless you head out away from the downtown area towards nicer, suburban neighborhoods, this is probably not an ideal spot for families. The parks are not particularly appealing, and you may have problems finding a safe place for your children to play.

Safety: Safety should not be much of a problem downtown in the daytime, when the area is bustling with people. However, watch out at night and in more secluded areas.

Entertainment: You'll find different cultural events popping up from time to time in the area. There are a few bars, but they are not very welcoming and might be a little scary for a woman by herself.

Restaurants: Jamaica has every kind of fast food, as well as an array of different ethnic cuisines. Just don't

THE PEOPLE

POPULATION	60,000
AGE	
0-18	27%
18-64	61%
65+	12%
ETHNICITY	
White	7%
Black	84%
Asian	4%
Spanish speaking	9%
Family households	35%
College educated	16%
HOUSEHOLD INCOME	
Below $25,000	38%
$25-40,000	23%
$40-60,000	20%
$60,000+	19%

WWW.ZANYS.COM
Find a NYC apartment now!

expect any fine dining, and you should be happy.

Parks & Gardens: King Park is situated near Jamaica Avenue. It features Rufus King's 18th century house, but is otherwise a rather run-down spot, where you'll see more menacing adults than frolicking children.

THE NEIGHBORHOOD

AVERAGE MONTHLY RENT

Studio	$300-700
1 br	$600-900
2 br	$800-1,200
3 br	$1,100-1,300

AVERAGE SALE PRICE

Studio	$30,000-45,000
1 br	$45,000-65,000
2 br	$50,000-80,000
3 br	$50,000-95,000

COMMUTING

The E, J and Z trains stop at Jamaica Center. The F train stops at Jamaica and 179th street.

DISTANCE

Time to midtown	30-50	min
Time to downtown	45-60	min

Shopping: Though its shopping heyday is over, you will still find quite a few shopping centers in Jamaica, including a couple malls and plenty of groceries.

Final Words: New York is constantly changing, but sadly, Jamaica has not changed for the better in the past fifty years. Revitalization is a slow process, but with new immigrants arriving here every year, nothing in this neighborhood will stay the same for long.

JERSEY CITY
• NEW JERSEY •

Some sympathy for Jersey City, please. Not only is the town totally eclipsed by its much larger, more important neighbor, but New Yorkers add insult to injury everyday with their countless putdowns and potshots aimed at the good folk of New Jersey. It is only an accident of geography and history that has kept New Jersey in New York's shadow for the past centuries. Today, Jersey City is getting a little bit of a revenge as an ever-growing number of Manhattanites are lured across the Hudson by the promise of more space for less rent.

In fact, it was New York speculators who originally founded Jersey City in 1804. Previously, the area had been the site of a British fort, which American General Henry Lee captured during the Revolutionary War. The town became a hub of transportation when the first railroad came to Jersey City in 1834. When Morris Canal was built to connect Jersey City to Newark, development really took off, and the next century was filled with a steady increase in industry and population.

However, in the mid-20th century, many of the dominant manufacturing industries moved away, and residents began migrating further inland to more welcoming suburbs. By the 1980s, Jersey City was in a period of major economic decline. Since then, however, many financial and real estate offices have been attracted to the city. Today, Jersey City's waterfront is full of expensive new office space and residential space, like a

> "A New Yorker looks to Neil Simon for cheering-up, Sigmund Freud for shocks of recognition and Sir Thomas Moore for Utopia."
>
> **NEW YORK TIMES EDITORIAL ON THE MOST FREQUENTLY STOLEN BOOKS FROM THE NEW YORK PUBLIC LIBRARY**

corcoran.com

For real estate
all around town,
we've got you covered.

the *corcoran* group gets results.
To feature your home on
real estate's hottest web site,
simply fill out the back of this
postcard and drop it in the mail.

where do you want to live?
corcoran.com
355-3550

☐ Please showcase my property on *corcoran*.com.

Name

Daytime Phone #   E-mail

Address/Property for Sale

No. of Rooms   Square Feet   No. of Bedrooms   No. of Baths

Special Features

Asking Price   Maintenance or CC   Taxes

☐ Please provide me with a complimentary market evaluation
   of my home.

☐ Please have a *corcoran* group representative contact me.

PLACE
STAMP
HERE

the *corcoran* group
660 Madison Avenue FL 11
New York, NY 10021-8405

miniature reflection of Manhattan's Financial District, which lies across the water.

Jersey City sits on a peninsula formed by the Hudson and Hackensack Rivers and New York and Newark Bays. Residents can easily travel to New York via the Holland tunnel or PATH train, which will get commuters to the World Trade Center in 15-20 minutes. Apartments on the waterfront feature gorgeous views of downtown Manhattan and the Statue of Liberty. Anyone can enjoy the views from Liberty State Park, which is even connected by ferry to Ellis Island and Lady Liberty, herself.

Jersey City contains a cross-section of two groups: emerging yuppie types and blue-collar workers, most of whom grew up in the area. Life moves at a slower pace on this side of the river, and as New Yorkers love to point out, residents aren't always as trendy as their Manhattan counterparts. For some who feel lost in the kaleidoscope of Manhattan style, this is a welcome reminder of what America is really like. Others find themselves longing for New York's hip yet tasteful displays of affluence. Jersey City is generally more middle-aged than its neighbor Hoboken; you'll see more families and can expect a more leisurely way of life. You should be able to find all the necessary amenities and then some, although it can be a bit of a walk to groceries and shops. Jersey City is built on a more sprawling, suburban scale than Manhattan, and most residents own their own cars.

Jersey City is becoming increasingly popular as a cheap alternative to Manhattan. People making the move across the Hudson include young professionals strapped for rent money as well as parents looking for a more family-friendly spot for the kids. Still, this is New Jersey, so you shouldn't have to worry too much about rents skyrocketing as they do when Manhattan neighborhoods rise in popularity. If you think Jersey City's the place for you, you will probably be able to find a reasonably priced apartment with much less difficulty than on that over priced island across the river.

THE PEOPLE

POPULATION	229,000
AGE	
0-17	30%
18-44	45%
45-64	15%
65+	10%
ETHNICITY	
White	48%
Black	30%
Asian	12%
Other	10%
Spanish speaking	24%
Family households	83%
College educated	25%
HOUSEHOLD INCOME	
Below $25,000	44%
$25-75,000	48%
$75-150,000	4%
$150,000+	4%

Noise: You shouldn't have any problems here.
Parking: There's parking everywhere, and most folks have their own cars. Also, New Jersey drivers usually don't have the cutthroat attitude of their New York counterparts.
Kids & Families: This is a popular spot for families looking for a laid back alternative to the big city.

WWW.ZANYS.COM
Find a NYC apartment now!

THE NEIGHBORHOOD

AVERAGE MONTHLY RENT

Studio	$500-1,500
1 br	$800-1,800
2 br	$1,100-2,400
3 br	$1,500-3,500

AVERAGE SALE PRICE

Studio	$75,000-130,000
1 br	$80,000-200,000
2 br	$90,000-350,000
3 br	$100,000-450,000

COMMUTING

If you don't have a car and don't want to take a shuttle bus home every day from the subway, you may find the distances daunting. The PATH train has wait times on the weekend, but it's significantly cheaper than the Long Island Railroad.

DISTANCE

Time to midtown	35-45	min
Time to downtown	15-25	min

Safety: Don't forget to use your New York street smarts, even over here in New Jersey. Although the city's relatively safe, residents should be especially careful walking around the empty streets at night.

Entertainment: There are lots of video stores and some nice movie theaters.

Parks & Gardens: Many houses have gardens and Liberty State Park is nearby.

Shopping: You can find everything you need here and indulge in the greatest pleasure New Jersey has to offer— the mall.

Final Words: For many who can't afford Manhattan rents, Jersey City is a pleasant alternative. Some yuppies are enchanted by the views of the Manhattan skyline, but others can't put up with living on the city's sidelines.

KEW GARDENS

• QUEENS •

Entering the neighborhood of Kew Gardens in Queens is like stepping out of New York City into an English country village—or at least some early twentieth century real estate developer's idea of what an English country village should look like. The Medieval-style storefronts and faux-Tudor cottages are a distinctly American attempt to create Old World atmosphere. Yet whatever it lacks in authenticity, Kew Gardens more than makes up for in genuine small-town charm.

Kew Gardens was originally the site of the Richmond Hill Golf Club. When the golf club closed in 1909, brothers Arthur and Alrick Man developed the area and named it after Great Britain's Royal Botanical Gardens in Kew. The Mans carefully created an exclusive neighborhood of large, expensive houses on winding, tree-lined streets. As the years went by, some apartment high-rises were built on the busier streets, along with commercial businesses. However, the Mans' designs for Kew Gardens remains largely intact.

Will Rodgers once called Kew Gardens home, as well as Rodney Dangerfield and UN Secretary-General Ralph Bunche, whose home is now a national landmark. The area gained unfortunate notoriety in the 1960s when Kitty Genovese was murdered on Austin Street. The incident brought national attention to this quiet neighborhood when it was revealed that dozens of neighbors had witnessed the crime but no one had taken any action to help the victim. However, that was long ago, and Kew Gardens has since regained its reputation as a safe, neighborly community.

Kew Gardens is located between Forest Park and Maple Grove Cemetery to the south of Flushing Meadows Corona Park. The neighborhood is bounded by Queens Boulevard, Lefferts Boulevard, Metropolitan Avenue and

Union Turnpike. Residents have easy access to the E and F subway lines, as well as the Long Island Rail Road.

There really are gardens here and lots of trees. All the houses are large and have nice, big yards to match. Boulevards of trees line the streets, which are all very clean and attractive, and the neighborhood borders the lovely Forest Park. In the small "downtown" commercial area, you will find cute cafés, markets, and an art-house cinema. Everything is on a small, friendly scale—people even say "hi" to one another as they walk down the street.

The houses represent a variety of early twentieth-century styles, but almost all are in lovely condition. The Tudor Revival style is quite prevalent, in both the houses

THE PEOPLE

POPULATION	58,700
AGE	
0-18	25%
18-64	66%
65+	9%
ETHNICITY	
White	63%
Black	18%
Asian	19%
Spanish speaking	26%
Family households	33%
College educated	17%
HOUSEHOLD INCOME	
Below $25,000	31%
$25-40,000	22%
$40-60,000	19%
$60,000+	28%

and strip malls of the commercial area. Most of the neighborhood's large apartment buildings date from the 1920s and remain attractive and well-kept. This neighborhood has not changed much in the past 80 years and shows no signs of changing anytime soon.

Noise: Kew Gardens is exceptionally quiet. Few cars drive through the residential streets, and everyone stays nice and quiet within their own homes.

Parking: Most people have their own driveways, but you will find plenty of space on the street or in lots.

Kids & Families: This is a great neighborhood for families. Kids have yards in which to play and streets on which they can feel safe walking.

Safety: The neighborhood is quite safe. At night, most everything shuts down, and people head to their own homes.

THE NEIGHBORHOOD

AVERAGE MONTHLY RENT

Studio	$900-1,100
1 br	$1,100-1,400
2 br	$1,300-2,400
3 br	$1,600-2,800

AVERAGE SALE PRICE

Studio	$50,000-70,000
1 br	$80,000-90,000
2 br	$90,000-200,000
3 br	$100,000-500,000

COMMUTING

The E and F trains stop at Kew Gardens and Union Turnpike.

DISTANCE

Time to midtown	30-45 min
Time to downtown	40-55 min

WWW.ZANYS.COM
Find a NYC apartment now!

Entertainment: You won't find much to do here at night, although there is a lovely movie theater, the Kew Gardens Cinema, which features a variety of independent, revival and mainstream films. There are a couple of "taverns," notably Austin's Ale House, which feature the largest variety of beer in Queens.

Restaurants: The selection is rather small, but you will find some nice options. There are a couple cute coffee shops, such as the Bliss Gourmet and some larger restaurants as well.

Parks & Gardens: Most folks have their own yards and gardens, but for those who don't Forest Park is right here and Flushing Meadows Corona Park is nearby, too.

Shopping: The commercial area has a couple supermarkets and drug stores, as well as specialty meat markets and bakeries.

Final Words: Kew Gardens is a lovely place for a family to settle down, but only as long as you are looking for small town charm rather than big city excitement.

LINCOLN CENTER AREA
→ MANHATTAN ←

Everyone has at least heard of Lincoln Center and knows it as one of the world's most famous locations for music and theater. But this is not the extent of what can be found here. If you are a true *artiste* at heart, the opportunities in this neighborhood are guaranteed to have your creative juices pumping. With musical and theatrical performances literally right outside your doorstep, how could you not be happy when there is so much going on here?

The boundaries of this neighborhood are a little hard to define, but it is basically situated between 57th and 66th Streets west of 5th Avenue. Since it is typically not known as a residential area, finding a place to live is a bit of a task. The living spaces are limited to generic looking buildings that are clustered in between all of the commercial establishments. Though the exteriors aren't beautiful, the interiors are quite spacious and modern. The infrastructure is left over from the 1970s, resulting in many tacky fountains, ferns, rocks and other adornments in the entryways. With Central Park nearby, some of the views here are the best in New York, but of course you will have to pay an exorbitant rent to see the park right from your apartment.

Residents here are typically stiff and middle-aged or older, including many who have recently retired from the entertainment business. They live in the area because it is comfortable, and all of their favorite entertainment spots are practically around the corner. Just like show biz itself, the residences tend to be exclusive, and the neighborhood has many social circles that aren't looking for change. If you are super-friendly and looking for a place where you can easily befriend your neighbors, you might be a little disappointed by the attitude here.

Those lucky enough to afford apartments here hardly have to leave the neighborhood. Everything you could ever want can be found within walking distance. On a commercial level, the area is hard to beat. There are shops and restaurants galore, and foot traffic at all hours of the day. Central Park is only a block away, and there is always a bevy of interesting characters perusing the area, such as homeless people, schizophrenics, exercise freaks and couples who seem to swear by PDAs. But you won't know how fortunate you are to have the park at your fingertips until you have one of those days when you can't stand the chaos of the city and need an escape. If you are stressed out, there is no better way to relax than by strolling into the park and communing with nature. Ok, it's not much of a forest, but it's as natural as New York gets.

> "The eternal man in the street says the street's no place for anyone anymore."
>
> NEW YORK TIMES EDITORIAL ON A SERIES OF UNPROVOKED ASSAULTS

For those looking to feel the cultural wealth of New York without the often annoying avant-garde and trendy qualities of most downtown neighborhoods, Lincoln Center is a perfect choice. You can expect to pay a lot for concert tickets, and apartments around here don't come cheap, either. Apparently, culture and refinement cost a lot.

Noise: During the day it's extremely hectic, but once the sun goes down a lot of the noise disappears.

Parking: There is no street parking whatsoever since Broadway runs right through the neighborhood. Garages are hard to find also, unless your building provides one.

Kids & Families: There are hardly any kids around, although it is a really safe place to raise them.

Safety: It is safe here, but don't travel alone at night since it is slightly more deserted after sunset.

Entertainment: Life doesn't get better than this. Plus, the Theater District is within walking distance.

Restaurants: There are some great, really expensive

THE PEOPLE

POPULATION	58,000
AGE	
0-17	9%
18-44	51%
45-64	20%
65+	20%
ETHNICITY	
White	87%
Black	7%
Asian	3%
Other	3%
Spanish speaking	9%
Family households	31%
College educated	68%
HOUSEHOLD INCOME	
Below $25,000	26%
$25-75,000	44%
$75-150,000	15%
$150,000+	15%

THE NEIGHBORHOOD

AVERAGE MONTHLY RENT

Studio	$1,400-2,000
1 br	$1,600-2,500
2 br	$3,000-4,800
3 br	$3,500+

AVERAGE SALE PRICE

Studio	$125,000-300,000
1 br	$210,000-500,000
2 br	$500,000-1,200,000
3 br	$600,000-1,200,000+

COMMUTING

The A, C, E, 1 and 9 trains all run through this small neighborhood. Buses are extremely helpful, and there are many that stop at locations all over midtown and downtown.

DISTANCE

Time to midtown	5-10 min
Time to downtown	20-25 min

places, but for something lighter and more casual, head further uptown.

Parks & Gardens: Two words: Central Park.

Shopping: Mainly brand-name retailers like Barnes & Noble and the Gap are here. Not higher-end stuff but definitely functional and mid-budget.

Final Words: If one word can describe this neighborhood: it would be "cosmopolitan." Those who long for an uptown environment (and can afford one) may want to try living here.

LITTLE ITALY
· MANHATTAN ·

Most people have a mental image of what Little Italy looks like—lots of vibrant people running around on the streets, food vendors galore and romance everywhere. If you want to experience this sort of environment firsthand, sans mobsters and the Godfather himself, Little Italy is the place to go.

One of New York's most popular tourist destinations, Little Italy has a charm that dates to the latter part of the 19th century, when a large wave of immigrants from Southern Europe settled in what was then a dirty, crime-ridden section of the city. A strong, self-sufficient community full of blue-collar workers rose from the slums on the strength of its native culture, introducing Italian food, character and style to the Manhattan landscape.

As immigrants began to assimilate into their new-found culture, the neighborhood slowly evolved from its blue-collar beginnings. As the population grew, many residents sought out more space in the Bronx, Brooklyn and Queens. Today's Little Italy exists as a tribute to this little-altered way of life, even if the neighborhood has seen better days.

The four north-south streets that comprise Little Italy—Mulberry, Mott, Elizabeth and Baxter—are lined with beautiful brick buildings built near the turn-of-the-century along cobblestone streets. The ubiquitous fire escapes are the result of laws passed in the 19th century after several fires destroyed large parts of the neighborhood and killed trapped residents in the buildings.

The majority of these structures are six-story walk-ups, although some have been renovated to include elevators and other modern conveniences. Interiors are typically accented with gorgeous details like fine wood moldings, marble floors and steel window frames. Rooms in most apartments range from small to modest, with only minimal space accorded for bathrooms and kitchens. Despite the small windows, most spaces receive lots of light since there aren't many large buildings around. Many of the streets are lined with small trees and adorable street lamps.

Sight, sound and smell—Little Italy is a delicious surprise for all of your senses. On weekend nights, its streets are mobbed with tourists from around the world delighting in the area's dozens of Italian restaurants. On warm evenings, diners can eat on sidewalk patios and pretend they're in Florence. Most New Yorkers, though, know these restaurants as tourist traps and do their best to avoid them.

Nonstop tourism means street congestion is a way of life. Residents in the neighborhood often complain of noise throughout the evening as waiters aggressively court patrons on the sidewalks. It might be easy to avoid the waiters, but the aroma from within the espresso bars and pastry shops claim many victims.

Hipsters and aspiring artists have recently rediscovered Little Italy as a wonderful place to live. The neighborhood's central location provides easy access to almost anywhere in downtown Manhattan. New venues and non-touristy restaurants and bars have been creeping into the neighborhood for some time. Rents are manageable, but be prepared to live in cramped quarters. Living rooms usually disappear when apartments are divided up among renters. Many newcomers choose to share two bedrooms among three people, with one person occupying what would otherwise be the living room.

Older Italian-Americans who still live here take a lighthearted, enthusiastic attitude to dealing with the crowds. Longtime locals appreciate the recent attention given to the neighborhood they love and enjoy the fact that many gems, like the Mott Street Church, the bar Mare Chiaro and markets like the Italian Food Center, still exist. It might be overrun with tourists at times, but Little Italy is still a far cry from Times Square.

Noise: Some delivery trucks, car alarms and restaurants create noise, but it's usually acceptable. The higher your apartment is above the street, the better. In the touristy

THE PEOPLE

POPULATION	23,000
AGE	
0-17	19%
18-44	46%
45-64	26%
65+	9%
ETHNICITY	
White	37%
Black	5%
Asian	58%
Spanish speaking	11%
Family households	38%
College educated	42%
HOUSEHOLD INCOME	
Below $25,000	17%
$25-75,000	52%
$75-150,000	30%
$150,000+	1%

parts of the neighborhood, street-level noise can be annoying. Careful telling anyone to be quiet, though, as you might end up with a fat lip.

Parking: Residents compete for a very limited number of spaces. Owning a car or bringing one here on the weekends is a bad idea.

Kids & Families: Most families left for greener pastures a full generation ago—these spaces are just too darn small and antiquated to raise families. Also, with escalating rents, even a modest two-bedroom place can be hard to afford. Kids won't find many local playmates.

Safety: Older residents go to bed early and so are not that helpful in spotting criminal activity. In keeping with

THE NEIGHBORHOOD

AVERAGE MONTHLY RENT

Studio	$1,100-1,600
1 br	$1,600-2,000
2 br	$1,800-2,700
3 br	$2,300-3,500

AVERAGE SALE PRICE

Studio	$170,000-300,000
1 br	$200,000-400,000
2 br	$250,000-600,000
3 br	$350,000-900,000

COMMUTING

The 6 train stops at Spring Street, the B, D, F and Q trains stop at Broadway-Lafayette Streets, and the J and M trains stop at Bowery Street.

DISTANCE

Time to midtown	10-15 min
Time to downtown	5-10 min

tradition, women are rarely seen walking alone at night. Streets have recently become even safer thanks to new nightspots opening in Nolita. Your biggest worry will be pickpockets.

Entertainment: The Little Italy nightlife is all about eating. Take a seat at one of the outdoor cafes or ristorantes and enjoy the people-watching as well as the enormous portions that Little Italy is famous for. In September, be sure to play some carnival games at the world famous San Genarro festival. The underground oasis Double Happiness is a yuppie watering hole in an old Prohibition-era speakeasy. Mare Chiaro is a perfect bar to enjoy a cigar and a scotch.

Restaurants: Until recently, Italian food was all that could be had in the neighborhood. Long-time residents know to avoid tourist traps in the southern part of Little

Italy, heading instead to the quality dining and selection found in next door Soho. Others stick to standards like the submarines at the Italian Food Center or the pizzas at Lombardi's. If you are craving the ideal Italian dining experience, Puglia's Ristorante makes the red, white and green flag proud.

Parks & Gardens: Local green space is nonexistent. Basketball courts can be found at Sara D. Roosevelt Park between Chrystie and Forsyth Streets.

Shopping: Hip fashions and accessories can be purchased in nearby Nolita boutiques.

Final Words: New York's reputation for unfriendliness can be redeemed by the guaranteed friendly people you are bound to find in Little Italy. It is a charming choice for couples or singles who don't have a family on the horizon. Its location and antique character are two of Little Italy's strongest selling points, balanced by small accommodations and tourist traffic.

LONG ISLAND CITY
• QUEENS •

There is one location in New York where you can get a full view of the entire Manhattan skyline from virtually any building—Long Island City. Real estate is booming at the moment with plenty of New Yorkers eager to take advantage of the views and excellent location. In the 19th century, Long Island City was once a full-fledged city and today it still retains its charm from a hundred years past. As the most high-profile neighborhood in Queens, it is both a residential and industrial haven, making it the most popular place in the borough.

The area forms a triangular shape on the western tip of Queens, bounded by the East River, Vernon Boulevard and Jackson Avenue. Residents here tend to be young creative types, beginning professionals and students, all of whom share one common goal: to make their homes as unique as possible. Most are drawn to the neighborhood because of the views, the enormous amount of cheap space and the opportunity to independently design their own living space. With so many available apartments and lofts here, it is a great place for people who don't have a lot of time to do an apartment search. There are also many former industrial warehouses that tenants have transformed into permanent residences.

Current inhabitants are thrilled that their beloved area has not yet been discovered by wealthier yuppies. As a result of Long Island City's relative unfamiliarity, there is a tremendous lack of commercial establishments. Restaurants, coffee shops and even diners are virtually impossible to find, and the ones that do exist are mostly

THE PEOPLE

POPULATION	61,000
AGE	
0-17	14%
18-44	48%
45-64	21%
65+	9%
ETHNICITY	
White	70%
Black	9%
Asian	12%
Other	9%
Spanish speaking	25%
Family households	56%
College educated	24%
HOUSEHOLD INCOME	
Below $25,000	44%
$25-75,000	50%
$75-150,000	5%
$150,000+	1%

WWW.ZANYS.COM
Find a NYC apartment now!

accessible by car.

Long Island City can be considered Manhattan's more avant-garde cousin. There are many landmarks that demonstrate the eccentricity of the area, such as the Socrates Sculpture Park that is home to some of New York's most provocative sculptures. Most famously it is the location of P.S. 1, a former public school that has been transformed into an artistic haven, with exhibit halls and classrooms. There is also an attached museum that displays some of the city's wackiest art.

Perhaps the most unique characteristic of Long Island City is its incredibly open landscape, attributable to the low story buildings. Unlike most cramped New York neighborhoods, there is a definite sense of spaciousness here. Just like the atmosphere, the residents here are also liberal and they pride themselves on it.

Many people claim that New York is beginning to

THE NEIGHBORHOOD

AVERAGE MONTHLY RENT

Studio	$600-900
1 br	$800-1,100
2 br	$1,000-1,700
3 br	$1,300-2,200

AVERAGE SALE PRICE

Studio	$50,000-70,000
1 br	$50,000-100,000
2 br	$55,000-150,000
3 br	$60,000-250,000

COMMUTING

The 7 train runs to Queensborough Plaza, and the E, F and G trains run to Jackson Avenue.

DISTANCE

Time to midtown	25-30	min
Time to downtown	15-20	min

become homogenous, which is why artists are getting out while they can. Although there are currently many real estate options in Long Island City, it won't last too much longer as more and more people find out about this uncovered secret. There is something truly special about the neighborhood that will never be diminished, despite the multitude of dirt and rundown buildings. But if you are a true artist, don't let a little filth stop you from creating the home of your dreams.

Noise: The only real noise comes from the subway.

Parking: Really easy to find since most people here don't use cars.

Kids & Families: Families are drawn here because of the space, even though the school system is a little behind.

Safety: Never travel alone since the area has a completely industrial facade.

Entertainment: The P. S. 1 Museum, and that's about it.

Restaurants: You'll find a few good ethnic spots around here, but choices are still limited.

Parks & Gardens: Long Island City has a great waterfront park with a view of the city.

Shopping: This isn't the best place to spend money, but expect at least the basics.

Final Words: Long Island City is definitely an acquired taste, but those who dig it absolutely love it and never want to leave.

LOWER EAST SIDE
MANHATTAN

he Lower East Side has changed a lot since its days as a teeming immigrant slum. Still, the turn-of-the-century image of tenements and urban squalor persists. Luckily, for this revitalized neighborhood, Manhattan's out-of-control real estate market is finally causing people to forget this old stereotype, and many who move here are finding themselves pleasantly surprised with their new digs.

WWW.ZANYS.COM
Find a NYC apartment now!

During the 1880s, religious persecution caused Russian and Polish Jews to immigrate to New York City. When they arrived, they were not as pleasantly greeted as they expected, as many Americans looked down upon them as uninvited guests. Eventually, they found their niche in the cramped but nevertheless cozy confines of the Lower East Side. The area became a vital working-class neighborhood, although living conditions were less than pleasant. During the 1920s-1930s, the Lower East Side had one of the highest population densities in the entire world. But after a while, inhabitants became fed up with their working class status and held many labor strikes to try and better their conditions.

The area bounded by Houston and Division Streets between the East River and the Bowery has significantly improved since the days of its Jewish forefathers, but it is still a little run down compared to wealthier New York neighborhoods. For some people, this sort of shabby chic is what makes the neighborhood so desirable. It is regarded as an affordable alternative to its downtown neighbors such as Soho and Tribeca.

As a general rule, buildings on the Lower East Side are six story walk-ups with apartments that are so small that it is common to find the bathtub in the kitchen! A lot of the living spaces here are not in good shape, to say the least. Yet despite these physical setbacks, the neighborhood has been infused with a younger crowd that is completely rejuvenating the area.

Since the Lower East Side's reinvigoration, many new bars, cafés, performance spaces and boutiques have begun popping up. These sorts of establishments are super trendy, so there's no telling how long they'll be around for. Some things are more old-fashioned and dependable, like the old-time vendors on Orchard Street, who still sell everything from fruit to hand-knit clothing.

"Everybody ought to have a Lower East Side in their life."

IRVING BERLIN

One unavoidable problem in the neighborhood is the lack of nearby public transportation. The only convenient way to get uptown is via the F train, but the stations are

THE PEOPLE

POPULATION	58,000
AGE	
0-17	22%
18-44	45%
45-64	23%
65+	10%
ETHNICITY	
White	59%
Black	33%
Asian	8%
Spanish speaking	42%
Family households	31%
College educated	21%
HOUSEHOLD INCOME	
Below $25,000	43%
$25-75,000	42%
$75-150,000	13%
$150,000+	2%

usually a hike from any Lower East Side location as they lie on the utmost northern boundary. The neighborhood certainly has a lot of drawbacks, but rents remain refreshingly low by Manhattan standards. You'd better believe it is a real treasure, one that many people find quite comfortable.

Noise: During the early morning, trucks are extremely loud and annoying, and at night the streets are usually packed with people. You'd better buy a set of earplugs if you ever want to sleep.

Parking: Given the narrowness of the streets, parking is extremely hard unless you're lucky enough to get a space in one of the neighborhood's sporadic garages.

Kids & Families: Not a good place to raise a family since living conditions are so cramped.

Safety: Giuliani has managed to up the cop quota here, making it a lot safer than it used to be. But don't travel alone and avoid traveling near the river after dusk.

Entertainment: The Lower East Side has recently become a hot late-night destination.

Restaurants: In the old days, the Lower East Side was dominated by Jewish gems like Ratners, Katz's and Russ and Daughters. Nowadays these legends have been joined by a host of young clubs, bars and restaurants that attract a younger crowd.

Parks & Gardens: Run-down Seward Park on the Lower East Side's south end provides residents with basketball and handball courts as well as a place to hang out. Your better bet is the East River Park, which sports green space, tennis courts and open amphitheaters.

THE NEIGHBORHOOD

AVERAGE MONTHLY RENT

Studio	$1,100-1,400
1 br	$1,200-2,000
2 br	$2,000-3,300
3 br	$3,400-3,700

AVERAGE SALE PRICE

Studio	$175,000-200,000
1 br	$250,000-300,000
2 br	$300,000-500,000
3 br	$400,000-900,000

COMMUTING

The F train stops at Delancey Street and 2nd Avenue, and the J, M and Z trains stop at the Delancey/ Essex station.

DISTANCE

Time to midtown	15-20	min
Time to downtown	5-10	min

Shopping: Blending old with the new, the Lower East Side has become one of the most unique shopping areas in all of Manhattan. Everything from hip boutiques to pickle stores can be found here.

Final Words: If you don't mind not having everything handed to you on a silver platter, then you will find the Lower East Side quite appealing. It is one of the best places for young people who want to be able to work and party all in one vicinity.

MIDTOWN CENTRAL
• MANHATTAN •

So you want to be right in the middle of things? Midtown Central is the literal middle of the world's busiest city. There is not a more central address than this. Everything you could ever imagine is right here, from huge department stores to world-famous restaurants to Central Park, which for some people is either a dream come true or a veritable nightmare.

As is true of most neighborhood beginnings, Midtown Central was not always a prestigious address. Around 1900, the area was an absolute war zone, messy, muddy and chaotic. But then rich folks like the Astors and Vanderbilts started to take over the neighborhood, building glamorous apartment buildings, immediately placing it at the top of everyone's real estate hot list.

Extending from Central Park South between 42nd and 59th streets, Midtown Central is among the most luxurious and expensive locations in Manhattan. Unless you are filthy rich, you will have a hard time moving into the beautiful, deluxe condos, really the only living spaces that can be found here. For the truly glamorous life, shell out the dough for a gorgeous place in Trump Tower.

Besides the exorbitance and baroque flavor of the neighborhood, you will also find a wealth of monumental architecture right at your doorstep, such as Rockefeller Center, St. Patrick's Cathedral, Radio City Music Hall, The

Plaza, and the Museum of Modern Art. If you live here, you undoubtedly have money to spend, so take advantage of nearby Saks Fifth Avenue, Bloomingdale's, Bergdorf Goodman's, and other fancy-schmanzy stores. If you have guests from out of town coming to visit, Grand Central Station is conveniently located in the neighborhood.

If you like peace and quiet, the incessant crowds and noise of Midtown Central will be a definite turn off. But the commotion definitely has its advantage. Wherever you work, Midtown Central is a good location to commute from as every subway line is within walking distance. And if you are one of the millions of people who actually work in the area itself, well, the commute couldn't be easier.

THE PEOPLE

POPULATION	40,000
AGE	
0-17	7%
18-44	55%
45-64	27%
65+	11%
ETHNICITY	
White	83%
Black	7%
Asian	5%
Other	5%
Spanish speaking	13%
Family households	38%
College educated	68%
HOUSEHOLD INCOME	
Below $25,000	36%
$25-75,000	44%
$75-150,000	12%
$150,000+	8%

Noise: The area is concentrated with traffic, especially taxis driven by raucous cab drivers, so it is usually quite noisy. But since most buildings have sixty floors or more, you probably won't be able to hear, let alone see, the street from your apartment.

Parking: All buildings here have parking of some sort, or at least a garage nearby.

Kids & Families: A terrific location for families if you can afford it and a private school tuition.

Safety: This area is generally very safe, given the high-profile people who come and go, but it does empty out after dark.

Shopping: Runs the gamut from the elite, expensive name-brand couture of Madison Avenue to clunky tourist traps selling souvenirs and discount electronics. Grocery stores are notably absent, but you can find little gourmand shops on every block.

THE NEIGHBORHOOD

AVERAGE MONTHLY RENT

Studio	$1,700-2,500
1 br	$2,300-2,700
2 br	$2,500-4,000
3 br	$3,200-6,000

AVERAGE SALE PRICE

Studio	$150,000-275,000
1 br	$240,000-400,000
2 br	$350,000-900,000
3 br	$650,000-1.000,000

COMMUTING

The entire transportation hub of New York runs through Grand Central Station. The 4, 5 and 6 trains all intersect Midtown Central, and the F train also runs through the neighborhood along Madison Avenue. Buses run up and down all of the main avenues.

DISTANCE

Time to midtown	15-20 min
Time to downtown	5-10 min

WWW.ZANYS.COM
Find a NYC apartment now!

Entertainment: Swank bars are plentiful, but there are absolutely no clubs.
Restaurants: All of the restaurants here are top notch, especially Cipriani's and Mr. K's.
Parks & Gardens: Hello—Central Park!
Final Words: Unless your yearly salary has six figures, look elsewhere. But if you are financially prosperous, it is one of the most fashionable addresses available, if a bit impersonal.

MIDTOWN WEST
• MANHATTAN •

Times Square—the first thing that may come to your mind is why on earth would anyone ever want to live in the world's most touristy area? True that it isn't exactly famous for its residences, but there are actually some hidden living spaces here that are rather lovely. If you are living in New York for the urban experience, you won't find a neighborhood more metropolitan than this.

If the 42nd Street that you are familiar with is filled with porn stores and hookers, you obviously haven't been here in a while. Ever since Giuliani and the turn-of-the-new-century corporations like Disney and huge chain restaurants arrived, the area has enjoyed a 360 degree cleanup. In between all of the megastores and movie multiplexes it is now hard to find an adult video store, though some still do exist.

Unlike the conformist commercial establishments, the residences located in the area are quite unique. Buildings are either quirky high rises or quaint brownstones. Since the number of actual buildings is few and a lot of people want to live right smack in the middle of things, the rents here have skyrocketed within recent years.

In the past, inhabitants were mostly people of Latin descent who were drawn to the area when it was a lot cheaper and more run down. But ever since corporate offices began springing up, such as MTV's headquarters, young professionals have taken over so they can be close to work. Of course, Midtown West is still overrun with tourists twenty four hours a day, so patience is high up on the virtue list if you choose to live here.

This is one of the better places in New York to encounter the up-in-your-face Manhattan attitude. For some people this is a perk, but if this sort of attitude scares you, don't worry because Times Square literally has cops on every block. Although you won't find hustlers and mobsters anymore, the area still has its fair share of wacky characters. Personality is one thing this neighborhood is not lacking.

THE PEOPLE

POPULATION	37,000
AGE	
0-17	8%
18-44	52%
45-64	23%
65+	17%
ETHNICITY	
White	78%
Black	8%
Asian	7%
Other	7%
Spanish speaking	18%
Family households	44%
College educated	52%
HOUSEHOLD INCOME	
Below $25,000	28%
$25-75,000	43%
$75-150,000	21%
$150,000+	8%

WWW.ZANYS.COM
Find a NYC apartment now!

THE NEIGHBORHOOD

AVERAGE MONTHLY RENT

Studio	$1,400-2,300
1 br	$1,600-2,700
2 br	$2,000-3,400
3 br	$3,200-3,800

AVERAGE SALE PRICE

Studio	$140,000-250,000
1 br	$175,000-400,000
2 br	$400,000-900,000
3 br	$700,000-2,000,000+

COMMUTING

The A, C, E, N, R, 1, 2, 3 and 9 trains all run through Midtown West. This neighborhood also has an incredible amount of buses running around Manhattan to many parts of the outer boroughs

DISTANCE

Time to midtown	5-10	min
Time to downtown	20-25	min

In order to live here and not commit suicide, you have to be a lover of constant commotion. It might be difficult to get friends to come visit you when you tell them that you live right by Times Square, but tell them to think of you as a new tourist attraction that is definitely worth seeing. Life is one big party here and you can act as one of its hosts.

Zanys.com user comments: Midtown West is "expensive, touristy, and stale."

Noise: Without question the loudest neighborhood in New York, and maybe even the world.

Parking: With the theater district right here, street parking is impossible but parking garages are numerous.

Kids & Families: Unless you want your kids to be absolutely petrified every time they leave the house, don't raise them here.

Safety: Even though it is police central both day and

night here, you will still want to be on guard at all times, especially on side streets. Lots of freaks still love to linger here.

Entertainment: *Les Miserables*, *The Phantom of the Opera*, twenty theater movie complexes—who could ask for anything more?

Restaurants: Midtown West is home to Restaurant Row, but most of the eateries here are overpriced with average food. They offer great aprés theater specials, though.

Parks & Gardens: The closest thing you'll find to greenery here is in Bryant Park, but you'll have to travel to the east side of 42nd Street even to find that.

Shopping: All shops here are geared towards tourists, making it extremely difficult to find basic necessities.

Final Words: As Reno Sweeney once said in her hit Broadway musical, "Anything goes!" You never know what to expect in Midtown West and you are guaranteed to never get bored here. Neon lights, crazy people and entertainment wait at every turn. This is what it is truly like to live in the Big City.

MORNINGSIDE HEIGHTS
→ MANHATTAN ←

New Yorkers frequently dismiss Morningside Heights as the no-man's-land between gritty, but colorful, Harlem and the increasingly hip Upper West Side. It's true—the area around Columbia University will never be called the most exciting neighborhood in Manhattan. However, there's certainly something to be said for living away from the hustle and bustle of downtown. Cheaper than the Upper West Side, but safer than most areas of the city, Morningside Heights is the practical choice for liberal intellectuals, students, families and elderly folks who enjoy the simplicity of community living.

Morningside Heights' most unusual feature is its

topography. It includes the second-highest peak in Manhattan, making it the obvious choice for the location of Columbia University. The historic dome roof of Lowe Library stands almost directly in the center of Morningside Heights, and the iron gates of Columbia University form a large rectangle in the center of the neighborhood. The land slopes down dramatically on the east, west and south sides of the campus.

Its character is largely shaped by the University, built over a century and a half ago. But to ignore other facets of the neighborhood would be tragic. In fact, it was a similar oversight by the University's administration that led to student protests in 1968 to keep the University from building an enormous athletic center directly on top of Morningside Park.

Columbia University owns most of the buildings in Morningside Heights, and the school exerts a fair amount of influence on the development of the neighborhood, especially when it comes to renting retail establishments and restaurants on Broadway and Amsterdam Avenue. When the academic giant's decisions come under criticism, students and other interested members of the community provide an important check on the school's power and have historically been successful in keeping the University from overstepping its bounds. Columbia shrewdly recognizes, of course, the value of a little local color, and neighborhood institutions such as The West End Diner, Koronet's Pizza, and Columbia Hot Bagels are hardly in danger of losing their leases.

Students from Columbia, Barnard College, Manhattan School of Music, Jewish Theological Seminary and other local colleges and universities are the most visible residents of Morningside Heights; however, the neighborhood remains surprisingly diverse, with its proximity to East Harlem contributing to a relatively high Latin-American population. Older families and upper-class residents fill the co-ops that line Riverside Drive, students and young professionals occupy most of the buildings between Riverside Drive and Amsterdam between 110th and 120th Streets, and Black and Latino families have settled east of Morningside Park. Shopping and nightlife are geared largely towards students, with a variety of cheap diners, bars and functional drugstores supplementing more upscale restaurants, stationery shops and clothing stores.

The peaceful Columbia University campus itself, standing in lush contrast to the grittiness of the city around it, may be the centerpiece of the entire neighborhood. In particular, the grandiose Lowe Library and the steps that lie before it are awe-inspiring and open to the entire neighborhood. Families with young children frequently play on the grassy Columbia and Barnard campuses, especially in the summertime. Other local sights include the Cathedral of St. John the Divine, which happens to be the largest Gothic cathedral in the world, and Grant's Tomb, America's second-largest mausoleum. Residents also take advantage of Riverside Park, a safe and beautiful sanctuary that borders the Hudson River. Morningside Park, a dangerous but picturesque, tree-bordered lawn, is also nearby. And, of course, Central Park is only a short walk away.

> "The word for New York is activity."
>
> **V.S. PRITCHETT**

Morningside Heights has always offered the convenience of Manhattan to those who can live without the crowds—and costs—of downtown. As rents increase, however, it is easy to see how the neighborhood may lose some of its appeal, especially for younger professionals who are looking for a little more edge. And keep in mind that while many love the community's laid-back atmosphere, others complain that the relatively monotonous layout of Morningside Heights lacks texture, that the commute downtown is too long, or that the nightlife options are too scarce.

Noise: Avenues like Columbus and Broadway see their fair share of traffic. Loud car alarms are unfortunately all too common. Side streets, as usual, are much quieter.

Parking: For Manhattan, the opportunities to snag a street spot are fairly good, especially along Riverside Drive, but be wary of theft. Professors often drive in from the suburbs and park in the area's many private lots.

Kid & Families: Families have long found Morningside

Heights to be a great place to raise children.

Safety: Cops, including Columbia and Barnard College security forces, are in full force. Women are advised to stay on the major streets at night or to walk with friends.

Entertainment: Miller Theater at Broadway and 116th Street and the Manhattan School of Music are two terrific venues to hear orchestral music. The Cotton Club at 125th Street is a swinging reproduction of the original Harlem nightspot.

Restaurants: Great local restaurants include Spoonbread Soul Food, Zula for Ethiopian cuisine and the Hungarian Pastry Shop.

Parks & Gardens: Riverside Park is beautiful, but Morningside Park is considered dangerous and is poorly

THE PEOPLE

POPULATION	47,000
AGE	
0-17	28%
18-44	34%
45-64	32%
65+	6%
ETHNICITY	
White	49%
Black	43%
Asian	8%
Spanish speaking	45%
Family households	47%
College educated	28%
HOUSEHOLD INCOME	
Below $25,000	44%
$25-75,000	34%
$75-150,000	20%
$150,000+	2%

lit at night. The park adjacent to Saint John the Divine is a wonderful place for a Sunday stroll.

Shopping: Most retail options are located on Broadway and around Columbia University. Many small boutiques have recently been threatened or replaced by larger retailers like FootLocker, RiteAid and Starbucks. Local bookstores like Posman, Papyrus and Labyrinth are among the best in the city.

THE NEIGHBORHOOD

AVERAGE MONTHLY RENT

Studio	$1,300-2,200
1 br	$1,500-2,800
2 br	$2,000-3,500
3 br	$2,800-4,000

AVERAGE SALE PRICE

Studio	$135,000-300,000
1 br	$175,000-400,000
2 br	$200,000-700,000
3 br	$250,000-1,000,000+

COMMUTING

The B and C trains stop at 110th, 116th and 125th Streets, the A and D trains stop at 125th Street, the 1 and 9 trains stop at 110th, 116th, 125th and 137th Streets, and the 2 and 3 trains stop at 110th, 116th and 125th Streets.

DISTANCE

Time to midtown	30-35 min
Time to downtown	40-45 min

Final Words: Morningside Heights should be high on anyone's list of desirable neighborhoods. It has all the essential services singles and growing families require.

WWW.ZANYS.COM
Find a NYC apartment now!

MURRAY HILL
◆ MANHATTAN ◆

Murray Hill is a tiny peace of heaven, slap bang in the middle of Manhattan. As the residents will no doubt tell you, there is something very special about being able to walk to work, eat at a variety of ethnic restaurants close to your door and enjoy many big city amenities without the drawbacks of other nearby neighborhoods. Bordered by bustling Midtown to the north and the chaos of Times Square to the west, this small East Side neighborhood offers more comfort than its immediate neighbors.

Many of the pre-war buildings here still retain their 19th century character. Residents tend to be older and professional, and many have lived here for years. This is an ideal neighborhood if you have the money to spend, like peace and quiet and are planning to settle in for the long hall. Although quite well-off, most of the locals have few pretensions, and it is pretty easy to make friends in any one of the cozy pubs or coffee shops that pepper the area.

Walk down Lexington, and you'll see plenty of shops, chains, drugstores, marts, markets and restaurants. If you can't find what you want right on your doorstep, then remember: it's only a short distance to Midtown. The many conveniences this neighborhood has to offer are a definite plus for those with not much time to spare.

If you're planning to live with any four-legged friends, then Murray Hill is an especially good choice because of its pro-pet atmosphere. There are quite a few veterinary clinics and adoption agencies around. The dog run at Madison Square Park is frequented by many pedigrees and their corporate owners who hail from nearby Murray Hill. On the other hand, if Rover is just a run-of-the-mill mutt, and you're not decked out in the latest from Armani, you may feel a little out of place.

While there is a definite lack of green space nearby, the neighborhood is situated only a few minutes from the East River, where you can walk, jog or bike for miles. It's not advised to venture there after dark, but during the day, the strip is packed and perfectly safe. Exercise lovers will find plenty of gyms around, but be prepared to pay high prices.

Though the streets in Murray Hill are not as well-kept as some of its more fanatical residents would prefer, it certainly is easy to see why people would be proud to call this neighborhood home. If your goal is to be in the epicenter of New York's thriving nightlife, then Murray Hill might not be the right place for you. But anyone seeking a quiet

THE PEOPLE

POPULATION	52,000
AGE	
0-17	7%
18-44	56%
45-64	25%
65+	12%
ETHNICITY	
White	82%
Black	7%
Asian	9%
Other	2%
Spanish speaking	10%
Family households	27%
College educated	60%
HOUSEHOLD INCOME	
Below $25,000	27%
$25-75,000	45%
$75-150,000	15%
$150,000+	15%

WWW.ZANYS.COM
Find a NYC apartment now!

safe haven apart from the hectic pace of the big city will like it in Murray Hill.

Noise: If you're on or near Lexington Avenue the noise is fairly constant.

Parking: There are several available parking garages just east of Lexington Avenue, and the further east you go the easier it is to find spaces.

Kids & Families: There are not many children around. Parents don't have to worry about their kids getting into much trouble around here, but they may feel a little isolated.

Safety: Murray Hill is regarded as a very safe neighborhood, although late at night the streets clear out completely. You would be prudent to take a cab home if you've been partying into the early hours.

Entertainment: This is a more reserved area—so no

THE NEIGHBORHOOD

AVERAGE MONTHLY RENT

Studio	$1,300-1,900
1 br	$1,700-2,600
2 br	$2,800-3,800
3 br	$3,500-5,500

AVERAGE SALE PRICE

Studio	$140,000-300,000
1 br	$190,000-400,000
2 br	$250,000-1,000,000
3 br	$400,000-1,000,000+

COMMUTING

The 6 train runs to 33rd and 42nd Streets. Buses are less plentiful.

DISTANCE

Time to midtown	5-10	min
Time to downtown	30-35	min

nightclubs or juke joints—but wander into Chelsea and you'll discover all the alternative amusements you could ever want.

Parks & Gardens: None in the immediate vicinity, unless you want to walk or jog down the East River.

Shopping: All of the basics are readily available, and if you're looking for haute couture Madison Avenue is only a small hobble away in those Gucci loafers.

Final Words: If you're looking for something cozy and conventional, then Murray Hill has what you're looking for. Those who prefer the dirt and grime of the urban experience might find it all a bit too sedate.

NOHO
• MANHATTAN •

Soho? No Noho. Yes it is an actual neighborhood, which can be considered Soho's Northern counterpart. Noho, which stands for "north of Houston," is a mini-neighborhood smack in the middle of Lower Manhattan. Debates rage on between lower Manhattanites about whether or not Noho actually exists, and there are many discrepancies about its boundaries. Officially, Noho runs from Houston to 8th Street and from Mercer Street to the Bowery.

The reason it's often dismissed by New Yorkers as fictitious is that it sits between two other well-known districts: Greenwich Village and the East Village. In many ways, Noho is the middle child between these two siblings. Then again, lots of folks simply consider the neighborhood to be part of the East or West Village.

Before waves of gentrification sent rents toward the stratosphere, Noho was known as a home to commercial and industrial trades like tool-and-die manufacturers, plumbing supply shops, photo processing labs, music recording studios and furniture shops. Noho took off as a residential location during the late 1980s and early '90s when New Yorkers recognized the potential of its centralized location, abundant loft spaces and, at the time, low rents. Prices have since skyrocketed, making Noho as expensive as Soho or Tribeca. As time passes, more landlords are converting their properties to residential dwellings simply because they can get more money for them.

This change has prompted service industries like bars and restaurants to open up on the ground floors of many buildings. The success of these businesses has turned the neighborhood from a barren no man's land to a thriving nighttime destination. Back when Noho streets were still deserted, few New Yorkers would risk the dangerous trek from East to West Village. Now clubs and busy restaurants like the Bowery Bar, Fez and The Time Café have literally paved the walk from between "villages."

When walking around the neighborhood, you'll find that most Noho structures are four to six-story loft buildings sporting large, turn-of-the-century proportions and massive windows on their front façades. Many of the side streets are paved with cobblestones, giving Noho a slightly European flavor. Residents who live in these lofts enjoy the large front-faced windows, but often complain that rear bedrooms lack natural light—just one of the drawbacks of living in formerly commercial dwellings.

If you're considering an apartment in Noho, it's essential to examine the quality of work done during the renovation process. Landlords often skimp on details like bathroom fixtures, recessed lighting, sound insulation and kitchen appliances. Be aware that once you sign a lease, your ability to get your landlord to correct these oversights evaporates. Make sure to negotiate all renovations or improvements before you sign on the dotted line. Noho is primarily home to childless couples in their late twenties and thirties. The prototypical Noho resident is young, maybe even famous and above all, wealthy enough to afford a place in the neighborhood—someone who will make you think Noho stands for North Hollywood.

The area is definitely one of the most up-and-coming in New York, and as it becomes more and more polished, even younger generations are starting to feel comfortable here. However, be aware that every avenue that bisects

Noho is a major traffic artery, and its central location attracts transients. The community board is doing its best to distinguish Noho from its neighbors and to create public spaces in the area where residents can congregate. As it stands, many Noho residents remain strangers to even their closest neighbors.

THE PEOPLE

POPULATION	17,000
AGE	
0-17	9%
18-44	49%
45-64	35%
65+	7%
ETHNICITY	
White	74%
Black	19%
Asian	7%
Spanish speaking	21%
Family households	11%
College educated	29%
HOUSEHOLD INCOME	
Below $25,000	33%
$25-75,000	37%
$75-150,000	28%
$150,000+	2%

Noise: Smack in the center of lower Manhattan, Noho sees more than its fair share of traffic. Although several streets are exceptionally quiet, noise from the busy avenues tends to bleed over.

Parking: For a traffic-heavy neighborhood, Noho has a decent amount of parking along its streets because most

WWW.ZANYS.COM
Find a NYC apartment now!

of the residential buildings don't house many tenants, and only a few people who do business in the area drive to work. Private lots are also available but are extremely expensive.

Kids & Families: It's not suggested that you bring up kids in the neighborhood. It could be done, but nothing about Noho says "family."

Safety: Lower Manhattan has never been safer, which is one of the main reasons neighborhoods like Noho have been resurrected. Twenty years ago, the only people you'd see walking the area at night were punk rockers and drug addicts. Nowadays you'll see more young professionals than anyone else in these parts.

Entertainment: The area is finally starting to see more than a few late-night venues and fine eateries. Karaoke bars on the Bowery have become a neighborhood specialty. The Noho Gallery is also worth visiting.

THE NEIGHBORHOOD

AVERAGE MONTHLY RENT

Studio	$1,600-2,000
1 br	$1,900-2,800
2 br	$2,200-3,400
3 br	$2,700-5,000

AVERAGE SALE PRICE

Studio	$140,000-250,000
1 br	$220,000-400,000
2 br	$300,000-1,000,000
3 br	$350,000-1,000,000+

COMMUTING
The A, C and E trains stop at West 4th Street, the 6 train stops at Astor Place and Bleecker Street, the N and R trains stop at 8th Street and the B, D, F and Q trains stop at West 4th and Broadway/Lafayette Streets.

DISTANCE

Time to midtown	15-20	min
Time to downtown	5-10	min

Restaurants: Plenty. Classic roadhouse food and rockabilly music can be found at the Great Jones Café. The Noho Star serves Asian-American fusion, and Marion's on the Bowery shakes up terrific cocktails in an intimate setting.

Parks & Gardens: The quality housing makes up for the lack of green space in the neighborhood. In this neighborhood you're about equidistant from Tompkins and Washington Square Parks.

Shopping: Until recently Noho didn't have much in the way of shopping. Now, it's a virtual mall, featuring everything from fancy furniture and home décor shops to bookstores and vintage clothing. Vintage hounds have long relied on Screaming Mimi's on Lafayette Street for antique clothing gems. The daily flea market on Broadway also draws a large crowd of shoppers to the area.

Final Words: Noho is the perfect neighborhood for the right type of person. It offers a convenient, central location, large loft residences and a cool nightlife just steps from your front door—for a price.

NOLITA
◆ MANHATTAN ◆

The name Nolita was only recently given to the tiny neighborhood north of Little Italy and is still unfamiliar to many New Yorkers. Hip city-dwellers know, however, that residents of this community have one of the trendiest addresses in Manhattan. The area used to simply be Little Italy, but as Soho's stylishness has rubbed off on this neighboring community, it has acquired an identity all its own.

A century ago, the neighborhood was packed with Italian immigrants, all in eager pursuit of the American dream. They lived in tenement buildings, which today have been converted into modern apartments. Little Italy has shrunk in the past decades and is now little more than a single street (Mulberry) of old-fashioned restaurants. To the south, it has been sucked into Chinatown and to the north it has become Nolita.

Nolita is also known as East Soho, and in actuality this title is perhaps a more fitting description. Today, the neighborhood is much more in the spirit of Soho than Little Italy. More and more fabulously hip and expensive boutiques are opening up along the streets, replacing the old family-owned meat shops and bakeries. Today, you are more likely to find actors and models living in these apartment buildings than old neighborhood families.

However, at the moment, residents of the area are lucky enough to enjoy the best of both worlds. Perhaps the neighborhood's most distinctive feature is that it provides easy access to a number of neighboring areas, while not really fitting into any of them. Nolita is a very trendy crossroads between Soho, Little Italy, Chinatown, the East Village, and the Lower East Side. The best of all these neighborhoods is within easy reach, along with the unique Nolita atmosphere, which is all its own.

The neighborhood is not as popular with shoppers as neighboring Soho and remains fairly quiet and low-key throughout the day. Local restaurants and shops offer a wide-range of food and services, ranging from ethnic and old-fashioned to stylish and cutting-edge. Mulberry Street is jam packed with cozy, old Italian eateries, and on the weekends with tourists looking for *Godfather*-like experiences, as well. All sorts of retail shopping is available on the Soho section of nearby Broadway, a short walk away.

Apartments consist mainly of small one to three-bedroom places often lacking conveniences like large closets, big kitchens and bathrooms. Lofts occasionally come on the market, but these are usually much smaller than their Soho or Tribeca equivalents. Quality of life for the few who can afford to live here is terrific, and above all, the neighborhood is charming and always rather surprising.

However, since the area's rediscovery in the past few years, prices have skyrocketed to ridiculous rates. The neighborhood is hot and does not show any signs of cooling down for quite a while to come.

Noise: Nolita's streets are too narrow for most trucks, but many businesses, like the restaurants and the fish and meat markets, receive early morning deliveries. Noise levels are usually bearable, but remember that the windows on these apartments often have little or no soundproofing.

Parking: This is not a good place to keep a car. It's very difficult to find parking spots along these popular streets, and nearby neighborhoods don't get much better.

Kid & Families: Nolita and Little Italy have been "dead"

THE PEOPLE

POPULATION	23,000
AGE	
0-17	19%
18-44	46%
45-64	26%
65+	9%
ETHNICITY	
White	37%
Black	15%
Asian	58%
Spanish speaking	11%
Family households	38%
College educated	42%
HOUSEHOLD INCOME	
Below $25,000	18%
$25-75,000	51%
$75-150,000	30%
$150,000+	1%

WWW.ZANYS.COM
Find a NYC apartment now!

neighborhoods for an entire generation, as kids left the small confines of the area's apartments when they could and the population continued to age. Newcomers are typically in their twenties and thirties but generally not family types. Apartments are so small and expensive that raising a family here would be a real burden.

Safety: The neighborhood is very secure during the day and night; you shouldn't have a problem now that so many stores line the streets. Nolita is so small that a scream could wake up the entire neighborhood.

Entertainment: Although much of the local atmosphere is dominated by a hipster aesthetic, Nolita is known more as a lunch-hour destination than a late-night spot. Midday people-watching is the best entertainment of all. You'll find a few bars and restaurants but may be better off

THE NEIGHBORHOOD

AVERAGE MONTHLY RENT

Studio	$1,400-1,900
1 br	$1,800-2,900
2 br	$2,000-3,500
3 br	$2,800-6,000

AVERAGE SALE PRICE

Studio	$150,000-300,000
1 br	$240,000-400,000
2 br	$300,000-1,000,000
3 br	$400,000-1,000,000+

COMMUTING

The 6 train stops at Spring Street, the B, D, F and Q trains stop at Broadway and Lafayette Streets and the J and M trains stop at Bowery Street.

DISTANCE

Time to midtown	10-15	min
Time to downtown	5-10	min

taking a short walk or cab ride to the Village at night.

Restaurants: Nearly every block has a half dozen wonderful places to meet, eat or drink, and you pay as much as you would in Soho. Lunch spots like Bread and Butter, Rice, Gitanes and the world-famous pizzeria Lombardi's are all terrific.

Parks & Gardens: Parks are limited to the asphalt-covered public space on Spring and Mullberry Streets. A private garden between Mott and Elizabeth Streets offers some relief from the concrete.

Shopping: Brand new, funky fashions are available from many lesser-known seamstresses. The boutiques themselves incorporate the beauty of the original spaces. Prices are moderate to very expensive.

Final Words: In New York, everything old really does become new again, and so it is with Nolita. It's become trendy for good reason—Old World charm, stylish boutiques, quiet streets, but prices are too high for any but the rich and famous to live comfortably here today.

PARK SLOPE
◆ BROOKLYN ◆

Ahhh Brooklyn. Perhaps New York's most precious gem at the moment, since it is the up-and-coming borough, and Park Slope is definitely the place to be once you cross over the Brooklyn Bridge. It has the landscape of Brooklyn and the energy of Manhattan—what could be better?

At the turn-of-the-century, immigrants, mostly Jewish, established themselves in Park Slope in walk-up brownstones with no elevators. These quaint, charming buildings remain as the majority of the infrastructure, inhabited by descendants of the original settlers. Park Slope is undeniably a place defined by family and tradition.

Bounded by Flatbush Avenue to the north, 15th Street to the south, Fifth Avenue to the west and Prospect Park to the east, Park Slope is really not that large of an area, although its population has momentously expanded within the past few years. What was once a quiet, strictly residential neighborhood has been transformed into a trendy, more commercial suburb by the onslaught of native Manhattanites who are seeking change. Needless to say, this influx of "foreigners" does not rest too well among Park Slope old-timers. Their peaceful haven has literally been invaded and metamorphosed. In fact many older residents have actually moved out to get away from all of wealthy, stroller-pushing youngsters.

Park Slope is not just a place to live for most inhabitants, but more of a way of life. Despite its modernization, it is ten times less noisy than Manhattan and hip but not too pretentious to be comfortable. As the most beautiful area in Brooklyn, residents take great pride in their beloved Prospect Park, which is considered to be the Central Park of the Big B. Once you move here, it is hard to imagine living anywhere else. For this very reason, newlyweds have settled down in the ornately decorated and spacious brownstones to begin their lives as parents. Apartments can also be found, but most of them are still in walk-up buildings, which is a bit of a turn-off.

While the architecture is breathtaking, the attitude of inhabitants is what really defines Park Slope. With academics, yuppies, multiracial couples and lots of lesbians, the area is extremely diverse. It is a prime place for people who work for themselves and who have a more laid back approach to life. Children also run rampant here, as it is one of the best places for kids. From The Children's Historic House Museum to the Prospect Park Wildlife Center, the young ones will never get bored. For adults, there is also plenty of entertainment such as top restaurants, diners, coffee shops, and boutiques.

On any day at any time, you will see all sorts of people insouciantly meandering up and down the hilly streets. This contented, carefree approach to life is at the heart of Park Slope's joy. For people who love life and want to enjoy it to its fullest, it is a great, old-fashioned choice.

Zanys.com user comments: Park Slope is "one of the largest, best-preserved, and most-noted historic districts in the United States."

THE PEOPLE

POPULATION	64,000
AGE	
0-17	18%
18-44	44%
45-64	27%
65+	11%
ETHNICITY	
White	71%
Black	12%
Asian	4%
Other	13%
Spanish speaking	25%
Family households	55%
College educated	46%
HOUSEHOLD INCOME	
Below $25,000	34%
$25-75,000	49%
$75-150,000	10%
$150,000+	7%

Noise: Hardly any, except at major intersections.

Parking: The only sure bet is Long Meadow, a 90-acre open urban parkland. But even here you can't keep your car all the time.

Kids & Families: Bring 'em on. It is the prime place to raise a family, even though the residents here have become more well-to-do.

Safety: Generally very safe. The area isn't patrolled that much, but it doesn't need to be. Before Giuliani's reign, cars were broken into occasionally, but this has slowed in recent years.

Entertainment: If you're looking for nightlife, hop on the D train to Manhattan. But Park Slope does have some wonderful restaurants and outdoor fairs.

Restaurants: The restaurants used to be largely of the ethnic and diner variety, but this has been changing. Great mom-and-pop establishments abound in the neighborhood, dishing up great cheap food and personal attention. Locals tend to be repeat customers.

Parks & Gardens: You'll find many small private gardens as well as the famous Prospect Park bordering Institute Park, graced with a Civil War Memorial Arch built in the 1890s. (The chariot driver on top symbolizes the Union cause.) Founded in 1910, the 50-acre Brooklyn Botanical Garden is near the Eastern Parkway by Washington and Flatbush Avenues.

Shopping: Great for day-to-day errands, with lots of little shops, grocery stores and family-run bodegas. Don't expect haute couture here, as stores here tend to be more functional than anything. Few chain stores have moved in yet, so for the higher-end goods you'll need to go into Manhattan like everyone else.

THE NEIGHBORHOOD

AVERAGE MONTHLY RENT

Studio	$1,000-1,500
1 br	$1,400-2,600
2 br	$1,700-3,000
3 br	$1,900-3,300

AVERAGE SALE PRICE

Studio	$90,000-160,000
1 br	$150,000-320,000
2 br	$200,000-700,000
3 br	$250,000-1,000,000+

COMMUTING

The F train runs to 7th Avenue and 9th Street, and the D and Q run to 7th Avenue and Flatbush. There are a couple of buses, but most residents commute by train.

DISTANCE

Time to midtown	10-15 min
Time to downtown	5-10 min

Final Words: There are few places in New York where you will be content with every aspect of your life, but Park Slope is one of these treasures. Treat the area with respect and you will be very happy with what it can give to you. When you tell people you live in Park Slope, they will be extremely jealous.

PROSPECT HEIGHTS
● BROOKLYN ●

rospect Heights is a small, lesser-known Brooklyn neighborhood, situated to the northeast of the Brooklyn Botanic Garden. The area's proximity to this wonderful oasis of natural beauty is enough to recommend it. But add to that lovely streets lined with trees and 19th century brownstones, and you've got a real gem of a neighborhood. Besides Prospect Park, the Brooklyn Museum of Art and the main branch of the Brooklyn Public Library are located in the area as well. Who needs Manhattan when you have all this culture lying at your doorstep?

The area was developed in the late 19th century, when Prospect Park was new and Brooklyn was booming. For the next few decades, people lived here happily enough, but as the economy shifted, so did the prosperous population of the area. Buildings were abandoned, and slowly Prospect Heights descended into urban decay and poverty. By the 1960s, the area became dominated by struggling African-Americans and was the site of riots after the assassination of Martin Luther King, Jr.

However, Prospect Heights was reborn in the 1980s, as New Yorkers began to once again realize the charms this neighborhood has to offer. The buildings were renovated, and a new, upper middle class moved into the once impoverished area. This yuppie population remains there today—along with reminders of Prospect Heights' less-affluent past.

Prospect Heights extends from Flatbush Avenue on the west to Washington Avenue on the east, and from the Botanic Gardens on the south to Atlantic Avenue on the north. The area has an exciting, still-evolving atmosphere, fueled by a diversity of residents from different ethnic and socio-economic backgrounds. Despite the waves of new people coming into the community, Prospect Heights retains a small-neighborhood feel. The residential streets are quite welcoming and a joy to walk through. Each row of townhouses is slightly different, and they are all adorned with lovely architectural details. There are lots of trees and many of the houses have gardens. Though they are not as elegant as neighboring Park Slope, the streets of Prospect Heights have a distinct beauty of their own.

Unfortunately, the avenues that cut through the area lack the charm of the residential streets. They are lined with run-down looking businesses and offer few opportunities for shopping or eating. It is not very far to more promising areas for restaurants, however, and the subway is nearby for anyone wishing to leave the area completely.

However, with Prospect Park and the Botanic Gardens so nearby, residents certainly do not need to go far in order to find a peaceful retreat from the hustle of city life. Anyone living in this area has an ideal opportunity to become a member of the Garden in order to enjoy its quiet beauty whenever she pleases. 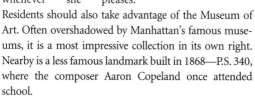 Residents should also take advantage of the Museum of Art. Often overshadowed by Manhattan's famous museums, it is a most impressive collection in its own right. Nearby is a less famous landmark built in 1868—P.S. 340, where the composer Aaron Copeland once attended school.

Rent in Prospect Heights has been going up for the last

twenty years, and there is no reason to think it is going to stop increasing anytime soon. It won't be long before the few brownstones and row-houses still in need of renovation receive the help they need and raise the neighborhood's prices even higher.

Noise: The residential streets are very quiet.

Parking: Street-side parking is your best bet, but as elsewhere in the city it can be challenging to find a spot.

Kids & Families: The park and garden are great places for children, and there are nearby schools.

Safety: The avenues should be avoided late at night, especially by women walking alone.

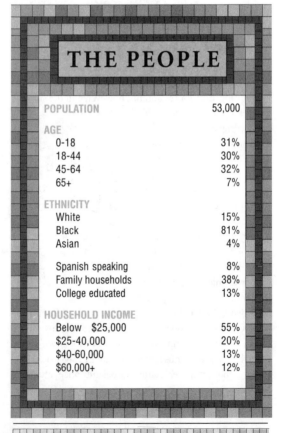

THE PEOPLE

POPULATION	53,000
AGE	
0-18	31%
18-44	30%
45-64	32%
65+	7%
ETHNICITY	
White	15%
Black	81%
Asian	4%
Spanish speaking	8%
Family households	38%
College educated	13%
HOUSEHOLD INCOME	
Below $25,000	55%
$25-40,000	20%
$40-60,000	13%
$60,000+	12%

Find a NYC apartment now!

THE NEIGHBORHOOD

AVERAGE MONTHLY RENT

Studio	$700-1,100
1 br	$900-1,800
2 br	$1,000-2,400
3 br	$1,200-2,800

AVERAGE SALE PRICE

Studio	$75,000-150,000
1 br	$150,000-300,000
2 br	$180,000-450,000
3 br	$200,000-700,000

COMMUTING

The F train stops at Prospect Park.

DISTANCE

Time to midtown	45-55 min
Time to downtown	35-45 min

Entertainment: Very little in the neighborhood itself but plenty not too far away.

Restaurants: Only a few on the avenues.

Parks & Gardens: Prospect Park and the Brooklyn Botanic Garden—as far as parks and gardens are concerned, it doesn't get much better than this.

Shopping: A few small, unimpressive delis and groceries.

Final Words: This is a charming residential neighborhood with easy access to some of the city's loveliest and most overlooked cultural resources.

RED HOOK
• BROOKLYN •

Like many areas in Brooklyn, Red Hook is currently undergoing a complicated process of reinventing itself. The neighborhood used to be home to one of the nation's most important ports, and ships from around the world found their way to Red Hook's docks. Twentieth century changes in the shipping industry seemed to strike the death knell for this Brooklyn neighborhood; however, Red Hook is once again struggling to assert itself as an attractive and imminently livable section of Brooklyn.

Red Hook is one of Brooklyn's oldest neighborhoods. The Dutch settled here in 1636 and named the spot after its red soil and odd hook-shape that juts into the East River. The neighborhood is actually a peninsula, surrounded by water on three sides. The water has always defined Red Hook, and it wasn't long before the neighborhood was a teeming port. In the 19th century, immigrants from all over Europe arrived to work on the bustling waterfront. All this hustle and bustle brought with it a dangerous organized crime element. Al Capone got his start here, as did countless other criminals.

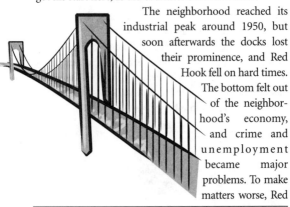

The neighborhood reached its industrial peak around 1950, but soon afterwards the docks lost their prominence, and Red Hook fell on hard times. The bottom felt out of the neighborhood's economy, and crime and unemployment became major problems. To make matters worse, Red

Hook became isolated from the rest of Brooklyn by the construction of the Gowanus Expressway and the Brooklyn Battery Tunnel.

Unemployment and poverty are still problems in this once bustling neighborhood. Still, Red Hook projects a proud, survivalist spirit. A new community of artists and poorer yuppie types has begun filtering into Red Hook. Residents enjoy simple pleasures like walking along tree-lined streets filled with young kids playing stickball, riding bicycles or taunting neighborhood cats. There's no shortage of prime real estate in these parts; were many of Red Hook's beautiful post-war homes transplanted to nearby Brooklyn Heights, they'd easily quadruple in value.

The sprawling neighborhood has three distinct sections. Red Hook proper, dominated by housing projects built in the 1960s, is bordered by Richards Street on the west, the Erie Basin to the south and the Gowanus Canal on the east. The area's reputation as a high-crime, low-income zone has been hard to shake. However, the neighborhood is also home to a recreational area featuring a half dozen baseball diamonds, basketball courts and an Olympic-sized public pool.

> "This is Red Hook… This is the gullet of New York swallowing the tonnage of the world."
>
> **ARTHUR MILLER**

Another area of Red Hook, "the Back," runs along the Atlantic Basin and ends at the Brooklyn Battery Tunnel to the north. The enchanting streets here were built during the neighborhood's heyday in the early 20th century, when grain boats docked regularly at the port. Artists began the first stage of renewal in the 1970s, when they discovered the neighborhood's inexpensive row houses. With care and patient renovations, these brick palaces have been saved as elegant vestiges of a bygone era. The only problem with the Back is the neighborhood's lack of public transportation

The final section of Red Hook is the piers. Dozens of

warehouses along the former docks have been transformed by clever architects into habitable lofts. Each space is unique, with glorious views across the bay to the Hudson River. Many residents choose to work at home or have private garages where they can store their automobiles. Other inhabitable docks like Pier 41 have become home to trades like glass blowing, etching and carpentry businesses. Today, residents can meander along a half-mile of waterfront esplanade, featuring many historical sites and cultural performances as well. The intention has long been to spur economic re-development along this port, including new housing, public services and perhaps

THE PEOPLE

POPULATION	32,000
AGE	
0-17	23%
18-44	47%
45-64	19%
65+	11%
ETHNICITY	
White	73%
Black	25%
Asian	2%
Spanish speaking	33%
Family households	42%
College educated	34%
HOUSEHOLD INCOME	
Below $25,000	42%
$25-75,000	45%
$75-150,000	11%
$150,000+	2%

WWW.ZANYS.COM
Find a NYC apartment now!

(though unlikely) expanded train service.

Red Hook has one of the best green-space-to-people ratios in the city, and many of the area's parks and playgrounds have been completely rehabilitated by the New York Parks Department. In an effort to dispel Red Hook's rough image, community boards have tried to accentuate the more positive aspects of the neighborhood. Now, when people think of Red Hook, they picture quaint Brooklyn streets, hard-working middle-income families and picturesque views of the Statue of Liberty from the piers. Red Hook has lots of potential as an exciting 21st century New York neighborhood, and developers and apartment-hunters alike are sure to take full advantage.

Noise: Screaming kids are your only worries; at night the streets are peaceful.

THE NEIGHBORHOOD

AVERAGE MONTHLY RENT

Studio	$700-900
1 br	$800-1,000
2 br	$1,000-1,300
3 br	$1,200-1,700

AVERAGE SALE PRICE

Studio	$50,000-90,000
1 br	$50,000-90,000
2 br	$50,000-100,000
3 br	$55,000-150,000

COMMUTING

The limited-service F and G trains at Smith and 9th Streets serve the entire community. Many residents rely on buses to connect with other area trains. Cars are also prevalent.

DISTANCE

Time to midtown	10-15	min
Time to downtown	5-10	min

Parking: Fabulous. Expect to find a spot in front of your apartment or house most nights. Parking is so plentiful that large, private garages are unnecessary.

Kids & Families: If you have a loose parental style, Red Hook is a perfect place to bring up kids. Children play all summer long like in the suburbs; however, commuting to private schools is difficult, and local public schools are notoriously poor.

Safety: Red Hook is safe during the day, but be wary at night. The quiet industrial blocks make for easy mugging avenues. Drug traffic has been present in the neighborhood for years, and ports are difficult for police to patrol. The Back is generally considered safer than Red Hook proper.

Entertainment: Nothing until recently except for the playgrounds and ballfields. Newcomers have opened a few cute bars and restaurant hangouts. Residents learn to make their own entertainment around here.

Restaurants: Defonte's Sandwich Shop, a family business open since 1922, is a typical Red Hook eatery. Ever since dockworkers began arriving in droves, food has been fast, cheap and transportable. Ferdinando's on Union Street is another local legend.

Parks & Gardens: Excellent, especially if you don't need a daily infusion of Manhattan to live a rich life.

Shopping: Pathetic. The only major merchant is the massive Home Depot. Supermarkets are small and retail stores offer slim pickings.

Final Words: If you're looking for privacy and an apartment that's bigger than you should be able to afford, Red Hook is perfect. Most people gripe about the inconvenient commute to the city, but car commuters do quite well.

ROOSEVELT ISLAND
— MANHATTAN —

They say beauty is in the eye of the beholder, and nothing exemplifies this better than Roosevelt Island. Due east of Manhattan, this 147-acre strip of land sits in the middle of the East River, extending roughly from 45th to 85th Street. Depending on who you are, Roosevelt Island may either seem creepily desolate and isolated or like the third bowl of porridge and just right.

Through the past centuries, Roosevelt Island has gone through a number of transformations and half a dozen name changes. The city of New York purchased it in 1828, and in the early part of the 20th century it became known as Welfare Island. The city built prisons, poor houses and nursing homes on the land, but soon most were relocated, and the island's buildings were destroyed or vacant.

A final name change took place in 1973 when Welfare Island became Roosevelt Island. The New York State Urban Development Corporation took control of the land and began building housing for a mixed-income community. Various apartment buildings were constructed, and residents began moving into this odd community stuck in the middle of the river. In 1989, luxury residences were built on Roosevelt Island in the form of five 21-story buildings dubbed Manhattan Park.

Roosevelt Island is divided into Northtown, the developed area of the island; Southtown, 19 acres of open space; Southpoint, 10 acres that have been abandoned for 40 years that make up the southern tip of the isle; and Octagon Park, 10 acres on the northern end. The island is under the political jurisdiction of Manhattan, but it receives its police, sanitation and fire services from Queens. Bridges connect the island to both Manhattan and Queens, and residents can travel by car, subway or bus.

Folks who want to raise their kids in a quiet environment with almost non-existent traffic will love Roosevelt Island. There isn't much to choose from as far as businesses go, although every weekend farmers and vendors gather to sell their goods. The island also has it's own post office and library. Residents enjoy Sportspark, an athletic center with a pool, basketball courts, squash courts, as well as other choices for fitness enthusiasts. There are pools in Island House (for apartment residents only) and Westview (open to all island residents). Manhattan Park has its own fitness facility.

About 30%-40% of the residents in Manhattan Park are affiliated with the United Nations, and a good number of Marymount Manhattan College students also live in Manhattan Park. However, the school is building dormitories for its students, and will not renew their leases as they expire within the coming year. Since one of the original uses for the Island was to provide housing and medical services for the disabled, many residents who are disabled or who have special needs find Roosevelt Island particularly attractive. There are various organizations like the Roosevelt Island Disabled Association ready to provide support. Residents do not have to travel far to access the few businesses, and it's common to see folks in wheelchairs or with other aids making their way around.

A lot of changes are about to take place on this quiet island. The untouched area of Southtown is scheduled to see the creation of 2,000 new apartments. In addition, there are plans to build new condominiums on the island. In late 1999, plans were set for a $100 million project to build the Engel Burman Eldercare Facility to provide long

"Not only is New York City the nation's melting pot, it is also the casserole, the chafing dish and the charcoal grill."

JOHN V. LINDSAY

term care for senior citizens. Meanwhile, Marriott wants to occupy Southpoint with a Hotel and Conference Center with approximately 350 hotel rooms. The proposed complex would also include a restaurant and ferry service. And in January 1999, Manhattan Park decided that all leases that are to come up for renewal will be brought to market rates. Rents could increase as much as 50% or as little as 5%, depending on when the initial signing of the lease for an apartment took place.

Residents have been naturally concerned that these developments will diminish their quality of life. With only one road leading into the island, construction traffic will likely create a very difficult situation that will try even the

THE PEOPLE

POPULATION	8,300
AGE	
0-17	16%
18-44	40%
45-64	24%
65+	20%
ETHNICITY	
White	64%
Black	26%
Asian	6%
Other	4%
Spanish speaking	15%
Family households	54%
College educated	41%
HOUSEHOLD INCOME	
Below $25,000	30%
$25-75,000	46%
$75-150,000	13%
$150,000+	11%

most patient of residents. Trips to the subway and tram that are now quaint and short walks, may not be so quaint, short—or quiet—anymore.

THE NEIGHBORHOOD

AVERAGE MONTHLY RENT

Studio	$900-1,400
1 br	$1,200-1,500
2 br	$1,700-2,400
3 br	$2,000-3,000

AVERAGE SALE PRICE

Studio	$125,000-150,000
1 br	$130,000-340,000
2 br	$150,000-500,000
3 br	$200,000-900,000

COMMUTING

The N train has one stop on Roosevelt Island, and the tram goes straight across to East 68th Street.

DISTANCE

Time to midtown	10-15 min
Time to downtown	5-10 min

Noise: If you listen closely, you just may be able to hear a pin drop.

Parking: Sparse street parking, but the Motorgate Garage has plenty of space.

Kids & Families: Small-town feel for your family if the big, bad city is too much for you. When your kids become teens, expect them to take the tram on afternoons and never come back home. You've been warned.

Safety: Residents should feel pretty comfortable and secure here.

Entertainment: You'll either have to go to Manhattan or be satisfied watching TV.

WWW.ZANYS.COM

Find a NYC apartment now!

Restaurants: Hungry? Here are your choices: (a) Capri Pizzeria and Italian Restaurant, (b) China 1 Kitchen or (c) Trellis Restaurant.

Parks & Gardens: There's Blackwell Park, just north of the subway station, that may give up a chunk to the planned apartments. There's Lighthouse Park at the tip of the isle. Octagon Field, Capobianco Field and the Octagon Pony Field are available for multi-sport usage. Also located in the Octagon area is the community garden where residents can exercise their agrarian tendencies. Be nice and share.

Shopping: Hardly any, although there is a large Gristedes supermarket.

Final Words: Roosevelt Island is in transition and about to undergo a major phase of development that will bring more people to the Island, thereby carrying out the original grand plan. Developers and some residents struggle over the possible impending identity crisis of Roosevelt. The question is whether these new digs will make this neighborhood more attractive than it is now to people across the river; and, whether the "New Roosevelt" will alienate those who have come to love it so.

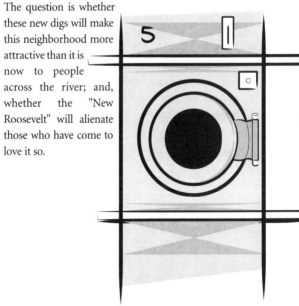

ST. GEORGE
→ STATEN ISLAND ←

Most Manhattan residents either treat Staten Island with disdain or simply forget about its existence. This suburban borough is, however, part of New York City, despite appearances to the contrary. St. George, the gateway to Staten Island from Manhattan, proves that it is possible to live in New York without living in the city. It is certainly not for everyone, but then again that is what keeps St. George a small town, even if it is part of the largest city in America.

Every day, hundreds of tourists ride the Staten Island Ferry for the magnificent views of lower Manhattan and the Statue of Liberty. Few ever venture out of the ferry terminal during their excursion, but if they did they would find themselves in the historic town of St. George. Situated on a hill overlooking the waterfront, St. George has a charming all-American feel and great views of Manhattan, Brooklyn and New Jersey.

Manhattan real estate developers first got the idea of creating a commuter community on this spot in the 1830s. St. George did not really take off, however, until after the Civil War. New York business was booming, and Staten Island offered a country retreat for middle and upper-class residents to build houses. When the many different ferry services to Manhattan were consolidated at the St. George Terminal in the 1880s, the town hit its heyday. St. George's appeal was

> "The voluptuous curve of the riverbank at 79th Street… escapes from the city's rigid grid of streets and avenues like a fat woman slipping out of a corset."
>
> **TOM BUCKLEY**

much the same in those days as in these: fast and easy transportation to Manhattan.

Though there is plenty of public transportation on Staten Island, the borough's suburban nature makes getting around without a car quite challenging. However, the ferry terminal is an easy walk from town, and ferries depart every fifteen minutes during rush hour. The ride takes about twenty minutes and features lovely views of New York Harbor. The ferry is usually about half full of sightseeing tourists and half full of those actually trying to get back and forth from between the two islands.

There are a few large apartment complexes in St. George along with rows of historic houses. Unlike other parts of the island, St. George is more small town than suburban in atmosphere. Though some of the old townhouses are rather shabby, they all have the potential to be very charming. The streets are lined with trees, and the houses have small yards and gardens. It is a very family-friendly atmosphere with ice cream trucks, children riding bicycles in the street and American flags waving from the porches.

In the historic district, there are many excellent examples of the shingle style of late 19th century architecture. Some beautiful houses have been well-preserved, although unfortunately they are mixed in with just as many that have been sorrowfully neglected. Reaching high above them all is the impressive spire of St. Peter's Catholic Church, a neo-Romanesque cathedral. Across from the ferry terminal stand two grand buildings from the same era; Borough Hall was built in the style of a Louis XIII chateau, while Richmond County Courthouse has a grand, classical design. And perhaps the most impressive building in St. George is Curtis High School. Built in 1902, this imposing structure was Staten Island's first public high school.

St. George Park is in the center of town and features a children's playground. A bit farther afield is Snug Harbor

Cultural Center, an impressive arts center that houses the Staten Island Botanical Gardens. For those who would rather look at skyscrapers than roses, there is the North Shore Esplanade with incredible views of the Verrazano-Narrows Bridge and Manhattan skyline.

THE PEOPLE

POPULATION	147,000
AGE	
0-17	28%
18-44	32%
45-64	24%
65+	16%
ETHNICITY	
White	76%
Black	18%
Asian	4%
Spanish speaking	13%
Family households	35%
College educated	24%
HOUSEHOLD INCOME	
Below $25,000	25%
$25-40,000	24%
$40-60,000	22%
$60,000+	29%

St. George has an active civic association that is quite busy promoting the town and planning improvements. If they have their way, many of the shabbier historic buildings will probably soon find themselves transformed and renovated, and New York families looking for small town peace and quiet will not even have to leave the city to find it.

WWW.ZANYS.COM
Find a NYC apartment now!

Noise: Hardly any except for children playing in the daytime.

Parking: There is plenty of streetside parking and a couple of parking lots. Many of the apartment complexes have garages available to residents.

Kids & Families: Families are very welcome here. Kids not only have access to playgrounds, but hopefully have their own backyards as well.

Safety: Don't become too enchanted by the small-time charm—it is good to remain cautious even in this suburban atmosphere, especially at night.

Entertainment: You'll have to get in a car or hop on a bus to find any.

Restaurants: An array of delis, different take-out options and fast food.

THE NEIGHBORHOOD

AVERAGE MONTHLY RENT

Studio	$500-800
1 br	$700-1,000
2 br	$900-1,800
3 br	$1,200-2,200

AVERAGE SALE PRICE

Studio	$20,000-40,000
1 br	$40,000-130,000
2 br	$50,000-150,000
3 br	$60,000-180,000

COMMUTING

The 1 and 9 trains go to the Staten Island Ferry. The Staten Island Railway runs from St. George to Tottenville

DISTANCE

Time to midtown	35-45 min
Time to downtown	25-40 min

Parks & Gardens: The small, kid-friendly St. George Park is here. Also nearby are Snug Harbor Cultural Center and the Staten Island Botanical Gardens.

Shopping: Local groceries and delis. You can take the bus to the Staten Island Mall. Or, you can just take the ferry to Manhattan.

Final Words: There is nothing hip or trendy about St. George, but if you long for a more suburban way of life, this is a commuter-friendly place to find it.

SHEEPSHEAD BAY
BROOKLYN

Sea breezes and fresh fish might seem the very opposite of what life should be like in New York, but Sheepshead Bay is the city's answer to its urban fishermen. Indeed, Sheepshead Bay offers not only fresh fish and tasty restaurants, but relative proximity to Manhattan, albeit at a price that is increasing as New Yorkers realize that water makes a better neighbor than a 54-story concrete chunk.

In the 1870s, Sheepshead Bay was a getaway for wealthy Manhattanites who ran from the hectic city lifestyle to the upbeat and risky business of horseracing. Yes, Ocean Avenue used to be home to a horseracing track. The affluent folks also would take full advantage of the many resorts and hotels in the area.

After gambling on horses was outlawed, the racetrack tried to switch to car racing, calling the once popular racehorse track "Sheepshead Speedway" in 1915. But it did not last for long. It was replaced by a commercial housing development in 1919. In the 1930s, the piers along Emmons Avenue were built as a result of a municipal building program. In the 1950s, with the opening of Beltway Parkway, came a steady flow of middle-class

Jewish and Italian families. Today, it remains very much a solid, middle-class locale. Most recently there has been an arrival of Russians into this area who have moved from nearby Brighton Beach.

Sheepshead Bay is located in Brooklyn along the Atlantic Ocean, just east of Brighton Beach. The area got its name from a once common fish in the area, the Sheepshead, now long gone due to city pollution. The inhabitants tend to be retirees, which adds to the feel of this locale, reminiscent of a small fishing town in New England. The people are laid back, but still quite dynamic.

Fishing boats and yachts along the piers are readily available for willing customers. It costs about 30 dollars per adult, though children under 12 get a discounted fare. Cruise along the inlet and enjoy the cool sea breeze atop one of these boats. If you are not the seafaring type, there are plenty of venders that sell fish fresh off the boat. Or, if you don't feel like lugging around a stinky fish for the day, you can still order them fresh off the boat at neighboring restaurants.

Lundy Brother's, an architectural presence in this locale, has been a popular seafood dinner destination as long as anyone can remember. With its stucco frame reminiscent of a Spanish house, it was booming as early as 1950. Though it closed in 1979, it has been restored and renovated and opened its doors once more in 1996.

Sheepshead Bay's claim to movie star fame derives from the fact that its comedy club, Pips on the Bay, was the location where Joan Rivers, David Brenner, Rodney Dangerfield, and Andy Kaufman performed their first gigs, before they were swept up by the masses and Hollywood. The cool ocean air sweeps over you as you walk along gazing at the docked boats along the piers and the small, rustic seafood restaurants that line the streets.

One subsection of Sheepshead Bay, Manhattan Beach, is an exclusive residential area that is stock full of luxurious homes, many with eye-catching views of the ocean or inlet. Apartments tend more towards scarcity, since most of the residents seem settled in their ways with no real intention to vacate their residences any time soon.

> "A town that has no ceiling price,
> A town of double-talk; A town so big that men name her twice, Like so:
> 'N'Yawk, N'Yawk.'"
>
> **CHRISTOPHER MORLEY**

Noise: Not overly loud or overly quiet. Water is the perfect neighbor, after all.

Parking: Parking is rather horrendous around Emmons Avenue. But otherwise, it is possible to find places on the street.

Kids & Families: This neighborhood will not strike you as the ideal breeding and developmental ground for children, though a child or parent who likes the fisherman's life may have his hands full with things to see and do. The children may also lack playmates and have to fill their days with original and new ideas.

Safety: Sheepshead Bay feels like a safe haven. It is the type of place where the routine is routine, and it doesn't really have too many surprises around the bend.

Entertainment: There are a couple of Russian nightclubs in the area that are stimulating. Other than that, there isn't a whole slew of activities to choose from. The kids get a kick out of Fun Time USA, a dingy amusement park that is reminiscent of the days of old (don't expect Six Flags Great Adventure or anything). There is always the comedy club, Pips on the Bay, that has a roster of hysterical and talented comics.

Parks & Gardens: Manhattan Beach Park is a favorite among families for a day of relaxation and fun; Gateway Recreational Area is a huge natural space where you can

THE PEOPLE

POPULATION	114,000
AGE	
0-17	20%
18-44	30%
45-64	32%
65+	18%
ETHNICITY	
White	82%
Black	9%
Asian	8%
Spanish speaking	6%
Family households	39%
College educated	24%
HOUSEHOLD INCOME	
Below $25,000	32%
$25-40,000	20%
$40-60,000	28%
$60,000+	20%

go bird-watching, stargazing or walking through the natural surroundings. Marine Park is Brooklyn's largest recreational area.

Restaurants: Lundy Brother's Restaurant is definitely worth a visit for its eats as well as its eccentricity. If you are in the mood for some greasy yet satisfying food, try your luck on Avenue U, a Chinatown right in Brooklyn.

Shopping: Don't count on finding much here, except if you're looking to buy fresh fish at rock-bottom prices.

Final Words: Three words: fish, fish, fish. This little fishing hamlet is a nice change of pace and scenery. Take a

THE NEIGHBORHOOD

AVERAGE MONTHLY RENT

Studio	$500-800
1 br	$600-1,300
2 br	$700-1,600
3 br	$900-1,800

AVERAGE SALE PRICE

Studio	$40,000-80,000
1 br	$60,000-150,000
2 br	$70,000-180,000
3 br	$80,000-220,000

COMMUTING

The D and Q trains stop at Sheepshed Bay

DISTANCE

Time to midtown	55-70 min
Time to downtown	45-60 min

stroll along the beach or go on one of the boats and enjoy the ocean air and panorama. You can definitely expect to clear your head of the worries that plague everyday NYC existence.

WWW.ZANYS.COM

Find a NYC apartment now!

SOHO
MANHATTAN

odels, actors, artists, art dealers – if these are the people you always dreamed of having as neighbors in NYC, look no farther than Soho. But remember that fame must always be accompanied by fortune, and if you don't have lots of excess capital lying around, you might be a bit disappointed by Soho's sky-high real estate prices.

When New Yorkers use big real estate terms like "rehabilitation" and "gentrification," Soho is the first neighborhood to come to mind. Named for its location south of Houston Street, which forms its border to the north, Soho has been transformed from what was once a purely industrial neighborhood into a luxurious outdoor mall.

The transformation of Soho began in the late 1960s, when artists first discovered the neighborhood's cheap rents and large loft studios. They quickly set about ignoring zoning regulations and converted many former factories, sweatshops and warehouses into personal studios and alternative galleries. Since a group of artists successfully petitioned the city in 1971 to rescind the zoning regulations regarding former warehouse spaces, Soho has thrived as an artistic community as well as a dynamic neighborhood full of expensive fashion boutiques, restaurants and hotels.

> "The two elements the traveler first captures in the big city are extra-human architecture and furious rhythm. Geometry and anguish."
>
> **FEDERICO GARCIA LORCA**

The neighborhood forms an almost perfect square directly in the center of downtown Manhattan. Delineated by Houston Street, Crosby Street, 6th Avenue and Canal Street, this central location makes Soho an ideal place to live or work. Transportation to and from the neighborhood is quite convenient.

Not only is Soho well-situated, but it has a unique charm. With its cobble-lined streets and boutiques full of imported goods, Soho is reminiscent of a bustling European city. Each street is loaded with terrific places to eat, shop or view some of the world's best art in one of a hundred galleries and museums. All of these fancy attractions make Soho incredibly high profile, so pay no attention to the affected, pretentious attitudes you will undoubtedly stumble upon.

Soho can feel like a vacation from anywhere else in the city. Leisure time seems to last all week long, even for those who only work in the neighborhood. Long lunches, late brunches and armfuls of shopping bags are common sights. Many residents and visitors enjoy having museums like the Museum for Contemporary Art, The Museum of African Art and the Guggenheim Soho all within a short walk.

The majority of Soho buildings are six-story lofts with huge windows facing the street. Interiors often follow a minimalist aesthetic that mirrors the white-walled art galleries downstairs. Most buildings have been retrofitted with at least a freight elevator, but several streets of nothing but walk-ups (Sullivan Street in particular) still exist.

While it's easy to enjoy the occasional visit to Soho, it's much harder to find a place to live. Recent years have seen rents skyrocket, pricing out many original residents. Most apartments are renovated lofts with high ceil-

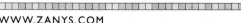

WWW.ZANYS.COM
Find a NYC apartment now!

ings. New residential spaces are rare, and if they are available, they're usually priced at over a million dollars per floor.

Your best bet continues to be subleasing. Many of the area's long-term tenants lease out apartments that they have had the wherewithal to hold onto. Such places are often not advertised but are certainly available if you keep your ears open. Brokers will also be helpful in landing a Soho loft, but expect to pay over $2 per square foot in addition to 15% of your first year's rent for their assistance. Because of such runaway prices, many New Yorkers fled to nearby Tribeca years ago. Others have converted part of their living quarters into home offices.

Since moving into Soho is a big investment, it's essential that you learn who your neighbors will be, as residents tend to be uptight about parties and other noise issues. Many older locals are bitter about the continually changing face of their once-quiet neighborhood.

Soho is expanding at a faster rate than most other New York neighborhoods, especially on a commercial level. Within the past year, Prada, Louis Vuitton, Gianfranco Ferre and other big fashion labels have all opened flagship stores on Soho's crowded streets, complete with cafes so you can shop and lunch in the same place. Spring Street is beginning to look more like Madison Avenue. It is up to you to determine if this is desirable or not.

Noise: Soho is relatively noisy due to constant delivery traffic on Canal Street and Broadway. Other streets, like Wooster, Greene and Mercer, are much quieter. At night the neighborhood is fairly still, except on weekends when jet-setters and fashonistas pile into the trendiest restaurants and nightspots.

Parking: Reliable parking is scarce unless you pay to park in a lot, which is very expensive. Residents eschew owning cars for this very reason.

Kid & Familes: Soho is an ideal place to raise a child, if you can afford it. To rear a large family, both Ma and Pa had better be working on Wall Street. One plus is that the excellent Stuyvesant High School is nearby.

Safety: Due to the large number of wealthy residents and tourists, Soho is a very safe place to live. Outsiders stick out like a sore thumb, and even the homeless are roughed up by the NYPD for begging on the sidewalk. You'd be hard pressed to find a safer place if you tried.

Entertainment: Soho style is all about black evening-wear and platinum credit cards. You don't go out to have fun here—you go out to be seen, and there are plenty of places to do both. Keep your eyes open for Leonardo DiCaprio and Kate Moss, who are both Soho regulars.

THE PEOPLE

POPULATION	84,000
AGE	
0-17	23%
18-44	42%
45-64	21%
65+	14%
ETHNICITY	
White	30%
Black	11%
Asian	43%
Other	16%
Spanish speaking	32%
Family households	82%
College educated	15%
HOUSEHOLD INCOME	
Below $25,000	23%
$25-75,000	20%
$75-150,000	41%
$150,000+	16%

WWW.ZANYS.COM
Find a NYC apartment now!

Restaurants: Too many to mention. Legends in the neighborhood include Spring Street Natural and Balthazar.

Shopping: Excellent, if pricey. Each street is filled with the best merchandise that the world has to offer. You'll love looking at all the things you can't afford, from priceless works of art to handmade gowns.

THE NEIGHBORHOOD

AVERAGE MONTHLY RENT

Studio	$1,600-2,200
1 br	$2,200-3,500
2 br	$2,500-5,000
3 br	$3,000-7,000

AVERAGE SALE PRICE

Studio	$200,000-350,000
1 br	$300,000-450,000
2 br	$500,000-800,000
3 br	$700,000-1,000,000

COMMUTING

The C and E trains stop at Spring Street. The N and R stop at Prince Street. The 6 train also stops here. Buses are not as useful in Soho as elsewhere.

DISTANCE

Time to midtown	15-20 min
Time to downtown	10-15 min

Final Words: If you have a bulging bank account, Soho is an ideal place to call home. Its quaint charm can't be beat, even as residents bemoan the proliferation of shops that make for unbearable weekend sidewalk traffic. Then again, most residents spend the weekends in the Hamptons anyway.

SUNNYSIDE
• QUEENS •

Residents are drawn to Sunnyside mainly because it's easy to leave the neighborhood and get to other places. This spot in western Queens is a perfect commuter community with access to trains, buses and plenty of highways. And as a middle-class suburban community, Sunnyside does have certain charms of its own.

In the 19th century, this area was the site of a farm on a small peak called Sunnyside Hill. When the Pennsylvania Railroad Company began constructing a train yard on the spot in 1907, the hill was leveled, and the neighborhood's name was shortened. The new railroad went through the first tunnel under the East River, which connected Manhattan to New England for the first time. The trains brought development, and Sunnyside became a popular community for working-class Manhattan families eager to escape from urban squalor.

Developers created one of the nation's first planned communities here, Sunnyside Gardens, a complex of small family houses and apartment buildings with courtyards. During the Great Depression, loyal Sunnyside residents barricaded their buildings with sandbags to try and evade eviction. Most didn't succeed, but the incident is telling of how strongly residents feel about their community. In the 1960s, however, many young families moved out to buy their American dream home elsewhere, leaving older residents to fend for themselves. Many low-income folks moved in during the 1970s and '80s, bringing crime and other statistics that clouded Sunnyside's reputation.

Today, residents are trying to restore their neighborhood's reputation. Sunnyside is still a little rough around the edges, having never quite regained its former glory. However, thanks to the Sunnyside Foundation (a not-for-profit group of committed residents), urban planning has returned as residents strive to continually improve services and the general state of their neighborhood.

Centered near Roosevelt Avenue and Queens Boulevard, Sunnyside is bordered by Queens Boulevard to the north and the Long Island Expressway to the south, and is split in half by the Brooklyn-Queens Expressway. Sunnyside Gardens takes up about 77 acres of the neighborhood between Skillman and 39th Avenues from 43rd to 50th Streets.

The Gardens, like Long Island City and other experimental settlements in Queens, were initially built to see how urban planning would work in the rapidly industrializing and expanding metropolis. Designers were more concerned with structure than aesthetics, so the architecture is unexceptional. Most houses face both the street and the back gardens, which sometimes border parks and other recreational areas. You'll be pleasantly surprised by how much you can get here for a small amount of money.

Sunnyside is a good, inexpensive alternative to many other areas of the city, without much remarkable in its make-up or amenities. The neighborhood is an interesting mixture of old and new, since it contains many cemeteries, industrial zones and abandoned railroad yards, alongside the many modern housing developments. Longtime residents feel a remarkable sense of pride in their little neighborhood. More recent arrivals came because the housing was cheap a decade or two ago when they couldn't afford something more beautiful. Hopefully, the community's efforts to better itself

> "People born in Queens, raised to say that each morning they get on the subway and 'go to the city,' have a resentment of Manhattan, of the swiftness of its life and success of the people who live there."
>
> **JIMMY BRESLIN**

will continue to reap good results, and Sunnyside will once again be a favorite commuter neighborhood.

Noise: Can be bad, depending on how close you live to the train line. Obviously, the closer you are, the cheaper your rent will be, but you'd better be an extremely heavy sleeper in that case.

Parking: Generally very good.

Kids & Families: This isn't the greatest neighborhood for older kids or teens, as there's not much to do around here except get into trouble.

Safety: The area has had some problems with crime, though it seems to be generally improving.

Entertainment: Mainly limited to people-watching,

THE PEOPLE

POPULATION	26,000
AGE	
0-17	16%
18-44	41%
45-64	22%
65+	21%
ETHNICITY	
White	70%
Black	2%
Asian	20%
Other	8%
Spanish speaking	23%
Family households	55%
College educated	27%
HOUSEHOLD INCOME	
Below $25,000	45%
$25-75,000	49%
$75-150,000	5%
$150,000+	1%

WWW.ZANYS.COM
Find a NYC apartment now!

dining out and video renting. Occasionally, this extends to watching a police bust, but that depends on where you live.

Restaurants: Very reasonable, but nothing to write home about.

Parks & Gardens: Sunnyside has lots of parks, great for pets and small kids.

Shopping: Most residents work in Manhattan and do their higher-end shopping there.

Final Words: In general, Sunnyside is a place to sojourn, not to settle down. On the other hand, it could ease your financial worries and free you up to live it up across the river on the spicier Manhattan scene.

THE NEIGHBORHOOD

AVERAGE MONTHLY RENT

Studio	$500-900
1 br	$700-1,200
2 br	$1,000-1,900
3 br	$1,200-2,400

AVERAGE SALE PRICE

Studio	$50,000-90,000
1 br	$70,000-250,000
2 br	$75,000-300,000
3 br	$85,000-350,000

COMMUTING

The 7 train goes to 40th and 46th Streets.

DISTANCE

Time to midtown	15-30 min
Time to downtown	35-40 min

TRIBECA
◆ MANHATTAN ◆

Mysterious, sunglass-wearing people dressed in head-to-toe black who go into a restaurant and seem never to come out. Edgy, brightly dressed characters carrying large parcels that look like paintings. If none of these images ring any bells, then think of slick inhabitants like Robert DeNiro, who also owns the trendy Tribeca Bar and Grill. Tribeca's name (which is an acronym for the Triangle below Canal) is a bit odd sounding itself, and just as it suggests, the area is home to the unordinary and the unexpected, the hip and the cool.

Like much of New York, Tribeca used to be eminently affordable, attracting many artists, social reformers and others looking to expand their expression and creativity. Then gentrification crept down the streets, inevitably changing the face and character of the neighborhood.

Like the Village and Chelsea, Tribeca has retained its bohemian feel while making way for the inevitable upper-middle class shops catering to antique collectors, decorators and gourmands. The streets, still some of the widest in the city, are beautifully lined with cobblestones.

Attractive people who are clear about their exact needs and wants are drawn to Tribeca. Residents generally want a space that will allow them to be high profile or low-key, depending on their mood. People here tend to be younger than other New Yorkers, but they are nonetheless well-established in their careers and want a living space that will complement their success.

For those looking to buy an older building or floor on a building and renovate, this is still a good area to search (although the East Village, Chelsea and Gramercy Park areas are also targets). "Tasteful" is a good word to describe Tribeca, but even this does not do justice to most of its apartments. The more tasteful and understated they look, the more they cost to put together. Shabby chic seems to be the décor of the moment. The height of the ceilings and layout of the buildings are an interior designer's dream come true.

Tribeca has a lot of quaint eateries, where style and grace are as important as the food. Big clubs and entertainment venues are hard to find here, and the ones that do exist don't need to advertise since their clientele

THE PEOPLE

POPULATION	23,000
AGE	
0-17	15%
18-44	60%
45-64	12%
65+	13%
ETHNICITY	
White	48%
Black	6%
Asian	45%
Other	1%
Spanish speaking	4%
Family households	52%
College educated	37%
HOUSEHOLD INCOME	
Below $25,000	45%
$25-75,000	38%
$75-150,000	6%
$150,000+	11%

THE NEIGHBORHOOD

AVERAGE MONTHLY RENT

Studio	$1,800-3,000
1 br	$2,300-4,000
2 br	$3,000-6,500
3 br	$3,600-8,000

AVERAGE SALE PRICE

Studio	$200,000-350,000
1 br	$300,000-450,000
2 br	$500,000-850,000
3 br	$700,000-1,000,000

COMMUTING

The N and R and the A, C and E lines run throughout Tribeca, with a busy nexus around Canal Street. Buses are useful for all commuters.

DISTANCE

Time to midtown	10-15 min
Time to downtown	5-10 min

is selective and self-selected. Besides, when you have a huge, lofty space to host parties in, who wants to go out?

This isn't exactly the warmest neighborhood in New York, so if you are looking for an ideal family destination don't stop here. Gen X-ers and their elders, however, seem to love it, and have solidly established it as a good choice in an understated way.

Noise: Noise isn't a problem, and things are pretty still at night.

Parking: There are some nearby lots, but expect to pay an arm and a leg.

Kids & Families: There aren't too many families around these parts, but good private schools aren't far away.

WWW.ZANYS.COM
Find a NYC apartment now!

Safety: Generally safe, although when out late at night, it's best to take a taxi home. Police presence is moderate—the residents don't like anything heavy-handed.

Shopping: Tons of little shops are situated here and sell higher-end goods to discriminating buyers. Clothes are correspondingly high-end boutique types, although there are a couple of chain stores in the neighborhood.

Entertainment: There are more places to hang out at and have a fine dinner than real party places. Most residents go elsewhere in the city rather than skip around the corner for what they're looking for. If you are easily star-struck though, you are guaranteed to see plenty of celebrities here.

Restaurants: There are plenty of great places to eat around here, particularly Continental cuisine and luscious Italian.

Parks & Gardens: Tribeca isn't known for its gardens. Residents tend to go elsewhere to get their outdoor fix.

Final Words: If you know you'll only be in New York a short while, this might be a great place to live while you get a real taste of the city.

> "Manhattan is a narrow island off the coast of New Jersey devoted to the pursuit of lunch."
>
> **RAYMOND SOKOLOV**

UPPER EAST SIDE
• MANHATTAN •

New York's Upper East Side is one of the wealthiest, most exclusive neighborhoods in the world. For over one hundred years, New York's richest have called this cozy residential neighborhood home, and the blocks to the east of Central Park haven't changed much in all that time. Wealthy folks are generally satisfied with their status quo, so don't expect to find anything edgy in the Upper East Side. Instead, look here for refinement, elegance and gorgeous old apartments.

As New York spread up the island of Manhattan during the 19th century, the city's elite kept getting driven north, as well. At one time, all of New York's high society lived downtown in grand townhouses. As immigrants poured into lower Manhattan, established society politely exited the area. When Central Park was constructed in the late 19th century, it was obvious that uptown was the perfect place for New York's moneyed families to settle down.

The grand houses and apartment buildings con-

structed here were built to be fit for kings— and after all, this collection of old money and robber barons was the closest thing America had to r o y a l t y . Through the years, new waves of New Yorkers have gotten rich and moved into the neighborhood, but few visible changes have taken place. People move here because they want to be a part of this exclusive community, and no one wants to rock the boat.

The Upper East Side is located east of Central Park, running from 59th Street all the way up to 96th Street. Only 4% of New York's households are located here, but the neighborhood is home to 18% of the city's lawyers, advertising executives and public relations managers, 21% of its management consultants, 14% of its entertainment promoters and 16% of its economists. This is some of the most expensive real estate in the world. Residents earn an average of around $200,000, and along Park Avenue and East End Avenue that figure rises to about $700,000.

To say that the Upper East Side has some nice museums would be an understatement of extreme proportions. The "Museum Mile," as it's called, stretches from 79th to 104th Streets and strings together the Metropolitan Museum of Art, the Guggenheim, the Whitney Museum of American Art, the Cooper-Hewitt, El Museo del Barrio, the International Center for Photography, the Jewish Museum, the Museum of the City of New York and the Frick Collection. The neighborhood also contains the city's most exclusive retail district—these stores sell just about everything money can buy. Some of the famous, outrageously expensive stores on the Upper East Side include Sotheby's and Christie's auction houses, Henri Bendel, Tiffany's and Louis Vuitton.

> "It is ridiculous to set a detective story in New York City. New York City is itself a detective story."
>
> **AGATHA CHRISTIE**

It seems that rich people enjoy raising children almost as much as they like shopping. The neighborhood is full of carriages, strollers and adorable little ones, dressed in designer school uniforms. Central Park is one giant backyard for all the families living in the neighborhood, and

what a backyard it is! In the park, residents can enjoy all
sorts of athletic activities, attend concerts, go to the zoo,
wander through the woods for a little privacy or simply
revel in the romance of one of the most beautiful spots in
New York.

Park Avenue is lined with million-dollar homes owned
by people with million-dollar habits and privacy requirements. More modest apartments along Second, Third
and Lexington Avenues are host to a majority of the
investment banking, finance and corporate types. Quite a
few bankers and Wall Streeters live up here, as well as corporate higher-ups who occupy homes in the city during
the week and retreat to the Hamptons for the weekends.

THE PEOPLE

POPULATION	57,000
AGE	
0-17	10%
18-44	51%
45-64	27%
65+	12%
ETHNICITY	
White	94%
Black	2%
Asian	4%
Other	3%
Spanish speaking	1%
Family households	56%
College educated	72%
HOUSEHOLD INCOME	
Below $25,000	19%
$25-75,000	45%
$75-150,000	11%
$150,000+	25%

WWW.ZANYS.COM
Find a NYC apartment now!

Some liberal-thinking folk are put off by the neighborhood's displays of affluence and exclusivity, while less high-minded people are attracted by these same qualities. The residents of the Upper East Side are usually quite fashionable but never trendy, and this is true of the neighborhood itself, as well. Don't expect any sudden changes to take place here in the years to come. Barring an unforeseen disaster, such as a meteor crashing into Central Park, the Upper East Side's real estate prices are going to remain out of reach for the vast majority of New Yorkers.

THE NEIGHBORHOOD

AVERAGE MONTHLY RENT

Studio		$1,600-2,200
1 br		$1,800-3,500
2 br		$2,200-4,500
3 br		$3,000+

AVERAGE SALE PRICE

Studio		$150,000-250,000
1 br		$200,000-500,000
2 br		$250,000-800,000
3 br		$600,000-900,000

COMMUTING

The 4, 5 and 6 trains all run to 86th Street, and the 6 train also stops at 77th, 86th and 92nd Streets along Lexington Avenue.

DISTANCE

Time to midtown	15-20 min
Time to downtown	30-35 min

Noise: You may hear some of this hustle and bustle down below if you live along Lexington or Park Avenues, as well as 59th and 86th Streets. At night, you shouldn't hear a thing except your spouse's snoring.

Parking: Don't depend on street parking, because there are many cars in this neighborhood. Luckily, there are plenty of garages and anyone seriously considering moving here shouldn't find them prohibitively expensive.

Kids & Families: There are tons of kids here, and the safe, private neighborhood is great for the families who can afford it.

Safety: This is one of the safest areas of the city.

Entertainment: Either throw your own swanky cocktail party or take a cab downtown for your thrills.

Restaurants: This neighborhood has many high-class restaurants, some middle-of-the-road eateries and a few diners.

Parks & Gardens: Central Park is right next door, and there's green space along the East River. On 63rd Street you'll find the Central Park Zoo and Castle Clinton, both popular destinations for kids.

Shopping: You'll lack for nothing living here as long as you've got your Platinum card ready.

Final Words: The Upper East Side is the epitome of elegance and sophistication. This neighborhood is a perfect place to settle and start a family, and nowhere else in New York has such a refined, sedate atmosphere. If you're part of the upper-class or aspire to it, then by all means move on up to the Upper East Side.

UPPER WEST SIDE
• MANHATTAN •

The Upper West Side was once regarded as the poor kid brother of the more glamorous Upper East Side, but the area has undergone a renaissance of sorts with restaurants, bars, comedy clubs and gyms springing up all over. No longer can snotty Upper East Side residents look down upon their western neighbors. Today, the main difference between the two areas is that West

Side dwellers tend to be younger and more socially active and artistic. For these residents, the neighborhood appeals because it combines the best of suburban living with all the amenities of upscale Manhattan.

In keeping with this new hip image, it has become de rigueur for celebrity darlings to call the Upper West Side Home. Helen Hunt and Meg Ryan have put down roots here. The West Side is where Jerry Seinfeld lives, on the TV show and in real life, and his cynical urban wit exemplifies the mood of the neighborhood.

Despite its wealthy status, the Upper West Side is not all fame and fortune. Due to its popularity, the boundaries of the neighborhood have been extended from 84th street up to 114th street on Riverside and Broadway, and 104th on Central Park West. There are still projects in these northern areas and some blocks show the scars of urban poverty. The current cultural cachet of the Upper West Side is linked to the buoyant status of the economy, making the long term stability of the neighborhood less secure than appearances would suggest.

> "New York… that unnatural city where everyone is in exile. None moreso than the American."
>
> **CHARLOTTE PERKINS GILMAN**

Critics get on the area's case, saying that residents have never met a cause they didn't like. Most locals truly care about the state of their neighborhood and community, and will organize others to change things. This is one of the best-educated areas in Manhattan, and as a result, there are always a lot of cultural activities.

The buildings may be prewar, but their inhabitants do not exemplify old-school Manhattan money. You will find few poodles here; though residents have enough disposable income to afford the best, they aren't so interested in stuffy pretensions. This is hardly a steady or staid neighborhood, and most who live here are too busy to sit around, so the streets are buzzing night and day.

As far as sights go, Central Park West is one big landmark, and the recently opened Rose Center for Earth and Science makes for a good conversation piece. There are also several nearby mansions dating to New York City's robber-baron period. Restaurants like Carmine's and Tavern on the Green are world-famous for the quality of their service and food, and Ollie's is an Upper West Side institution that serves Chinese and American food. H&H Bagels, which ships their dough around the world, is considered by many to make the best bagel-maker on the planet.

Part of the Upper West Side's draw is that it has become known as the starting point for new ventures appealing to Generation X-ers and older crowds. The Reebok gym is just one example, famous for spurring national fitness trends such as spinning, rock climbing and kick boxing. Residents are comfortable with themselves, and are adventurous enough to still want to go out, even though they aren't the party animals they used to be. Unattached locals have many places to go to meet other singles; the coffee shop Drip has gained attention for its singles books where you can leaf through pages of descriptions of eligible mates and choose a potential partner as you sip your java.

Economic forecasts aside, the Upper West Side can be a reassuring blend of old and new, and for those who are just a little too settled for Tribeca or the East Village, the Upper West Side offers a great alternative to the more established neighborhoods like the Upper East Side and Midtown.

WWW.ZANYS.COM
Find a NYC apartment now!

THE PEOPLE

POPULATION	166,000
AGE	
0-17	13%
18-44	52%
45-64	23%
65+	12%
ETHNICITY	
White	71%
Black	16%
Asian	4%
Other	9%
Spanish speaking	21%
Family households	40%
College educated	60%
HOUSEHOLD INCOME	
Below $25,000	34%
$25-75,000	43%
$75-150,000	10%
$150,000+	13%

Noise: Considerable around Broadway and on 72nd and 96th Streets. The neighborhood is extremely quiet if you live off of Broadway.

Parking: It depends where you look. Some streets have free parking for most of the week, but the major roads are congested 24/7. If you can't find a good place, however, garages abound.

Kids & Families: The Upper West Side is known as one of the best places to raise kids, with many exceptional public and private schools nearby. There are more children here than in most other areas of New York, so younger kids will have plenty of playmates.

THE NEIGHBORHOOD

AVERAGE MONTHLY RENT

Studio	$1,500-2,100
1 br	$1,800-2,700
2 br	$2,000-4,000
3 br	$2,900-5,000

AVERAGE SALE PRICE

Studio	$130,000-300,000
1 br	$220,000-500,000
2 br	$300,000-1,200,000
3 br	$400,000-1,400,000

COMMUTING

The 1, 2, 3 and 9 trains run up and down the West Side. The local 1 and 9 have stops at 59th, 77th, 86th and 96th Streets, and the express 2 and 3 have stops at 96th Street. There are plenty of buses that run to midtown and downtown from this area.

DISTANCE

Time to midtown	10-20 min
Time to downtown	30-40 min

Safety: This area is generally extremely safe, but things do get progressively sketchier the further west and north you wander.

Entertainment: The Upper West Side is known for its comedy clubs, as well as some good live performance places. There aren't a lot of nightclubs yet, but this is changing.

Restaurants: This neighborhood harbors some of the city's best restaurants. Locals don't lack in expendable income, and most spend it on good food and wine.

Parks & Gardens: The Upper West Side is right next to Central Park and near the river, so there's more greenery here than you can shake a stick at. Riverside Park, which starts at 72nd and Riverside, boasts multiple gardens, vistas and free-range dog parks.

Find a NYC apartment now!

Shopping: Shopping can be adventurous, since there is more fun and trendy stuff available than you'll find in most neighborhoods. A proliferation of stores appeal to the well-heeled more than to the student set.

Final Words: The Upper West Side is a great middle ground for people who are tired of the hostility of the busier sections of New York. This neighborhood combines sophistication with earthy activism—a balance not easily found in this sometimes cynical town.

WASHINGTON HEIGHTS
• MANHATTAN •

Washington Heights has so much potential as a residential neighborhood that it's a shame that crime and neglect have ruined its reputation. The neighborhood has a rich history, some architectural gems and access to incredible park space, yet it still remains one of Manhattan's least desirable addresses. Hopefully, the current real estate boom will help Washington Heights out of its slump, but don't hold your breath since it can take quite a while to reverse decades of urban decay.

The Heights really are quite high; in fact, the neighborhood is built on one of Manhattan's tallest hills, which spreads out between the Harlem and Hudson Rivers. Evidence of the region's once pristine natural condition is still evident in the lovely parks. Washington Heights was named, of course, for George Washington, but was in fact the site of one of the American army's worst defeats during the Revolutionary War. The neighborhood remained a rural farming community throughout the 19th century, made up of large estates

> "Anything that's ever happened on the planet can happen in New York City."
>
> **DICK WOLF**

overlooking the Hudson River. But as soon as subways were built connecting Washington Heights to the rest of Manhattan, attractive apartment buildings went up, and people, mostly Jewish immigrants, moved in. Today, the neighborhood is dominated by African-Americans and Hispanics.

Washington Heights runs from West 154th Street north to West 173rd Street and is bordered by the Hudson and Harlem Rivers on either side. Beautiful vistas await at the top of the Trinity Church, an imposing gothic edifice on West 155th Street. Broadway forms the spine of Washington Heights, and also serves as the main drag for all restaurant, retail and transportation needs. Store after store sells almost identical brand-name merchandise to local hip-hop consumers. Times have been so hard in recent years that most of the businesses off Broadway have had to shut their doors. For safety during the day or at night, most residents only feel comfortable walking on this main street's well-lit sidewalks.

> "What the New Yorker calls home would seem like a couple closets to most Americans. Yet, he manages not only to live there but also to grow trees and cockroaches right on the premises."
>
> **RUSSELL BAKER**

The neighborhood's gorgeous infrastructure stands as a testament to what Washington Heights could be. Today, Washington Heights is a very low-income area; many residents have been out of work for years. Understandably, the community has a noticeably low collective morale. The streets are often in need of a serious cleaning, as are many of the windows and building facades.

The completion of the George Washington Bridge in 1931 was an impressive feat of engineering. The bridge, which connects Washington Heights to New

WWW.ZANYS.COM
Find a NYC apartment now!

Jersey, today makes the neighborhood an ideal pipeline for illegal goods to enter the city. So, despite steady efforts by the NYPD Blue, Washington Heights still sees significant drug trafficking.

One bright spot in the midst of this rather grim neighborhood is Fort Tryon Park, a large hilly natural area overlooking the Hudson River. The park is a lovely place to relax and play, and features one of Manhattan's cultural treasures, the Cloisters, which house the Metropolitan Museum of Art's collection of Medieval works. Here, you can step back in time and enjoy the garden and impressive artworks from a bygone era.

Unfortunately, though, dismal 21st century reality awaits outside the park. You can find amazing fixer-uppers here, but must walk alone down the street at your own risk. Virtually every apartment has some vacancies, and entire streets are filled with boarded-up brownstones begging for rehabilitation. The great thing about Washington Heights is that if you establish good credit, you can basically live anywhere you like. Phenomenal spaces are available with high ceilings and majestic views of downtown or the Hudson River—all at prices more befitting Cleveland than Manhattan. Conscientious landlords are renovating spaces in hopes of luring wealthier residents; however, affluent individuals still feel insecure in these parts. Washington Heights may still turnaround, but chances are it won't be any time in the immediate future.

Noise: Washington Heights is plagued by car alarms, police sirens, ambulances, helicopters and the occasional gunshot.

Parking: Parking is available along most streets, with

THE PEOPLE

POPULATION	33,000
AGE	
0-17	32%
18-44	38%
45-64	22%
65+	8%
ETHNICITY	
White	39%
Black	58%
Asian	3%
Spanish speaking	71%
Family households	65%
College educated	22%
HOUSEHOLD INCOME	
Below $25,000	42%
$25-75,000	44%
$75-150,000	13%
$150,000+	1%

street-side cleaning rules always in effect. Better long-term parking is available on Riverside Drive. Safety is always a concern. Private garages are the only way to really protect your car from being vandalized.

Kids & Families: Many children call Washington Heights home, although some probably wish they didn't have to. This is a tough place to grow up, where kids are exposed early and often to evils absent in other neighborhoods.

Safety: Washington Heights has had one of the highest crime rates in Manhattan throughout the 1990s, as much of the big-time drug dealing pushed out of Harlem

THE NEIGHBORHOOD

AVERAGE MONTHLY RENT

Studio	$400-700
1 br	$500-1,100
2 br	$600-1,300
3 br	$1,000-1,700

AVERAGE SALE PRICE

Studio	$40,000-90,000
1 br	$60,000-150,000
2 br	$60,000-200,000
3 br	$65,000-300,000+

COMMUTING

The 1 and 9 trains stop at 125th, 137th, 145th and 157th Streets.

DISTANCE

Time to midtown	10-15	min
Time to downtown	5-10	min

wound up here. Much of the crime is drug and gang-related, although a good set of deadbolt locks on your door won't hurt.

Entertainment: Local hangouts are mostly members-only clubs. Many of the dance clubs and bars court a dangerous element. You're best off to party at home or go downtown for your entertainment.

Restaurants: The standard fare includes inexpensive Spanish diners and restaurants serving staples like rice and beans, plantains and chicken. Food is well-priced but selection is limited. Jamaican restaurants offer some much-needed variety.

Parks & Gardens: Riverside and Fort Tryon Parks offers some solace from this neighborhood's rough atmosphere. For summer relief, there's a huge swimming pool on West 173rd Street and Amsterdam Avenue.

Shopping: You should have no problem finding grocery stores, beauty salons and 99-cent shops.

Final Words: Washington Heights is still too bedraggled to make the extremely affordable and large apartments worth the risk. Once personal safety is no longer such a big concern, it might be worth a shot. If you're gutsy, you can live like a king here on a pauper's budget.

WILLIAMSBURG
— ● BROOKLYN ● —

These days, it seems like everybody's moving to Williamsburg. The West Village, the East Village and Manhattan in general have become passé for young hipsters, and the word on the street is that Williamsburg is where it's at. But what wonders actually await those shopping for apartments across the East River? Happily, the hype about this neighborhood is justified, and most residents are loving their trendy new Brooklyn lifestyle. Williamsburg is a diverse and bustling neighborhood, where stylish young people mix with the remains of old-fashioned industry and ethnic communities.

Until the mid 19th century, Williamsburg was its own city, independent of the rest of Brooklyn. The neighborhood began as a farming community; however, the opening of the Erie Canal in 1825 turned New York into one of the world's most important ports, and Williamsburg's location on the East River made it an important new center of commerce. The community's population grew rapidly, as did the businesses along the waterfront.

Even more people were attracted to the neighborhood in 1906, when the Williamsburg Bridge connected it to Manhattan. Tenement buildings went up, and the neighborhood became known for terrible living conditions and general urban squalor. In the 1930s, Williamsburg served as a refuge for Jewish immigrants fleeing Nazi-controlled Germany, who began self-sufficient communities in the southern section of the neighborhood. New York's first housing project was built in the neighborhood during this era and efforts to alleviate the neighborhood's housing problems continued into the 1950s. Unfortunately, in 1954, the Brooklyn-Queens Expressway was constructed and cut right through the heart of Williamsburg. Thousands of residents lost their homes, and it seemed that the neighborhood's spirit had been totally destroyed.

However, concerned residents refused to give up on Williamsburg, and many began working to give their neighborhood new life in the past few decades. Artists discovered the neighborhood's charms in the 1980s and began converting abandoned lofts and storefronts into studios apartments. The neighborhood is home to a rich diversity of residents, dominated by a large Hispanic community and the ever-growing ranks of yuppies. The far south end is still dominated almost exclusively by an insular Hasidic community. Though historically there have flare-ups between Puerto Rican residents and the Hasidic community, tensions seem to have cooled down in recent years.

> "There's a tree that grows in Brooklyn. Some people call it the Tree of Heaven. No matter where its seed falls, it makes a tree which struggles to reach the sky."
>
> **BETTY SMITH,**
> **A TREE GROWS IN BROOKLYN**

Williamsburg is a large area, stretching from the East River to the Queens County border on the east. As the neighborhood's reputation has grown, rents have correspondingly skyrocketed. The neighborhood is now considered one of the most desirable rental markets outside of Manhattan. The northern section, divided by the Brooklyn-Queens Expressway, has recently become crowded with predominantly white residents in their 20s. Many abandoned warehouse spaces initially offered terrific lofts and live/work studios, but many of these prime spaces have been snatched up already.

Thankfully, as Williamsburg's popularity has grown, more developers have started converting unused commercial spaces into habitable residential lofts. Most of the facilities and services are located around the main drag on Bedford Avenue, so rental properties closest to the first stop on the L train are in the hottest demand. Spacious apartments can also be found inside the large pre-war buildings that line Metropolitan Avenue and Grand Street. You can expect prices in this Brooklyn hotspot to only get worse, and you'd better have some inside connections if you hope to score a good deal on one of these popular apartments.

Noise: Moderate on the main avenues; elsewhere you could hear a mouse squeak. A large bus port, subway trains and cars traversing the Williamsburg Bridge make for loud mornings and rush hours.

Parking: Plenty, but be wary of leaving nice cars in unprotected lots and desolate streets. The lack of sidewalk traffic makes Williamsburg a carjacker's dream.

Kids & Families: Williamsburg isn't very family-friendly, offering few opportunities for the wee ones. Outside of the insular Puerto Rican and Hasidic communities, family-oriented renters look elsewhere.

Safety: Cops are hard to find if you need one. Patrol cars do semi-routine sweeps through the warehouse areas and the projects. Despite this lack of attention, the streets are generally safe, although they can become empty quickly.

Entertainment: In recent months many new bars and restaurants have opened in the area. Rowdy crowds hang out at the Sweet Water Tavern, while hipsters like The Abbey and Enids and older crowds congregate at the Brooklyn Ale House, Teddy's and Muggs.

Restaurants: Aside from the legendary Peter Luger's Steak House, and near the trendy area near the first L subway stop, restaurants are hard to find.

Parks & Gardens: Residents love nearby McCarren Park in Greenpoint, which has tennis courts, baseball diamonds, an all-purpose running track, a soccer field, basketball courts and a children's playground.

Shopping: Varies greatly, depending on the area in question. Northern Williamsburg has seen a host of new retail additions, including bookstores, coffee shops, video rental stores, music shops and a small but diverse collection of eateries. Southern Williamsburg is dominated by kosher

THE PEOPLE

POPULATION	77,000
AGE	
0-17	37%
18-44	37%
45-64	16%
65+	10%
ETHNICITY	
White	81%
Black	15%
Asian	4%
Spanish speaking	49%
Family households	30%
College educated	5%
HOUSEHOLD INCOME	
Below $25,000	61%
$25-75,000	36%
$75-150,000	2%
$150,000+	1%

THE NEIGHBORHOOD

AVERAGE MONTHLY RENT

Studio	$800-1,500
1 br	$1,100-1,900
2 br	$1,200-2,500
3 br	$2,100-3,000

AVERAGE SALE PRICE

Studio	$80,000-100,000
1 br	$125,000-180,000
2 br	$140,000-400,000
3 br	$150,000-800,000

COMMUTING

The L train stops at Bedford, Metropolitan, Grand and Graham Avenues, and the G train stops at Metropolitan and Lorimer Streets.

DISTANCE

Time to midtown	10-15 min
Time to downtown	5-10 min

markets and other stores appealing to the Hasidic community. Manhattanites love scavenging the bins of thrift clothes at the enormous Domsey's Warehouse.

Final Words: Williamsburg is still on the rise. As renters continue to get priced out of Manhattan and seek refuge in this up-and-coming East Village look-alike, the neighborhood will only become more popular.

WINDSOR TERRACE

BROOKLYN

Windsor Terrace has been a residential area for well over a hundred years, and time has only increased the neighborhood's charm. In the early 19th century, there were more cows in this section of Brooklyn than people. That began to change in 1849 when John Vanderbilt sold the farmland to developers, one of whom, William Bell, began laying out plans for much of what comprises Windsor Terrace today. In the years to come, Bell laid out streets and built dozens of houses, a school and a firehouse. Over time and with much care, the area became an attractive neighborhood filled with tree-lined streets and well-sized row houses.

Windsor Terrace is tucked in between Prospect Park to the west and Greenwood Cemetery to the east, south of Caton Avenue and north of Prospect Park West. The neighborhood is only nine streets wide, split down the middle by the Prospect Expressway. For years, Windsor Terrace was forgotten by the majority of New Yorkers in their search for attractive, livable real estate. The rising popularity and reputation of neighboring Park Slope has meant a surge of interest in Windsor Terrace, a nearby, lower-cost alternative.

> "New York is a granite beehive, where people jostle and whir like molecules in an overheated jar."
>
> **NIGEL GOSLIN**

Residents find the neighborhood an ideal place to bring up a family. Like Brooklyn Heights, Windsor Terrace's streets are well isolated from outside traffic, making perfect places for children to play stickball, hopscotch and other games. Windsor Terrace is also home to some of the highest-rated public schools in the borough, and is close to several renowned private institutions in Park Slope and Brooklyn Heights. Prospect Park is nearby, offering a lovely, peaceful place to picnic, play or find seclusion.

Until very recently, the neighborhood has been home to a tight-knit community of families who have lived here for generations. Families tend to hand down homes through generations, making it difficult for outsiders to gain a foothold. Only as housing demand has grown in recent decades has Windsor Terrace truly begun to change. New public housing projects were begun in the area, designed to bring moderate and middle-income families to the neighborhood. Soon, many landlords began chopping up homes into multiple family apartments.

Buildings in Windsor Terrace are mainly brick or limestone row houses. Many have been converted from single-family dwellings into multiple-family homes, and some feature circular facades. A handful of warehouses have also been made into homes. Windsor Terrace is home to a healthy mix of friendly people. Residents belong to a variety of ethnic groups, but all share a strong commitment to keeping their neighborhood beautiful. If local real estate continues to boom, expect prices to climb well past their current reasonable levels. Local sons and daughters dread the day when Windsor Terrace prices climb out of the reach of their children. Already the neighborhood isn't quite what it used to be. This is good news if you want to move into Windsor Terrace but bad news for the locals who would like to hold onto the community their parents helped create.

Noise: The residential streets of Windsor Terrace are almost as quiet as nearby Greenwood Cemetery, but not nearly as eerie.

Parking: Plenty of spaces are usually available on the streets, but you'll have to compete for them with your neighbors. Plan on racking up a good share of parking tickets from the unreliable meters.

Kids & Families: Windsor Terrace is one of best places in New York to raise a family. Similar to nearby Park Slope, Windsor Terrace has all of the necessary facilities for parenting and child rearing.

Safety: A surprising number of at-home mothers form an unofficial neighborhood watch. Women are safe walking the streets of Windsor Terrace. Residents avoid Prospect Park at night.

THE PEOPLE

POPULATION	63,000
AGE	
0-17	25%
18-44	41%
45-64	19%
65+	15%
ETHNICITY	
White	70%
Black	18%
Asian	12%
Spanish speaking	23%
Family households	37%
College educated	25%
HOUSEHOLD INCOME	
Below $25,000	39%
$25-75,000	52%
$75-150,000	8%
$150,000+	1%

THE NEIGHBORHOOD

AVERAGE MONTHLY RENT

Studio	$700-1,200
1 br	$800-1,400
2 br	$900-2,000
3 br	$1,000-2,600

AVERAGE SALE PRICE

Studio	$80,000-100,000
1 br	$130,000-170,000
2 br	$150,000-300,000
3 br	$180,000-600,000

COMMUTING

The F train stops at Prospect Park.

DISTANCE

Time to midtown	45-50	min
Time to downtown	35-40	min

Entertainment: Dinner and a movie are your only local options. Locals do their daily duty in Manhattan and then come home to enjoy peace and quiet.

Restaurants: Diners and modest family restaurants provide decent meals.

Parks & Gardens: Prospect Park has everything you'd ever need to maintain an active and healthy lifestyle, and the Brooklyn Botanical Gardens are only a short bike ride away.

Shopping: Expect to travel to find retail items other than hardware and groceries.

Final Words: Although a little out of the way for those who work in Manhattan, Windsor Terrace is a terrific place to look if you plan to start a family or if you need a little peace and quiet.

WWW.ZANYS.COM
Find a NYC apartment now!

WOODHAVEN
• QUEENS •

I n the early 19th century, developer John R. Pitkin came up with a secret plan to turn the Queens neighborhood now known as Woodhaven into a new city, which would become as big and important as Manhattan and Brooklyn. The plan didn't work out. Woodhaven is no major metropolitan area; however, it does have certain small-town charms, which residents have worked very hard to cultivate. And it's probably for the best, anyway. How many Manhattans does New York really need?

Woodhaven is located south of Forest Park and north of Atlantic Avenue. Jamaica Avenue has cut through the neighborhood since Colonial times and been attracting travelers and settlers ever since. The neighborhood first rose to prominence in 1821, when Queens County lifted its ban on horse racing and the Union Course Race Track opened. The racetrack brought in visitors from all around the young nation, and it was this new commerce that gave John R. Pitkin his ideas of developing a metropolis.

Unfortunately for Pitkin and his city-to-be, in 1837 the country's economy entered a recession. However, a few years later, a chisel factory opened in the area and brought in new residents. Sometime in the mid 19th century, the neighborhood began to be recognized as Woodhaven, and the name has stuck. It wasn't until an elevated train was built along Jamaica Avenue that the neighborhood really saw much development.

Woodhaven has the looks of an all-American small town that has fallen on slightly hard times. The streets are lined with cute wood-frame houses from the turn-of-the-century, with small yards and trees lining the sidewalks. American flags wave in the wind; however, most houses appear rundown and the yards are fenced-in.

Jamaica Avenue is crowded with shops and businesses of all sorts. There are lots of discount stores and delis, as well as a variety of businesses offering different services. It's not Fifth Avenue, but residents should be able to find what they need.

The people of Woodhaven have made efforts to have

THE PEOPLE

POPULATION	58,000
AGE	
0-17	27%
18-44	33%
45-64	34%
65+	6%
ETHNICITY	
White	59%
Black	18%
Asian	13%
Spanish speaking	26%
Family households	33%
College educated	17%
HOUSEHOLD INCOME	
Below $25,000	31%
$25-75,000	22%
$75-150,000	19%
$150,000+	28%

WWW.ZANYS.COM
Find a NYC apartment now!

certain residential blocks listed as historic landmarks and some creative fixing-up could turn these old houses into lovely residences. One landmark that visitors can check out is Neirs Tavern, an 1838 general store that was turned into a tavern in the 1850s. Mae West began her performing career here as a child, and Martin Scorcese used it in *Goodfellas*.

Woodhaven is a cute neighborhood with a slightly seedy edge. It wouldn't take much to turn it into an adorable town, but it's impossible to know how development trends will flow in the city. The best sign for Woodhaven is that concerned residents are determined to keep the neighborhood's charms intact.

Noise: The neighborhood stays pretty quiet except around big streets like Jamaica Avenue.

THE NEIGHBORHOOD

AVERAGE MONTHLY RENT

Studio	$400-600
1 br	$500-800
2 br	$600-900
3 br	$700-1,500

AVERAGE SALE PRICE

Studio	$45,000-85,000
1 br	$50,000-90,000
2 br	$55,000-100,000
3 br	$60,000-120,000

COMMUTING

The J and Z trains stop at Woodhaven Blvd.

DISTANCE

Time to midtown	50-70	min
Time to downtown	45-60	min

Parking: Parking isn't a problem here, although safety is a concern.

Kids & Families: Lots of families live in these small houses and most do have access to a small yard of their own.

Entertainment: You won't find much to do on a Friday night, although there are some local dives you could venture into for a little excitement.

Restaurants: There's an assortment of diners and various ethnic cuisines on Jamaica Avenue. Don't expect anything fancy.

Parks & Gardens: Forest Park is nearby and provides lots of trees, grass and room in which to play.

Shopping: You can find all the necessities on Jamaica Avenue as long as your tastes aren't too uppity.

Final Words: Woodhaven has small town charms but has been somewhat neglected in the past decades. A little effort could return the neighborhood to its glory days, but at the moment it's a rather run-down slice of Americana on the outskirts of the city.

WWW.ZANYS.COM
Find a NYC apartment now!

WOODSIDE
• QUEENS •

Queens is not up to par with the rest of New York City, according to the majority of elitists that live in Manhattan. But the offbeat neighborhood of Woodside deserves far more credit than the rest of the admittedly mundane borough.

Woodside was established by a diverse group of immigrants at the turn-of-the-20th century. What makes the neighborhood so unique is that most of its current residents are also from a range of ethnic backgrounds, one of the most mixed groupings in all of New York City actually.

Woodside's boundaries are Woodside Avenue on its western side to 34th Street on the east. Its northernmost point is the tip of Saint Michael's Cemetery, and to the south it is defined by the Mt. Zion and New Cavalry Cemeteries. Sound a little spooky? Yes, cemeteries are a bit of a turn-off, but the community is nonetheless vibrant.

> "The $100-plus dinner in New York is a major speculative undertaking akin to going after sunken treasure.... The cost of the expedition is going to be steep [and] you'll come out of it enriched or just soaked."
>
> **ROSS K. BAKER**

The apartment buildings here are not very large, but serve their purpose. Most are six-story buildings from the 1950s and 1960s, which offer conveniences like elevators, security systems and basement laundry facilities. What make these buildings so appealing, though, are their excessively detailed rooms.

For all of these luxuries, Woodside is inexpensive,

THE PEOPLE

POPULATION	66,000
AGE	
0-17	37%
18-44	37%
45-64	16%
65+	10%
ETHNICITY	
White	67%
Black	17%
Asian	16%
Spanish speaking	18%
Family households	33%
College educated	18%
HOUSEHOLD INCOME	
Below $25,000	42%
$25-75,000	51%
$75-150,000	6%
$150,000+	1%

especially if you consider that it is a mere thirty minute drive from Midtown Manhattan. Though a Woodside address isn't posh, residents marvel at what they pay compared to their Manhattan brethren.

This neighborhood isn't all perks, though. The noise here in the morning and evening can be unbearable, as Queens is part of many commuter routes into Manhattan. Since Woodside is up-and-coming, many of its buildings are run down and its landlords don't always put their money into overdue repairs. But, if you have a good head on your shoulders and are aware of any potential scams, Woodside will do the job.

THE NEIGHBORHOOD

AVERAGE MONTHLY RENT

Studio	$700-1,100
1 br	$800-1,300
2 br	$1,000-1,900
3 br	$1,200-2,400

AVERAGE SALE PRICE

Studio	$50,000-75,000
1 br	$55,000-100,000
2 br	$60,000-120,000
3 br	$70,000-150,000

COMMUTING

The 7 train stops at 46th, 52nd and 61st Avenues.

DISTANCE

Time to midtown	20-25 min
Time to downtown	35-40 min

Noise: In the morning and late afternoon, you can hear the sounds of trucks, subways and car stereos just about anywhere in the neighborhood.

Parking: Street parking is not hard to find, but you're probably safer using a garage.

Kids & Families: Woodside is a great place to raise a family, as it is cheap and most apartments here offer a lot of space.

Safety: The only real threat here is crazed drivers on their way home from work.

Entertainment: Woodside is a little lacking in this department, but Karaoke, drinking and Ping-Pong are fun sometimes.

Restaurants: There are also many different ethnic cuisines from Thai to Korean to Ecuadorian. Best of all, local eateries are exceptionally affordable, and many are BYOB.

Parks & Gardens: Despite its arboreal name, there aren't many trees in Woodside. The largest green space you'll find is New Calvary Cemetery to the south, but it's not open to the public. Residents make do with what they have; many play dominos on the curb or organize asphalt softball leagues in the makeshift public park that has evolved underneath the highway.

Shopping: Merchants focus on supplying residents with the essentials. Hardware stores, appliance dealers and various forms of discount stores make up the shopping scene. There isn't a big demand for luxury goods here.

Final Words: Woodside is a little rundown, true. But for young families who don't have a lot of money to spend, it's a great place to start off.

YORKVILLE
• MANHATTAN •

When people dream of living in New York City, Yorkville is probably the quintessential neighborhood that they conjure up in their minds. Situated in a quiet little corner of the Upper East Side, it is one of the few neighborhoods that has almost as many trees and flowers as it does apartments.

As a product of the late 1840s, its old buildings and pavement give Yorkville a Western European feel, which can be attributed to its foundation by German, Czech and Hungarian upper-middle-class immigrants. Foreigners came here to find better living conditions of course, but also to establish themselves politically. Books and newspapers were their main outlets of expression. Yorkville is still home to a handful of Hungarian publishing firms, the result of early 20th century political activism here. In some of the current European coffee shops that populate the neighborhood, politics remain a hot topic of conversation. This shouldn't be surprising given that the New York Mayor's office and home, Gracie Mansion, has been located in Yorkville since World War II.

York runs eastwards, parallel between East End and First Avenues right through Yorkville. The neighborhood is tiny, situated between 77th and 86th streets east of Lexington Avenue.

With the original residents' political freedom came financial prosperity, resulting in a massive build up of the infrastructure, most of which still stands strong today. As a quiet, quaint, mostly residential neighborhood, Yorkville almost feels suburban. The only annoying noises that you might hear are raucous schoolgirls. The Brearley School and the Chapin School, New York's top two elite, private girls schools, are a block away from each other on East End Avenue. If East End doesn't ring any bells, it's probably because it runs only through Yorkville, but it is among the most beautiful streets in New York directly overlooking the East River and the FDR Drive.

> "No other city in the U.S. can divest the visitor of so much money with so little enthusiasm. In Dallas, they take it away with gusto; in New Orleans, with a bow; in San Francisco, with a weak and a grin. In New York, you're lucky if you get a grunt."
>
> **FLETCHER KNEBEL**

The architecture here is both beautiful and historic. Five-story brownstones from the early 1900s make up the majority of buildings, with lovely details like wrought-iron railings, intricate moldings and interior gardens. Queen Anne and Tudor style brick buildings are most common. Originally, there were thirty-two buildings built by the architect John C. Henderson, twenty-four of which still remain. Henderson used features such as wide arched entryways, terra cotta plaques, windows divided into tiny square panes and projecting bays and oriels. Current inhabitants are all members of New York's upper-upper-class, and each brownstone is worth several million dollars. There are also several apartment buildings in Yorkville, but they are equally as expensive, given the area's peacefulness and prestige. While brownstones are mostly occupied by large families, well-off singles have been flocking to the gorgeous apartments.

> "Little has changed in our New York neighborhoods except the faces, the names, and the languages spoken. The same decent values of hard work and accomplishment and service to the city and nation still exist."
>
> **DAVID DINKINS**

No matter where you live in this utopian part of town, you will be in close proximity to Carl Schurz Park (sort of a smaller Central Park), and the boardwalk that runs directly parallel to the East River. On any given day you will see a slew of yuppies jogging, well-dressed women walking their poodles and good-looking men spending the afternoon with their newborns. Everyone who lives here seems to be living life to its fullest.

Despite the residential emphasis of the neighborhood, in recent years restaurants and little shops have popped up everywhere. Early Yorkville settlers have left their marks here, as the neighborhood offers some of the best European candy shops, bakeries, and butchers in the city, including many that have been around since the turn-of-the-20th-century. There are also many family-run diners that are perfect for any meal. For more trendy restaurants, the new-ish Penang is a great place for Malaysian food and a hot meeting spot for Yorkville's plethora of singles.

WWW.ZANYS.COM
Find a NYC apartment now!

THE PEOPLE

POPULATION	108,000
AGE	
0-17	9%
18-44	46%
45-64	27%
65+	18%
ETHNICITY	
White	93%
Black	2%
Asian	4%
Other	1%
Spanish speaking	4%
Family households	36%
College educated	70%
HOUSEHOLD INCOME	
Below $25,000	19%
$25-75,000	43%
$75-150,000	10%
$150,000+	28%

As increasingly more wealthy people discover the gem that is Yorkville, the area is becoming one of New York's most affluent. It's up there with nearby Park Avenue real estate. What distinguishes Yorkville, though, is its self-sufficiency, which is a rare quality to find amongst the normal hustle and bustle.

Noise: Complete silence is common here, unless you live on or near 86th Street, which is congested with buses and trucks.

Parking: Really hard to find. The neighborhood's overabundance of kids means lots of parents looking for parking spaces so they can drop off and pick up their young ones safely. Let's face it—Suburbans were not designed for city life.

Kids & Families: Expecting parents will find this to be an ideally quiet and restful place to raise a family.

Safety: The area is generally very safe, but it shuts down after midnight, thus making it an ideal target for the notorious East Side Rapist. You'll be fine if you don't walk alone at obvious hours.

Entertainment: Comedy clubs and a few yuppie bars like Who's On First exist here, but that's about it.

Restaurants: Pastries, baked goods and meats galore are available from the local European eateries.

Parks & Gardens: Carl Schurz Park borders Yorkville along the river. The park was named after an illustrious German immigrant and boasts one of the city's longest

THE NEIGHBORHOOD

AVERAGE MONTHLY RENT

Studio	$1,500-2,300
1 br	$1,700-3,300
2 br	$2,000-4,000
3 br	$2,500-5,000

AVERAGE SALE PRICE

Studio	$150,000-250,000
1 br	$180,000-450,000
2 br	$200,000-500,000
3 br	$300,000-700,000

COMMUTING

The 6 train will drop you off at 68th Street and Lexington. There are several bus lines running up and down Lexington, 1st and 2nd Avenues to midtown and downtown.

DISTANCE

Time to midtown	10-15	min
Time to downtown	5-10	min

WWW.ZANYS.COM
Find a NYC apartment now!

dog runs. Free concerts are often held there Wednesday nights.

Shopping: A mix of bourgeois house and home stores, and discount chain stores are located in Yorkville.

Final Words: Yorkville is a great representation of old world New York, as its name suggests. It is one of the few neighborhoods that has managed to maintain its original state, without being completely overrun by huge corporations. Despite the high rents, everything else in the neighborhood is moderately priced, making it a great location for people who have their priorities straight and know how to manage their money well.

> "Give me your tired, your poor, your huddled masses yearning to breathe free."
>
> **EMMA LAZARUS, INSCRIPTION ON THE STATUE OF LIBERTY**

"It is a great monument to the power of money and greed… a race for rent."

-FRANK LLOYD WRIGHT ON NEW YORK CITY

272

WWW.ZANYS.COM
Find a NYC apartment now!

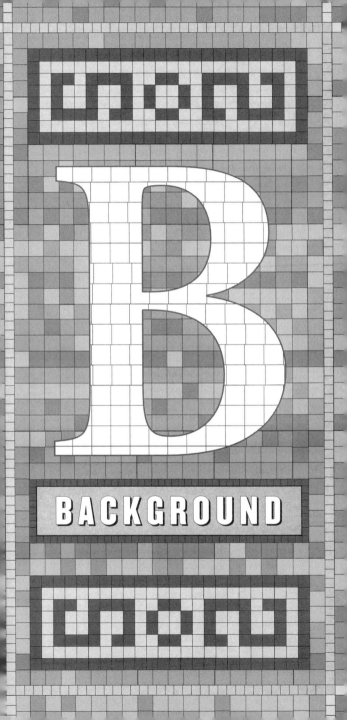

B

BACKGROUND

BROKERS & FEES

NEW YORK HAS MANY QUIRKS, BUT ITS MOST ONEROUS TRADITION IS THE BROKER FEE SYSTEM—A MIXED BLESSING THAT'S HEAVILY RIGGED IN EVERYONE'S FAVOR BUT YOURS. IF YOU NEED TO FIND AN APARTMENT QUICKLY IN NEW YORK, YOU TRADITIONALLY HAVE HAD TO GO THROUGH A BROKER. THE ADVANTAGE IS THAT THEY TAKE CARE OF A LOT OF THE HEADACHES FOR YOU. LIKE A REAL ESTATE AGENT, THEY SEPARATE THE WHEAT FROM THE CHAFF AND TAKE YOU TO ONLY THOSE PLACES THAT MEET YOUR RENT AND QUALITY-OF-LIFE REQUIREMENTS.

andlords prefer this system because brokers filter applicants ahead of time, screening their credit and renting histories and generally sorting out the flakes and weirdos. However, be advised that most brokers are in the Manhattan area, so the apartments they list won't be cheap. If you have some ready cash, great credit and want the convenience of someone else to do the dirty work for you, then the broker system is probably more help than hassle.

If you decide that you have the money and could use a broker's services, you need to do some homework. First, ask if your company has a broker of choice, since many do (particularly high-flying law firms and investment banks), which they either pay for or arrange a deal through—generally about 3% off the regular fee.

> "Why, if you're not in New York you are camping out."
>
> **THOMAS W. DEWING**

Second, you should interview a prospective broker, because not all are created equal. The "best" broker you hear about may not be the best one for you. Many people choose several brokers in the hope that one of them will find the perfect place. Try to narrow your broker list to two at the most and get to know them—and vice versa—so they become crystal clear about what you like and dislike. This will save you from the nightmare scenario of a broker who you don't know very well deciding to take you all over town and showing you places that you have zero interest in or can't afford. It pays to invest a little time up front to avoid wasting a lot of time later.

WWW.ZANYS.COM
Find a NYC apartment now!

Third, find out how long a broker has been in business and how knowledgeable she seems to be about the neighborhood or area you're interested in. If you're interested in Tribeca but your broker lives and works on the Upper East Side, chances are he won't know the neighborhood nearly as well as a broker who operates locally.

Fourth, you need to choose between brokers with more listings and sophisticated web pages, or smaller brokers with more personal service and deeper ties to the community of choice. If possible, ask around about the reputation of a broker before choosing. The older, bigger, slicker operations like Corcoran have an established clientele and tons of testimonials. Searching the internet or calling the Better Business Bureau will give you a better idea of what a broker's reputation is. There are also newer brokers on the block, but their reputation and repeat business rate aren't usually as good as others who charge higher fees.

Fifth, be very honest in dealing with your broker. If your credit is bad, or you don't make over $30,000 per year, or you have a criminal record, let them know. They'll either tell you to get a co-signer, refer you to somewhere else, or tell you to take a hike.

Let the broker know how much money you make, not only how much you can afford to spend. They are pros at the apartment rental numbers game, and can easily calculate what you can afford while still maintaining the lifestyle you prefer. Also, they know how much landlords will require you earn to rent a particular apartment. You might be clear that you're willing to live on macaroni and cheese and put most of your salary towards rent, but most landlords aren't willing to make that kind of judgment call. They are after the sure buck, and don't take many chances.

Broker's fees are generally 15% of your first year's rent.

For example, if you're going to pay $1,000 per month, that will mean you have to pay $1,800 up front to a broker, plus your first month's rent and a deposit to the landlord—about $3,800 all told. If this makes you feel a little nauseous, don't give up hope. You can do it on your own, but it might take much more time, persistence and cunning.

If you choose to forego a broker and try to find an apartment yourself, the first thing to do is to hit the internet, because if you wait around to find your dream apartment in the print versions of the *The Village Voice* or *The New York Times*, chances are it'll be gone by the time you call. *The Voice* comes out on Tuesday evening, so if you log onto their website on Monday night and hit the phones first thing Tuesday morning, you'll have a much better chance of finding something than the chumps who wait around for the printed version. *The New York Times* doesn't have many bargains, so don't waste much time looking there if your resources are severely limited. Finally, if you can make do temporarily with some of the low-cost options (see "Low-Cost Living Options"), you can buy yourself a little time as you wander through the apartment jungle.

> "No place has delicatessens like New York."
>
> **JUDY BLUME**

If you're doing it on your own, set aside as much time as possible to look at places. Schlepping around New York is no fun at all, but don't cut corners here—remember, you're competing with thousands of other apartment-seekers, so you get what you put into your search. It's easiest if you aren't working when you first arrive, but if you are, then you need to get creative about setting aside time to look. Take a long lunch, go before or after work, or be prepared to walk your tootsies off over the weekend.

In general, once you locate an available place (say, on the internet), the sooner you get off the couch to go look at it the better. Prime places have been known to go on and off the market in a matter of minutes. Also, don't spend a lot of time traipsing around if you don't actually have the money in hand to put down a deposit. A landlord isn't going to keep a place on hold for you out of the goodness of her heart. "Winner Takes All" holds truer in New York than in most places, and in the world of apartment hunting the winner is the one who shows up first and plunks down cash or a cashier's check on the spot. If you can't afford to do this when you first arrive, find someplace you can crash temporarily until you can earn or borrow the cash.

Another way out of the broker/fee/deposit quandary is to move in with someone who already has a lease under his belt. There are benefits and liabilities to all of the above options. Think clearly about what you want and what you're willing to sacrifice to get it before you start your search. It will save you a lot of time and money in the long run.

BUDGETING

UNLESS YOU'RE A TRUST-FUNDER OR A LOTTERY WINNER, YOU MOST LIKELY DO NOT HAVE THOUSANDS OF DOLLARS AT YOUR ELBOW TO PLUNK DOWN IN DEPOSITS AND FEES FOR AN APARTMENT, ESPECIALLY IF YOU'RE COMING STRAIGHT FROM COLLEGE. WELCOME TO NEW YORK. IDEALLY, YOU SHOULD PLAN ON SAVING AT LEAST $3,000 BEFORE YOU MOVE HERE.

I f you're in the unenviable but often-unavoidable position of arriving with barely enough cash for your first month's rent, though, you have fewer options. Once you've navigated the shark-infested rental waters of New York and have found your dream (or at least survival) apartment, you need to start thinking ahead all over again. Many people who move to New York find themselves grabbing the first expensive, overpriced place they find without considering the implications of their choice on their subsequent lifestyle. The stress and adrenaline that often accompanies apartment searches doesn't usually lend itself to wise decisions in terms of future spending potential.

The main point to remember is that what you set aside for rent you simply cannot blow on other things like restaurants or clubs. Far too many New York newbies find themselves "apartment-poor," meaning they have spent so much money finding, paying for and maintaining their homes that they have nothing left over for fun or savings. Below are some guidelines that will help you avoid jumping into something that may easily become an economic albatross.

#1 DEFINE YOUR PRIORITIES In an ideal world you could have it all: a great job, time and money to go out all the time, fun-filled weekends adventuring around town and opportunities to meet new people left and right. Given the expensive reality of life here and a limited budget, though, you need to get a clear idea of what things are really important to you, and in what order.

If your priority in New York is to party as much as possible, you probably can't afford to live in Manhattan unless you have a millionaire uncle who just died and left it all to you. Keep in mind every activity has its costs, and in this town they are anything but cheap. For the party-going crowd, cover fees at clubs typically run $15-25 per place, plus $10-15 per person for drinks, and $10-20 for a cab ride home. Also, you'll spend more cash on the trendy outfits you need to get into the clubs in the first place.

If you're the type that likes to throw lots of parties, you'll need a larger, expensive space, plus you'll have to shell out for booze and refreshments, which can run in the hundreds for a single soiree. All told, you're looking at only having enough money to live in Brooklyn or Queens—if that—left over from an average New York starting salary.

Even homebodies must factor in the costs of home videos (which aren't cheap here), takeout food and incredibly expensive grocery bills for choice fruits and vegetables. If you expect your job to be very demanding (in New York terms, that means 80-100 hours per week), it won't matter where you live, because you'll never see your apartment anyway. If you choose an expensive apartment and can't really afford it, you'll find yourself taking on a second job or other wage-generating activities to fill in the gap—and even then you'll have no spark left over on weekends to enjoy the wonderful place you spent so much time, energy and money to find.

#2 SET UP A MONTHLY BUDGET Once you've aligned your priorities (work, fun, travel or peace and quiet), start setting up a monthly budget based on how much you earn. First of all, figure that between local, state and federal taxes only about two-thirds of your paycheck will ever reach your wallet. Your rent ideally shouldn't be more than one-third of your salary, but if you want to live on more than Ramen noodles and a futon, plan on spending closer to half of your salary on rent.

Utilities, depending on the apartment and whether you live alone, will run you $100-400 per month. You know if you're a gabber and how much your average phone bill is—if you have lots of college friends and family out of state, consider using e-mail instead, or having people call you as much as possible. Going out depends on your preferences—maybe a few beers one night a week, or perhaps dinner and club-hopping from Thursday through Saturday. Count on spending $300-700 for food—no kidding—per month, depending on whether you're the rice-and-beans or Tavern-on-the-Green type. You can get an unlimited Metro pass for around $65 per month.

Line by line, break down what you want, subtract it from your tax-adjusted salary, and be honest about how much you really have to spend on rent once all of your other lifestyle choices are factored in. This is a serious business—you won't want to be calling your friends and relatives for cash if you spend yourself into a hole. A few tough, honest decisions will make your choice of apartments that much easier by eliminating those you can't afford by the sheer, cold numbers. Some people even go as far as to put the money they have for food, going out, clothes, etc. into separate bank accounts (or even envelopes) to keep their expenses straight.

As an example, Sally makes $3,000 per month, meaning she takes home $2,000 after taxes. She likes to party, so she has budgeted $400 per month for hair, make-up, shoes, pantyhose and everything else. She also likes to go out to eat, so she factors in $400 for food. Sally spends on average about $150 per month in phone charges. Give her an unlimited Metro card at $65, student loan payments of $200 per month and a health-insurance premium of $150 per month, and that leaves her only $635 per month for her apartment—a far cry below her $3,000 salary. With the numbers in front of her, Sally realizes she can either share an apartment, which doesn't bother her because she's never home anyway, or a shoebox in Queens barely big enough for all her clothes and Ricky Martin posters.

While this example might be extreme, it does show how these numbers add up quickly. Do your own math, and if you can't handle the facts, reconsider your priorities until you have a financial plan you can live with.

BUYING

IF YOU'RE CONSIDERING BUYING AN APARTMENT IN NEW YORK, MANY PEOPLE WOULD TELL YOU THAT BUYING INTO A CO-OP IS THE BEST WAY TO GO—IF YOU CAN PULL IT OFF. A COOPERATIVE, OR CO-OP, IS A RESIDENTIAL BUILDING THAT IS OWNED AND MANAGED BY A CORPORATION MADE UP OF ITS RESIDENTS. MEMBERS HOLD PROPRIETARY LEASES TO THEIR APARTMENTS AND OWN SHARES IN THE CORPORATION THAT CORRESPOND TO PARTICULAR UNITS.

C o-ops are owned jointly by all residents of a building, similar to shareholders who own stock in a company. Larger, more expensive apartments entitle their owners to more shares in the co-op, which in turn determines not only how much maintenance they pay on their apartment, but also how many votes they have in co-op decisions. A board of directors oversees the management of the building, which includes duties like allocating funds to pay for the building's expenses, mortgage payments, taxes, insurance and upkeep of the facilities. The co-op board also has responsibility for approving or denying prospective tenants from joining the co-op, decisions which are usually based on prospective tenant's credit history and current finances, and all too often on intangibles like the individual's lifestyle choices. The board can reject an applicant for any reason other than those protected by discrimination laws.

Co-op boards also rule on all renovations made to the building. Typically, if you choose to go through a commercial broker and are looking for a Trump Tower-style condo, there are a number of new listings on the market, since demand has made it easier for new construction to sprout up all around the New York area. You'll find listings in every price range except the lowest ones, so be prepared for six and seven-figures. In other words, unless you make a lot of money, the vast majority of condos and co-ops will be out of your price range.

Another thing to consider is how long you plan to stay in New York. If you're thinking of a condo or co-op as merely a good investment opportunity, think twice, because the hassle, paperwork and legal expenses involved in securing a place are considerable. If you're not going to be here for more than two or

> "Traffic signals in New York are just rough guidelines."
>
> **DAVID LETTERMAN**

three years, buying may be a bad choice. On the other hand, if the thought of dishing out a grand or three for rent every month makes your stomach churn, then buying may be the lesser of two evils. Think clearly about what your priority is, and be prepared to wait a long time while the process runs its course.

Unlike condominiums, co-ops entail more responsibility for owners. If tenants in the building do not pay their mortgage, or if apartments are left vacant, then other shareholders in the building are required to pick up the slack. In a worst-case scenario, if a co-op is unable to cover its mortgage, it may be given over to a bank or private owner, who can then change the property over to a rental arrangement, thereby erasing the shareholder's entire investment. For this reason, co-ops are typically very strict regarding who they allow in. It's best to be aware of the many rules and regulations you are agreeing to before buying into a co-op. Discuss the ramifications of the purchase agreement with a lawyer and thoroughly investigate the financial situation of the building before making a final decision. If you ever want to move out of the co-op, you can usually sell your shares to an incoming tenant.

The co-op route is often the most cost effective, but also the most time-consuming. If you're applying to co-ops and need a place to stay fast, consider short-term housing for up to a year (see "Low-Cost Living Options") while you jump through the various hoops. Co-ops only want members who they'll feel comfortable rubbing elbows with in the decades to come. Co-op residents tend to stay a long time, and there usually aren't a whole lot of openings at any given moment.

For various zoning, regulatory and financial reasons, it has become harder to get into a co-op than it was a generation ago. If you decide that this is still the route for you, be ready to submit more paperwork than it takes to get a top secret security clearance at Los Alamos. They'll rake your credit history over the coals and interview your past landlords intensively. There are many celebrities who move to New York and think they can buy their way into a co-op, but most places actually prefer to avoid the aggravation and exposure that high-profile people bring to the table. Julia Roberts couldn't get into one, if that gives you any idea.

One benefit to owning part of a co-op or condominium is that mortgage payments can be deducted from your federal income tax, whereas apartment rent cannot. Also, if the property value of your condominium or co-op appreciates faster than inflation, you stand to make a profit when you sell your property. You may also use co-ops and condos as collateral for future purchases. Home ownership is not for everyone, however. Unless you plan to stay in your home for more than five years, you're better off renting, because mortgage payments for the first five years do not substantially reduce the loan principal.

> "Don't you see, the rest of the country looks upon New York like we're left-wing, communist, Jewish, homosexual pornographers? I think of us that way sometimes, and I live here."
>
> **WOODY ALLEN**

Currently, the cheapest condos for sale are in the Wall Street area downtown, along the East and Hudson Rivers (which can be dicey in spots), and in the outer boroughs and New Jersey. For many, buying a condo in New Jersey means a much shorter commute, a better view and much lower taxes, all for one-third to one-half the price of a comparable place in Manhattan.

The best way to find a condo is to go through a broker (see "Brokers and Fees"). Although luck will get you by in most cities, it's all about the numbers in New York. Your income should be about 50 times your monthly mortgage, although there are buildings that will be a little looser about that, so determine up front with a reputable broker what you can comfortably—repeat, comfortably —afford. There's nothing worse than buying a great place in the center of everything and not being able to afford any of the many perks of living in this unique city.

COMMUTING

LOCAL TRANSPORTATION, AND ACCESS TO IT, IS AN IMPORTANT FACTOR IN CHOOSING WHERE TO LIVE IN NEW YORK CITY. LUCKILY, THE CITY HAS ONE OF THE BEST PUBLIC TRANSPORTATION NETWORKS IN THE COUNTRY, WITH A MOSTLY SOLID NETWORK OF BUSES, SUBWAYS, TRAINS AND TAXIS TO GET YOU WHERE YOU NEED TO GO. EVEN BETTER, EVERYTHING—WITH THE EXCEPTION OF TAXIS—IS REASONABLY PRICED.

First, you can't discuss subway access and commuting costs without first considering how much money you have to spare (see "Budgeting"). Unless you live out in the middle of nowhere, commuting costs will be fairly standard—about $3 per day or $65 per month for buses or the subway, and about $2 per day or $45 per month for the New Jersey Transit Authority's PATH system. Taxis are exponentially more expensive, and only practical for last-minute rush travel, especially when you can share them with someone else.

Costs start to climb quickly if you like to party hearty and take cabs home late at night, or if you work late and your company doesn't send you home in a company car. As the city has become safer under Mayor Giuliani's administration, you'll find more and more women travelling home alone late at night on the subway, saving money in the process.

> "After all, the three major sources of apartments are death, divorce and transfer."
>
> CORNELIUS GALLAGHER, REALTOR, ON READING OBITUARIES FOR LEADS IN THE TIGHT MANHATTAN HOUSING MARKET

As far as where to live, if you decide you want—or—have to live in one of the outer boroughs, then there's not much choice when it comes to commuting (aside from working at home). You'll certainly get to know the sights, sounds and smells of the city as you speed through town for hours every week. On the other hand, if you're the type who hates to commute, you should find a neighborhood closer to your workplace.

If you work on Wall Street, for instance, living in New

Jersey is a good option because you can hop on a train and be there in minutes. If you work in Midtown, commuting to certain parts of Brooklyn, Manhattan or Roosevelt Island would cut down on your commuting time, especially on the east side.

If you can't afford to live in Manhattan, you'll need to look at how much time you have or are willing to spend getting yourself to and from the subway, in all kinds of weather, wearing whatever it is you wear to work. If you have to get up at 6 a.m. to get to work by 8 a.m., you had better be a morning person, because facing the occasionally obnoxious subway rider after a sweaty 20-minute walk to the subway will not start your day off on a cheerful note. If you regularly get off work late and like nothing better than to hop off the subway and slip into your slippers, then a long trek home from the station is not going to sit well after a few weeks.

You should also look at how often the trains run and, if you live further out, whether there are express trains that can cut a lot of time out of your commuting schedule. For instance, if the N and R trains are the only ones in your neighborhood, then you should take into account that this is probably the slowest and most infrequent train in New York—you have to be a very patient person to depend on the N and R regularly. If, on the other hand, you work or live near the 4, 5 and 6 line, you can hop onto an express night or day and be where you want to go in no time.

Take the subway or bus to visit apartments to try out the route you'd be taking if you lived there. For instance, if the L train is the only one that services your neighborhood in Brooklyn, you should know that there are many neighborhoods that are a

long way from a station, and that your fellow subway riders will include a more financially diverse crowd than most other lines.

On the other hand, if you work regular hours and like taking the bus, then grab a map at a subway station and eyeball the bus routes. For many, taking the bus is a more civilized, interesting and comfortable way to get where you're going while being able to read, talk or knit at the same time.

If you're new to New York and don't know the city that well, it would behoove you to consider how much commuting time you can live with, and carefully weigh what options are available. If you choose to live in Manhattan, virtually everything is at your doorstep, but that convenience jacks up rent accordingly. Time, distance and price start to vary widely if you start to look at Queens, Brooklyn and New Jersey.

"URBANITY, n. The kind of civility that urban observers ascribe to dwellers in all cities but New York. Its commonest expression is heard in the words, 'I beg your pardon,' and it is not consistent with disregard of the rights of others."

AMBROSE BIERCE, THE DEVIL'S DICTIONARY

WWW.ZANYS.COM
Find a NYC apartment now!

WORKPLACE   QUICKEST COMMUTE

THIS TABLE LISTS THE MOST CONVENIENT COMMUNING OPTIONS FOR WORKING IN PARTICULAR NEIGHBORHOODS:

Workplace	Quickest Commute
MIDTOWN EAST	Brooklyn
	Roosevelt Island
	Murray Hill
UPPER EAST SIDE	Astoria
	Muray Hill
	East Village
	SoHo
	Little Italy
MIDTOWN CENTRAL	Murray Hill
	Tribeca
MIDTOWN WEST	Times Square
	Clinton
	Lincoln Center
	Upper West Side
	Flatiron
	Greenwich Village
DOWNTOWN	East Village
	New Jersey
	Brooklyn
	West Village
	Chelsea
	Nolita
	TriBeCa
	Little Italy
	Staten Island
	Northern New Jersey

DEMOGRAPHICS

MORE THAN ANY OTHER CITY IN THE COUNTRY, NEW YORK IS A TOSSED SALAD OF PEO-
PLE FROM ALL BACKGROUNDS, PHILOSOPHIES, ETHNICITIES, RELIGIONS AND SEXUAL
PROCLIVITIES. GIVEN THIS, YOU CAN LIVE AMONG AS MUCH DIVERSITY AS YOU
CHOOSE—OR NONE AT ALL, THOUGH THAT WILL BE HARDER TO FIND.

The typical cycle has run for centuries. Since the early days of Ellis Island, countless ethnic and racial groups have moved in, found themselves at the bottom rung of the social and economic ladder and spent the subsequent decades climbing to the next level while their own place has been taken over by newer, poorer groups. New York neighborhoods traditionally have attracted particular immigrant communities, eventually becoming dominated by certain ethnic or religious groups. As the communities prosper and their residents age, many people tend to move farther away when they can afford to purchase a dream house in the suburbs.

> "He speaks English with the flawless imperfection of a New Yorker."
>
> **GILBERT MILLSTEIN**

This cycle has changed somewhat as many urban yuppies decided that they didn't care who was in a neighborhood so long as the price was right (or that living among a rainbow of people was actually kind of neat), and as distinct groups began to intermarry and break the unspoken barriers of social access and assimilation. Slowing immigration rates have changed things, too. Now you'll find people of all backgrounds in many New York neighborhoods, but certain trends tend to persist, as described in the individual neighborhood write-ups.

If you love salsa and meringue music and the lilting sounds of Spanish, then look at neighborhoods that have large Hispanic populations. If you love peace and quiet and would prefer to live with older, settled folks, then Murray Hill or the Upper East Side would be a good choice for you. If you adore Indian cooking, move near

WWW.ZANYS.COM
Find a NYC apartment now!

Little India in the East Village.

Whatever your bag is, some place in New York will surely accommodate it. There's no reason not to explore and infiltrate other cultures during your stay. Given that most people couldn't care less where you come from, what your name is or what your preferences are, in New York you can become someone completely different like nowhere else in the world. If you grew up in Iowa and want to pierce your eyebrows, dye your hair black and serve coffee in the East Village, nobody here is going to blink an eye, so go for it. If you have interracial children and want them to be more exposed to both cultures, with a little research you can choose the neighborhood to best suit your dreams.

In each section of this book, you'll find a short description of the ethnic makeup of each neighborhood's residents, and info on what doors this will open should you choose to move there. Decide up front what you're looking for in terms of demographics, because next to financial and commuting considerations, this may be one of the most important factors about where to live. If you have kids and want a quiet, more suburban neighbor-hood for them, the demographic information provided in the Neighorhoods section can help you pick and choose what will work for you.

DOORMEN

AS LONG AS UPSCALE MANHATTANITES HAVE EARNED ENOUGH TO PAY SOMEONE ELSE TO DO ALL THE LITTLE THINGS THEY DON'T WANT TO BE BOTHERED WITH, DOORMEN HAVE BEEN HIRED TO TAKE UP THE SLACK. DOORMEN COME IN ALL SHAPES AND SIZES, BUT GENERALLY WEAR A DISTINCTIVE UNIFORM COMPLETE WITH CAP, MILITARY-STYLE JACKET AND WHITE GLOVES. AS THE NAME IMPLIES, THEIR JOB IS TO STAND INSIDE THE MAIN ENTRANCE TO A BUILDING AND MAKE SURE ANYONE ENTERING HAS A GOOD REASON TO DO SO—BUT THEY CAN DO MUCH MORE THAN THAT.

For people who work long hours, or who don't like to run errands, choosing a building with a doorman will be important. A helpful doorman can save you many hours each week since they can help arrange everything you formerly did yourself on frantic Saturdays. For instance, a doorman can receive packages for you so you don't need to go to the post office or the FedEx office to pick them up. They can accept your dry cleaning, laundry or groceries if you order them over the phone. They can also keep items at their desk to be picked up if your neighborhood has services that pick up clothes, furniture, shoes and the like for cleaning.

Most doormen have sweet dispositions, but cross one and you could find your packages getting misdirected or lost, or your friends getting hassled about coming up to your apartment. Doormen are invaluable to your comfort and convenience as an apartment dweller—in effect, they're the secretaries of the building—so it's a good idea to treat them with respect. Try to find buildings with doormen who seem to enjoy what they do and whom they do it for. That will speak volumes about the management of the building and the value they put on satisfied employees.

Buildings with

doormen are concentrated in the Upper East Side, Upper West Side and near Wall Street and Battery Park City. Most large apartment buildings anywhere in the city will have doormen, but the service won't be as personal as they are in smaller, more expensive buildings, since they're providing service to thousands of people and not just a select few. Their service will also add to the cost of an apartment, but for many this is worth it.

Finding a good-priced doorman building is often difficult, and many people (women in particular) consider themselves lucky if they happen on one. Life can be much more comfortable and worry-free if you know someone is downstairs 24 hours a day to help with the little things.

ENTERTAINMENT

NEW YORK COULD BE CALLED THE CAPITAL OF ATTENTION DEFICIT DISORDER—IF YOU LIVE TO BE ENTERTAINED, THIS TOWN OFFERS WHATEVER IT IS YOU'RE LOOKING FOR, NO MATTER WHAT IT ENTAILS, IN EVERYTHING FROM MOMENTARY BITES TO EXCESS.

◆ ◆ ◆ ◆ ◆ ◆ ◆ ◆

The neighborhoods with the most club action are located near the heart of Manhattan: Greenwich Village (particularly the East Village), SoHo, Flatiron and TriBeCa. If you're into people-watching, these neighborhoods offer endless opportunities. If you love trying out hot new restaurants, look to trendy neighborhoods listed in this book and rest assured that the restaurants and cafes that line their streets will ooze up-to-the-minute hipness. Comedy clubs and bars are located all over the map; you can find one in or near most neighborhoods.

Before you look at neighborhoods, it's a good idea to consider what you can afford (see "Budgeting"). Once you've established your budget, you can move on to what types of entertainment you will be able to afford in a given neighborhood. If going out to eat four or more times a week is your preference, for example (and you can afford to do so and still live in Manhattan), choosing neighborhoods with a wide variety of cuisines will work for you. If you want to eat in, then living anywhere and ordering out for the food of your choice would work just as well. Night owls thrive in clubby neighborhoods, and they also save money on the cabs they don't have to take home at 4 a.m.

If you have kids and are looking for things to entertain them, living near Central Park or an area with a lot of other children would be best. The Upper East Side also has a full supply of bookstores, clothing stores and the like that cater to kiddie consumers and their parents. Children living in or near Battery Park City also have plenty of parks to enjoy. If you're into the sexier entertainment zones like Greenwich Village, Times Square or Chelsea, then living down the block from your favorite club, shop or dungeon of choice always makes life easier. All things being equal, most people new to New York or renting for the first time choose neighborhoods with great restaurants and a park nearby.

The best advice is to figure out what your priorities are, and to do your research—which is where this book comes in. If you're in your early to mid 20s, then living in the center of all the after-dark fun is probably just what the doctor ordered. If you're in your late 20s to early 30s, then you probably still want to have access to the action, but aren't as interested as being in the middle of it, so living on the outskirts of Manhattan would work for you.

Those in their mid 30s to mid 40s, including (but not limited to) committed couples, are probably looking for more peace and quiet, in which case a neighborhood in the outer boroughs would work well. Older arrivals can usually live quite happily in more sedate neighborhoods. Consider the financial, ethnic and social makeup of a neighborhood (see "Demographics" and the various neighborhood sections) to get a good indication of the types of entertainment available wherever it is you're thinking of living.

FAMILY & SCHOOL ISSUES

WHEN MOVING TO NEW YORK WITH CHILDREN IN TOW, EITHER AS A SINGLE PARENT OR AS A COUPLE, THERE ARE SOME SPECIFIC REALITIES YOU'LL HAVE TO FACE WHEN FIGURING OUT WHERE TO LIVE. THE GOOD NEWS IS THAT IF YOU'VE ALWAYS WANTED YOUR KIDS TO BE BILINGUAL, MULTICULTURAL AND ARTISTICALLY LITERATE, THIS IS THE PLACE FOR YOU. PLUS, GIVEN THE EXCELLENT PUBLIC TRANSPORTATION SYSTEM, YOUR KIDS ARE ONLY A SUBWAY RIDE AWAY FROM THEIR SCHOOL OF CHOICE. THE BAD NEWS IS THAT YOU'LL HAVE TO TRAVERSE A FEW MORE MINEFIELDS IN NEW YORK THAN MOST OTHER CITIES IN SHEPHERDING KIDS THROUGH CHILDHOOD AND ADOLESCENCE.

◆◆◆◆◆◆◆◆

First, it is a good idea to determine your tolerance for schools that have problems with funding, safety and community support. Children grow up very quickly in New York, and if your kids have lived a comparatively sheltered life so far, they may be in for a few rude awakenings their first year in a public school. Your child will be exposed to locals who may be jaded by the violence, aggression and economic hardship many face on a daily basis, so they might well develop a thicker skin than what you're used to.

Schooling quality varies widely from district to district, and it's beyond the scope of this book to give you all the ins and outs of which are the "best" school districts. That really depends on what grade level your child is in, and where exactly within a neighborhood you live. Each chapter in the Neighborhoods section has a brief description of the general quality of schooling in the area, but it's always best to ask around and get the dirt in person.

For all of the challenges that New York public schools face, there are many talented, devoted and tireless educators who only want the best for their students. If you decide to go with a public school, for economic or other reasons, be forewarned that some face huge shortages of computers, books, equipment and other basic necessities. This is particularly true of under-funded districts on the outer edges of the Bronx, Queens and Brooklyn.

One good idea in scoping out a school district is to talk with brokers—ideally those who are parents themselves—when looking for an apartment or condo. Parents in Brooklyn seem to be proudest of their schools, as are many who send their kids to specialized high schools like Stuyvesant or the science, music and technical schools in Manhattan.

Take time to weigh the benefits and economic implications of private schools. The level of education is almost universally higher, but New York private schools run upwards of $10,000-15,000 per year unless your child is eligible for the very few scholarships that are available. Most parents who can afford to send their children to a private school bring home two incomes in the six figures. If this is the route for you, there are many schools in New York with alternative educational styles, like the Montessori or the International School, so there's bound to be one to fit your standards.

As always, it pays to do your homework. Although the challenges that public schools face are fairly uniform, no two New York schools are alike. Each neighborhood has its own ethnic and cultural dynamic that is reflected in its schools. Nothing compares with a personal visit to the school to get a sense for the teachers and the administration before committing yourself to living in an area for the duration.

If you choose a private school, look into all the options, because you could be opening up educational doors that would not be possible anywhere else, for a price. New York has fantastic resources for kids, from museums to free programs at libraries and other public venues. Chances are your child will thrive among all these new opportunities.

INSURANCE

RENTAL INSURANCE IS NEVER A BAD IDEA SINCE IT PROVIDES A WELCOME BUFFER IF YOUR APARTMENT IS ROBBED, FLOODED OR GOES UP IN FLAMES. THE WAY IT WORKS IS THAT YOU PAY A RELATIVELY SMALL MONTHLY OR QUARTERLY PREMIUM AND GET REIMBURSED FOR THE COST OF YOUR DECLARED PROPERTY IF ANYTHING HAPPENS TO IT.

Before you decide whether to fork out the money, though, you should do a cost-benefit analysis of your own. Most rental-insurance policies start out insuring you for a minimum of $10,000, so if your stuff is worth much less than that, or coming up with the necessary $400 or so per year is going to leave you eating pasta every night, then it's probably not a good idea. If you have lots of expensive possessions, or you're earning enough to make the premiums negligible, then why not? If you run your own business out of your apartment, insurance is recommended, since you'll have all your assets in one place.

If you go the insurance route, it's very important to thoroughly catalogue and photograph your possessions—and keep the list somewhere else—in the event of loss or damage. Some policies supply supplemental housing if you are displaced for any reason, and others will help pay you to rebuild or remodel, or reimburse you for the damaged rental property. Renter's insurance should cover you if someone else gets injured in your apartment (this is called "Guest Medical Protection"), and most policies cover engaged couples.

Most rental policies carry a hefty deductible, which you can reduce if you're willing to pay more in premiums. Coverage limits are also important:

> "It's one of those New York questions, like 'Why don't you ever see baby pigeons?'"
>
> **ANONYMOUS**

the higher total coverage you request, the higher your premiums will be. Make sure to read the fine print: if you're most concerned about your stuff, as opposed to the place itself, make sure that your policy includes "Personal Property Protection." Jewelry in particular may have caps for insurance coverage. You may also opt for "Family Liability Protection," which kicks in if you damage somebody else's property.

LEASES & SUBLETS

SHOULD YOU BE LUCKY ENOUGH TO FIND A WONDERFUL APARTMENT IN NEW YORK CITY, YOU'LL WANT TO ACT QUICKLY TO SECURE A LEASE. EXPECT THE REAL HEADACHES TO BEGIN WHEN YOU START NEGOTIATING THE DETAILS WITH YOUR PROSPECTIVE LANDLORD OR MANAGEMENT COMPANY. MANY WOULD-BE TENANTS END UP LOSING THEIR CHANCE TO LIVE IN THEIR DREAM APARTMENT BECAUSE THEY FOUL UP THE LEASE-SIGNING PROCESS. HERE ARE THE HOOPS YOU'LL HAVE TO JUMP THROUGH TO MAKE SURE YOU DON'T BECOME ANOTHER VICTIM OF THE PROCESS:

◆◆◆◆◆◆◆◆

#1 ACT FAST When you see a place that you like, count on a half dozen other people trying to swipe it out from under you. When visiting apartments, either with a broker or alone, it's smart to carry your checkbook, several forms of personal identification (including pay stubs from your employer), and the phone numbers of personal and professional references. Landlords and real estate management companies are very particular about whom they rent to, so the more organized you appear, the better impression you'll make.

#2 ASK QUESTIONS Just because you're dying for the place, don't be foolish and sign a lease before negotiating the best deal possible. This is the time to ask every question you can think of, and to insure that all commitments made by the landlord or the management company will be put in writing. All matters not already outlined on paper should become addenda to your lease.

#3 FINANCIAL INFORMATION Most landlords run a credit check on every tenant looking to rent one of their apartments. Expect to pay anywhere from $25-100 for these credit checks. You'll also be asked to give phone numbers of your present and previous landlords. Landlords rarely rent to individuals with poor credit unless they are able to provide a secure guarantor. Make sure to bring identification, including a driver's license, social security card, birth certificate or passport.

#4 THE LEASE Most landlords use a standard lease that outlines the contract between the tenant and building owner guaranteeing the right of the tenant to occupy the unit in exchange for a specific amount of money due on the first day of each month. You can usually obtain a standard copy of a rental lease at an office supply or stationary store. The contents are fairly simple to understand and include basic information like names, dates, addresses and a Social Security number. After the lease is signed, make sure to keep a copy for your records. Any riders to the lease should be dated and signed by all participants—do not rely on oral promises made by the landlord. Be aware of restrictions regarding home improvements, pets and occupancy allowances.

> "New York now leads the world's great cities in the number of people around whom you shouldn't make a sudden move."
>
> **DAVID LETTERMAN**

#5 SECURITY DEPOSIT Most landlords require a full month's rent to be paid at the signing of the lease to serve as insurance for the property owner in case the tenant damages property or defaults on rent. In most cases, tenants can reclaim their security deposit at the end of their lease. Many landlords, though, have made a fine art of keeping these deposits for no real reason at all. Before signing, make certain to define the stipulations for getting your deposit back, and the time limit within which it must be returned. You'll usually have to repaint walls back to their original color, patch any dents or holes you made in the walls, and clean the floors, kitchens and bathrooms until they sparkle. Make a careful examination of the apartment before you sign the lease so you won't be responsible for damage from previous tenants, and note any imperfections you find—just like when you rent a car.

6 SUBLETTING If you decide to break your lease for any reason of your own choosing, you remain liable for all unpaid rent until the end of the lease. Many New Yorkers who have to leave early choose to sublet their apartment to other tenants for the duration of their lease. Most leases allow subletting, but you should check carefully before handing your keys over to someone else. Leases often have built-in qualifications that require subletters to be personally approved by the landlord. Some leases, especially in co-ops, don't allow subleasing at all. Remember that subletting your apartment to someone else doesn't erase your responsibility to pay the rent should your subletter fail to pay. The next best option if you're quitting town early is to sign your lease completely over to another person. Your landlord must approve this, since they are entitled to increase the rent whenever leases change hands.

WWW.ZANYS.COM
Find a NYC apartment now!

LOFT LIVING

WHEN YOUR NEED FOR LIVING SPACE GROWS BEYOND YOUR MEANS, YOU HAVE TWO OPTIONS IN NEW YORK: YOU CAN EITHER MOVE FARTHER AWAY FROM MANHATTAN TO FIND LARGER SPACES FOR LESS MONEY, OR YOU CAN HUNT DOWN A PRIZED LOFT. LOFT LIVING HAS BEEN IN STYLE SINCE THE '60S, WHEN ANDY WARHOL AND HIS ARTISTIC CRONIES SET UP THE LEGENDARY FACTORY LOFT SPACE AS THEIR HUB FOR WORK, PLAY AND PARTYING.

The variety of ways you can use the space in a loft remains the main reason why so many find them desirable. Loft living often requires that you convert the space yourself. Many of the most beautiful lofts were once dingy factories or empty garages, and as manufacturing continues to drift off our shores, more and more warehouses are becoming available to those in search of living space.

Lofts have many unique benefits, but also many drawbacks. Obviously, a loft will provide more space than most apartments. Not only will you enjoy more floor space, but the high ceilings (usually 8-12 feet) allow you to construct raised platforms (lofts) that greatly increase your living space.

It's up to you to design the interior according to your tastes. Lofts occupied by roommates are most often divided up with drywall dividers. A well-designed loft can convert effortlessly from workspace by day to living space at night. They can also allow for activities like painting or carpentry, and for large objects like pianos and pool tables, unlike apartments. Another benefit is the natural light streaming in through large windows and skylights. Some lofts, however, are little more than caverns with light available only on the side facing the street.

On the negative side, lofts are expensive. Most people moving into "raw" spaces, as unconverted lofts or warehouses are called, should budget about three month's rent just to get the place going. Then there's the issue of living in the space in the first place: housing codes prevent individuals from living in unimproved spaces, but many New Yorkers—both landlords and tenants—ignore these regulations. Squatters (those who illegally inhabit dilapidated or unused buildings without paying rent) and others living in places that aren't zoned as residences can be evicted at the drop of a hat, even if they're paying rent.

Once you've found your place, get ready to spend many long, hard hours getting the space into habitable condition. This usually involves adding kitchens, shower facilities and interior walls in addition to refurbishing the ceiling, floors, windows and electrical and plumbing systems. These projects can eat up time and money like a drug habit, even if you're doing the work yourself.

Even after your loft is livable, there are still drawbacks to such large spaces. Heating is particularly expensive. Despite paying two or three times as much in heating bills as you ever have before, you're still liable to feel chilly in the winter. If your loft comes with gas blowers (a standard feature in many former commercial spaces), you're essentially trying to heat a massive space with what amounts to a gigantic hair dryer. For lofts with many windows, heating costs are even greater.

When finding and setting up a loft, be curious and ask questions. Landlords who have been renting to commercial businesses for a lifetime are often aware of their property's potential as a living space. Before you sign into any loft lease, you should be clear with your landlord about your intentions to build within the space. It's advisable to include clauses in your lease with explicit agreements about interior constructions. Without such protection, you could miss out on another significant benefit of loft living: flexibility.

If you're considering rehabilitating a raw space, you should negotiate for rent-free building time. It's often in the landlord's best interest to offer a period of free rent while the work is being completed, because in the end they'll have a habitable space that they can rent. However, it's a bad idea to try and move in until the bulk of the work is complete. The most important consideration when thinking about renting or owning a loft is whether or not you really need the luxuries that lofts provide. A loft is much more of a responsibility than a comparable sized apartment would be. You should need the space that a loft provides, not merely crave the comforts it affords. Having a Foosball table in your living room is not reason enough to own or rent a loft.

In Manhattan, you'll find a host of luxury lofts (meaning that the conversion work has already been done for you) in Tribeca, Soho, Wall Street and the western part of Chelsea. In Brooklyn, raw lofts are plentiful in many areas, most notably Dumbo, Williamsburg, Bedford-Stuyvesant and Prospect Heights. Long Island City in Queens has many former commercial spaces available for do-it-yourselfers.

> "This is New York, and there's no law against being annoying."
>
> **WILLIAM KUNSTLER**

LOW-COST LIVING OPTIONS

THIS CHAPTER COVERS TWO ALTERNATIVES FOR FINDING A PLACE TO LIVE RIGHT NOW, WHEN YOU DON'T HAVE TIME TO SHOP FOR YOUR DREAM HOME, JUST YET. IF YOU'RE NEW TO NEW YORK AND NEED TO WORK A BIT TO SAVE UP FOR YOUR PAD FROM HEAVEN, THESE CAN BE EXCELLENT TEMPORARY BRIDGES UNTIL YOU'RE ABLE TO COUGH UP THE REQUISITE DEPOSITS AND RELATED MOVING COSTS.

SHORT-TERM OPTIONS

There are about half a dozen short-term residence options available to you as you begin to live (and hopefully work) in New York. The list of names, phone numbers and addresses that follows will get you pointed in the right direction, although there's no guarantee that any but the best known, like the 92nd Street Y, offer decent facilities.

SHORT-TERM LISTINGS

92ND STREET YMHA
1395 Lexington Ave.
(800) 858-4692
Rates:
$945/month

WEST END STUDIOS HOTEL
850 Western Ave.
and 101st St.
(212) 749-7104
Rates:
$85/night

WESTSIDE INN
W 107th St. and
Broadway
(212) 866-0061
Rates:
$89/night

MURRAY HILL INN
143 E 30th St.
Between 3rd Ave.
and Lexington Ave.
(212) 683-6900
Rates:
$75/night

HOSTELLING INTERNATIONAL NEW YORK
19 W 103rd St.
(212) 678-0491
Rates:
Dorm beds
$27-32/night
Family room
$75/night

BIG APPLE HOSTEL
119 W 45th St.
(212) 302-2603
Rates:
Shared room
$33/night
Private room
$85/night

LONG-TERM OPTIONS

I f you need to camp out a little longer, you have two basic options. You can pay to stay as long as you want at one of the above places, or you can scout *The Village Voice*, *The New York Times* and other publications for sublets. Sublets are historically thought of as a summer-only option, but they're actually available year-round as New Yorkers get job offers, assignments and sabbaticals all over the world.

Most sublets run for about three months, but some range from as little as one month to up to a year in length. In taking on a sublet, however, you'll have to abide by certain inconveniences—the most important being that it is not your place, so you can't disturb anything that belongs to the owner. As a result, you can't get too settled in, because you're going to have to leave eventually. You'll also have to keep the place impeccably clean, which is harder for some than others, and keep everything alive—pets, plants and the like—until their owner gets back.

As if all that wasn't enough, you usually have to go through an extensive background check before someone will let you in the door. This can take some time, depending on when the owners plan to leave. Sublets aren't that common, and it's hard to get one unless you know someone who knows someone, so it is not recommended that you count on this option until you have the key in your hand.

Often the best way to get something short-term is to swallow your pride and pick up the phone. Call up your Uncle Nester, Auntie Em or whomever, and find someone who knows someone with an extra room you can stay in until you get on your feet. If you just graduated from college, go through your school's alumni files to find out who is in the city and start cold-calling people ("Remember me,

> "It couldn't have happened anywhere but in little old New York."
>
> **O. HENRY**

BACKGROUND 303

from biology class . . ?"). Brace yourself up for some rejections. More likely than not, though, you'll end up uncovering somebody who has something just for you. Remember—if you can make it here, you can make it anywhere.

NOISE

IN NEW YORK THE ADAGE IS SIMPLE: NO NOISE IS GOOD NOISE. UNFORTUNATELY, IT'S NOT ALWAYS THAT EASY. NOISE POLLUTION STILL RANKS AS ONE OF THE MOST COMMON COMPLAINTS YOU'LL HEAR IN THESE PARTS, AND IT CAN BE HARDER TO AVOID THAN A SUBWAY PANHANDLER.

Noise pollution comes in various forms, but the most common is street traffic. Major avenues of transit are particularly loud. Although it's technically illegal to honk your horn repeatedly in New York, drivers tend to disregard this law—especially, it seems, when you're trying to sleep. For this reason, veteran New Yorkers know to avoid street-level or second-floor apartments. Even if you're looking at living in a walk-up, you're better off tackling four flights of stairs than trying to get to sleep over the sidewalk and street-level noise. If a terrific street-level apartment does present itself, make certain that it's on a quiet side street or that the windows (if there are any) are well insulated from noise. Landlords should offer discounts on noisy apartments.

When shopping for an apartment, remember to consider the noise level at night. Often, an apartment will be quiet during the day, but directly in the path of delivery trucks in the wee hours of the morning. Try to visit more than once to find out how noisy things are at different times of the day. For instance, if you're looking in Sunnyside you should linger long enough to hear what it's like when a DC-10 flies overhead on its way to LaGuardia.

Other sources of noise include those from within your building, like rowdy neighbors, clanging pipes or obnoxious pets. Be advised that once you sign on the dotted line, there's very little you can do about neighbor noise. Make sure to read the fine print of your lease regarding such issues as pets, loud music and apartment parties, since this might be your only source of leverage for controlling noisy neighbors. Typically you'll experience more problems with neighbor noise in newer apartment buildings since the walls are thinner and less sound absorbent. The worst noise problems are in Manhattan neighborhoods where the streets are wide enough for trucks to travel. Brooklyn, Queens and especially Staten Island tend to be better in terms of noise pollution. High-crime areas in any borough are rife with car alarms and police sirens wailing throughout the night.

There are many options for insulating your place from noise. Check the yellow pages for companies advertising insulated window replacements. If you play loud music or have a neighbor who does, try lining your walls with soundproofing materials. Wherever you live in the city, noise will always be a concern. If you can't afford a penthouse suite, do your best to make your situation tolerable, and don't expect New York to quiet down any time soon.

PARKS & GARDENS

MORE PEOPLE MOVE TO NEW YORK FOR THE PURPOSE OF MAKING GREEN RATHER THAN PLAYING ON IT, SO IT OFTEN COMES AS A PLEASANT SURPRISE THAT THERE'S ACTUALLY A GREAT AMOUNT OF PUBLIC GREEN SPACE IN THE FIVE BOROUGHS. THANKS TO THE FORESIGHT AND CAREFUL PLANS OF ARCHITECTS LIKE FREDERICK LAW OLMSTED AND CALVERT VAUX, NEW YORK IS BLESSED WITH MARVELOUS PUBLIC PARKS.

The list begins with Central Park, created in 1863 to keep Manhattan from becoming paved over completely. Central Park sees over 20 million visitors a year, and includes such diverse treats as an outdoor

Shakespearean amphitheater, a merry-go-round, an ice skating rink and a zoo. It is without question the largest and most expensive plot of land set aside for public enjoyment in the world.

Central Park and other flagship greens like Prospect Park, McCarren Park, Thompkins Square Park and Riverside Park have the New York City Parks Department to thank for their continued existence. The department oversees the parks' upkeep and coordinates their schedule of events. Although public spaces, these parks can be rented for events like concerts, bicycle rides or marathons. Central Park is also home to institutions like the legendary Tavern on the Green restaurant.

Proximity to both parks and gardens will probably be a consideration when considering where to rent or buy in the city. Not only will they provide room to exercise and relax, but the city's parks are also a great source of free entertainment, with outdoor concerts, impromptu soccer games and opportunities for people-watching. Each has its own unique topography and features. Some offer public tennis courts, basketball courts and baseball diamonds, while others have lush community gardens or wide green spaces offering a welcome break from the otherwise endless acres of asphalt.

Consider what features you would use most in a nearby park and choose your neighborhood accordingly.

WWW.ZANYS.COM

Some Manhattan neighborhoods, like Midtown and Murray Hill, don't have much in the way of quality green space. Other locations, like Central Park West, Battery Park City and Gramercy Park, have direct access to open fields. If you exercise but don't live near a park, you'll probably have to factor in the cost of a gym membership to your monthly bills if you want to stay in shape. One thing is for sure—there are few if any drawbacks to living close to the city's parks.

If open public space is a big priority, consider neighborhoods in Brooklyn, Queens and Staten Island that are adjacent to immense but relatively uncrowded public parks. Park Slope, Williamsburg, Greenpoint, Prospect Heights, Red Hook and Windsor Terrace are all great choices in Brooklyn. Queens offers lush parks in Corona Heights, Flushing, Astoria and along the water in Long Island City. Many New Yorkers consider Staten Island to be one big, park-filled suburb. For happiness in the Big Apple, follow this tried-and-true formula: make your financial green during the week, and enjoy the other kind on the weekends.

> "That enfabled rock, that ship of life, that swarming, million-footed, tower-masted, sky-soaring citadel that bears the magic name of the Island of Manhattan."
>
> **THOMAS WOLFE**

PETS

SINCE THERE AREN'T ANY CITYWIDE REGULATIONS REGARDING PET OWNERSHIP IN APARTMENTS OR CONDOS, RULES FOR OWNING PETS VARY ACCORDING TO THE INDIVIDUAL POLICIES OF LANDLORDS OR MANAGEMENT COMPANIES. PET OWNERS WILL FIND THAT MANY PLACES ARE NOT PET FRIENDLY, AND THAT FINDING A BUILDING THAT ALLOWS ANIMALS OF ANY KIND WILL BE AN ADDED CHALLENGE IN AN ALREADY DIFFICULT PROCESS. WHEN SEARCHING, IT'S BEST TO BE UP FRONT ABOUT ANY PETS YOU OWN TO KEEP FROM WASTING EVERYONE'S TIME. AND "NO PETS" MEANS JUST THAT; LANDLORDS REGARD ALL PETS EQUALLY, FROM IGUANAS TO DOBERMANS, AND BREAKING THIS RULE IS GROUNDS FOR EVICTION.

◆◇◆◇◆◇◆◇

uildings are usually pet-friendly or have a no pets policy from top to bottom. In places where pets aren't explicitly banned, though, it's often a matter of semantics as to whether or not your pet will be allowed. For example, landlords tend to be more accepting of older animals who presumably won't soil or gnaw up the apartment as much as kittens or puppies. Even if your dog is only a year old, it's best to depict it as a mature animal with a calm disposition. Landlords are often loathe to allow large pets, particularly dogs, in the building.

It's also a good idea to check on your neighbors' feelings about pets before you sign a lease. Even if your landlord agrees to let your pet in the building, it will be the other tenants who complain if your pet is a nuisance. According to most leases, you can be evicted from a property if you deprive fellow tenants of their right to "quiet enjoyment of the premises." Asking your future neighbors about their feelings regarding your pet can prevent many headaches.

There are many benefits of having pets in the city. Large dogs can provide a great deal of protection from personal assault, and can also discourage robberies. However, many dog owners find that having large breeds in the city only facilitates more scuffles and headaches. Owners are liable for their dog's behavior, so if your pooch takes a bite out of an innocent bystander instead of a bite out of crime, expect to pay for the victim's medical and legal fees. Furthermore, city laws require that dogs that are repeat "bite-offenders" be euthanized.

> "Young singers ask me, 'Do I have to live in New York?' I say, 'You can live wherever you want—as long as people think you live in New York.'"
>
> **BENITA VALENTE**

WWW.ZANYS.COM
Find a NYC apartment now!

PRE-WAR VS. POST-WAR APARTMENTS

APARTMENTS BUILT BEFORE AND AFTER WW II DIFFER IN TWO MAIN WAYS: THE AMOUNT OF WEAR AND TEAR THEY'VE ACCUMULATED, AND THE DISTINCTIVENESS OF THEIR DECOR AND EXTERIORS.

◆ ◆ ◆ ◆ ◆ ◆ ◆ ◆

Pre-war apartments have many advantages. Most of them are built in interesting architectural styles, including Tudors and brownstones, and many have incredible detailing like scrollwork, ceiling frescoes and working fireplaces. They also have thick walls, which you'll appreciate if you're a light sleeper or like to throw parties.

On the other hand, most pre-war apartments have accumulated more grime and ragged edges than those built later. Many renters don't maintain their apartments as well as they could, and over the years this neglect takes its toll. If you have allergies, dusty older building can drive you crazy. If you rent a pre-war building, try to find one whose landlord is attentive to any repair needs or structural problems.

The main advantage to post-war buildings is that most have been built or renovated recently, which can save lots of time and money in cleaning bills over the years you'll live there. Post-war buildings often have great floors that have been refinished (watch out for splinters, though). Many detractors consider post-war buildings ugly, pointing out that they often lack gardens and have paper-thin walls.

This may not be your main factor in deciding where to live (and it shouldn't be), but the age of your building is something to consider. If you'd like a building with more flair, then pre-war is probably for you if you can stand the accumulated dirt and grime. If you like buildings that were built more recently, post-war structures offer less history, but also fewer surprises.

RENOVATED APARTMENTS

THE MAIN DIFFERENCE BETWEEN A RENOVATED APARTMENT AND ONE THAT HASN'T BEEN DONE OVER RECENTLY IS TIME, MEASURED IN THE AMOUNT OF DIRT THAT HAS BEEN ABLE TO ACCUMULATE IN ALL THE CRACKS AND CREVICES.

You would do well to consider a newly-renovated apartment if you can find one, if you:

1. Love to spend a lot of time cooking or entertaining,
2. Consider yourself a Neat Freak or Clean Queen,
3. Have kids,
4. Work out of your apartment,
5. Enjoy taking baths or spending time primping in your bathroom,
6. Spend more time outside of your apartment than in it, or
7. Want a totally dingy, dirty New York apartment experience.

If you don't fall into one of the above categories, then choosing an apartment that hasn't been renovated in ten or more years would work just fine for you—plus, they're a heck of a lot cheaper. If you're coming to New York straight from the college frat house, then little things like bathroom fixtures might not matter that much. If you don't like to clean and don't necessarily care how many other organisms already inhabit your apartment, then an unrenovated apartment will fit your needs and your pocketbook quite well.

If, on the other hand, you're used to white-on-white quarters kept antiseptically clean, then living in an apartment that hasn't been renovated in

> "New York, New York, it's a helluva town.
> The Bronx is up but the Battery's down.
> The people ride in a hole in the ground.
> New York, New York, it's a helluva town!"
>
> **BETTY COMDEN & ADOLPH GREENE**

four or more years could easily push you over the edge. No matter how much you work at cleaning an older apartment, many somehow always end up looking and feeling dirty. This is a law of nature and has nothing to do with how your mother brought you up.

One thing to consider, if you're handily inclined, is to choose an older, unrenovated apartment and fix it up. If you do this, be sure to negotiate a rent discount with your landlord, even if it's something you would enjoy doing—you could even end up making some money off the deal in the long run. Older apartments always need fixing, and one major disadvantage to an older place is that New York landlords are seldom good at keeping ahead of the forces of entropy.

If you have an unrenovated apartment, expect that things will break down more often, that the paint will most likely peel sooner or later, that bugs might someday climb out of your drains, and that tiles will soon start to chip and drip in your bathroom.

Another place you might find all these household nightmares is in a badly-renovated apartment. In this case, the landlord probably had his brother-in-law do the carpentry and got the plumber's number off a telephone pole. The result is often not much better—and occasionally worse—than whatever it was supposed to improve upon. The best renovations are usually done either when landlords want to increase the rent in a building and attract a more upscale clientele, or when the owner of a building wants to build a loft or convert a warehouse into luxury condominiums. In both cases, the effect is thoughtful, deliberate and gorgeous. You'll pay for an apartment with these amenities, however.

If you're looking for a completely renovated f o r m e r ware- house turned into a luxury apartment, check the area around Broad and Wall Streets. The rents there are still fairly reasonable, given the astronomical turnover the area has seen, and the apartments are beautiful. There won't be much going on outside, but that's also goes for many places where condominiums and the like have gone up. Decide what your priority is and be warned that it's extremely difficult and astronomically expensive to have your cake and eat it too when it comes to settling in New York.

RENT CONTROL
VS.
RENT STABILIZATION

RENT CONTROL WAS AN INITIATIVE FIRST BEGUN IN NEW YORK CITY IN 1943 IN RESPONSE TO A SERIOUS HOUSING SHORTAGE FOLLOWING THE END OF WW II. DEMAND SO FAR EXCEEDED AVAILABLE HOUSING THAT LANDLORDS WERE GOUGING TENANTS FOR EXTREME RENT INCREASES OR THREATENING EVICTION. THIS UNSCRUPULOUS BEHAVIOR ON THE PART OF LANDLORDS LED TO LEGISLATION THAT PROTECTED TENANTS FROM EXCESSIVE RENT INCREASES.

◆◆◆◆◆◆◆◆

About 100,000 apartments are protected by rent control measures to this day. Residents are called "statutory tenants" and do not require a lease to remain in their apartments. Tenants who live in a rent controlled apartment in New York began renting their apartment before 1971, when rent control protections were rescinded.

It's rare, if not impossible, to get an apartment that is under rent control these days. Families that have rent-controlled apartments wisely pass them down to succeeding generations. When such apartments aren't passed on, they're usually reclaimed by the owner of the building, who can then start charging fair market value. It should be obvious why landlords dislike the rent control system.

Rent stabilization is a compromise between the city's landlords and tenants, enacted in the late 1960s, limiting the amount a landlord can increase rent when a lease comes up for renewal. In theory, this was supposed to allow landlords to receive fair market value for their property without letting them overcharge long-term tenants. It also grants the tenants more security against evictions and requires landlords to play active roles in the upkeep of their properties.

Every July, the New York Rent Guidelines Board decides the appropriate percentage that landlords may increase rent, starting the following October. Typical rent increases range from 2% for a one-year lease to 4% for a two-year lease. However, when the market demand is high, rent increases can be anywhere from 5% for a one-year extension to 7% for a two-year extension. Such incremental rent hikes can also be applied to vacant apartments and renovated apartments when capital improvements are added.

ROOMMATES

SO YOU AND YOUR COLLEGE BUDDIES HAVE DECIDED TO MOVE IN TOGETHER? SOUNDS GREAT! AFTER ALL, HAVING ROOMMATES IS A GREAT WAY TO SHARE EXPENSES WHILE YOU GET YOUR FEET ON THE GROUND. IT'S ALSO AN IDEAL WAY TO FEEL SAFE AND AVOID LONELINESS IN WHAT CAN OTHERWISE BE A COLD AND HEARTLESS CITY.

There are many things to consider, though, before you jump into a roommate situation. First, ask yourself if you are truly compatible with the people you're considering living with. It's essential to find roommates who will respect your privacy, your need for quiet and your cleaning habits. Many times, good friends do not make good roommates. Living alone is always an option, albeit an outrageously expensive one, since you'll have to pay for everything, including all the bills, yourself.

Another concern before choosing a roommate is that person's financial situation. By sharing expenses, you're also agreeing to share responsibility for the total rent of the apartment. This means that you will ultimately be responsible for the total rent should your roommates fail to come up with their share, or you'll both be out on the street. Your best protection against this is to secure each portion of the rent with a lease guarantor, such as each person's parents. For your financial safety, it's also wise to put every roommate's name on every utility bill, so no one can duck his or her responsibility for phone and utility charges.

Other issues to address before signing any agreement to live with someone else are rules regarding individual property. How do you feel about letting your roommate use your bicycle? Will it annoy you if your roommate drinks your last beer and doesn't buy any more? Who will let their stereo become the "house" stereo and risk the abuse that roommates give to consumer electronics that aren't their own? All of these questions are worth airing before deciding to live with someone else. No matter how casual you are, you'll undoubtedly have some differences with your roommates on many lifestyle choices, both large and small.

Roommates typically squabble over who gets which bedroom and how rent will be divided. If bedrooms are unequal in size—and they most often are—it is only fair to charge more rent for more space. Ideally, this will prevent resentment by the roommate with the dinky bedroom with a view of a brick wall.

If you're in need of a roommate but don't know anyone to share a place with, there are many services that match up roommates for a small service fee. Most roommate services advertise in

The Village Voice and other local papers. They are generally trustworthy, though they should be considered a last alternative to finding someone you know. The danger of consulting roommate services is that usually people who register with them couldn't find a roommate any other way—get the idea?

SAFETY

IT'S NO SECRET THAT NEW YORK IS FAR FROM THE SAFEST CITY IN THE WORLD. LATELY, THOUGH, THANKS TO THE EFFORTS OF THE NEW-AND-IMPROVED NEW YORK POLICE DEPARTMENT, NEW YORK IS THE SAFEST IT'S BEEN IN YEARS. BY PUTTING MORE COPS ON THE STREETS AND ACCOSTING PEOPLE FOR THE SLIGHTEST OFFENSE, THE NYPD HAS SENT CRIME STATISTICS THROUGH THE FLOOR (EVEN AS THEIR DRACONIAN MEASURES HAVE RAISED AN UPROAR.)

Since January 1994, felonies have declined by 28 percent and homicides have plummeted by 38 percent. In the past two years, about 118,000 less people have found themselves the victims of crimes. So-called "quality-of-life crimes" have been a major focus of the NYPD, and the petty theft rates have plummeted in the last eight years under Rudy's thumb.

For women, more police officers cruising the streets has meant a whole new freedom to take the subway at three in the morning, walk around their neighborhoods after dark and feel like they're not in danger of imminent attack. If you visited New York in the 1980s, particularly around Times Square, you probably remember streets filled with trash, porn shops, squatters and hookers galore. No more—not only has Disney bought and cleaned up much of that prime real estate, but since the early '90s, the city has

made a concerted effort to root out people with no legal residence and move them either into shelters or at least out of their normal haunts.

What has always been true about New York—and still is—is that if you do get into a jam, chances are it will take a while for someone to come to your aid, if they do at all. Most New Yorkers just don't want to get involved in anything that looks like trouble, an attitude which occasionally results in much-publicized cases of people being attacked or even killed within earshot of fellow citizens who choose to mind their own business instead of help. This is just another good reason not to venture into areas you're not familiar with after dark. Many women carry cell phones for protection if something goes wrong, but the police can still take a while to find you, depending on which borough you live in (response time for Manhattan is the shortest).

One other thing to be warned about, ladies, is the occasional person who will try to follow you home. This rarely happens, but in general it's always a good idea to refrain from handing out your phone number and address, to pay attention to who is in and around your personal space, and to take action if you feel at all uncomfortable. The longer you live here, the more finely tuned your radar will become to situations that make you uneasy or scared.

Although things are safer now, the random street types didn't disappear into the earth—rather, they shifted to neighborhoods where it's harder to get busted. On any given Friday or Saturday night at any major social thoroughfare in the city, you'll see officers in cars, on motorcycles and patrolling the streets looking for signs of trouble.

> "I moved to New York City for my health. I'm paranoid and New York was the only place where my fears are justified."
>
> **ANITA WEISS**

This is good news for would-be victims, and not-so-great news if you're a member of a minority who fits a suspicious profile. There's a reason why the NYPD has had a record numbers of court cases brought against them recently for discrimination—many people feel as though they are being specifically targeted for no other reason than the color of their skin or the clothes they're wearing.

Shopping

IF YOU'RE THE TYPE OF PERSON WHO NEEDS IMMEDIATE PURCHASING GRATIFICATION AT YOUR FINGERTIPS, THERE ARE SEVERAL NEIGHBORHOODS IN MANHATTAN THAT CAN INDULGE YOUR NEED FOR FINE DINING, MAKE-UP, ICE CREAM, HAUTE COUTURE, OR WHATEVER YOUR FIX MAY BE. SHOPPING FOR FOOD AND CLOTHES IS A BIG REASON WHY PEOPLE MOVE TO NEW YORK, FOR HERE YOU CAN TRULY FIND THE BEST THE WORLD HAS TO OFFER AT YOUR VERY DOORSTEP. FROM THE BIG SPENDERS TO THE BARGAIN HUNTERS, NEW YORK CAN DRIVE EVEN THE MOST SEASONED SHOPPER A LITTLE OVER THE EDGE.

One caution to shopping in New York: this is the fad capital of the world, and many people new to New York tend to go crazy in their first few months here. Much of what you buy on impulse can be extremely trendy (i.e. out of style in six months and not worth a fraction of the hundreds of dollars you spent on it). It's good to consult people whose opinion you respect to help narrow down your options and decide where best to invest your limited time and budget, rather than wander all over the city in search of stores that carry just your style.

Before embarking on a quest for the best shopping and food in the city, be realistic about what you can spend. If shopping and going out to eat are a priority, it's going to put a big dent into your budget, so you will need to watch your spending in other areas accordingly. In other words, if you get New York's coolest apartment but then can't afford to go out in your newly arrived cool neighborhood, then you've already defeated your purpose in moving to New York. Be clear about what it is you want and how much you're willing to spend for rent, food and clothing in any given month.

> "As only New Yorkers know, if you can get through the twilight, you'll live through the night."
>
> **DOROTHY PARKER**

To find the best in food and clothing, you'll need to live fairly centrally in Manhattan, which will be expensive. Most neighborhoods outside of Midtown tend to have the best shops for restaurants and clothes centered in one convenient area. The Garment District offers the hottest clothes in the world, with more variety than you'll ever see in Milan or Paris. If you're into trendy threads, move to Soho, Tribeca or Chelsea. For designer labels, move near Midtown, and for sexy or grunge duds, move to Greenwich Village.

In terms of food, you'll find a wide variety of restaurants all over the city. Wherever you live, takeout is only a call away. Food options are generally top-notch anywhere in Manhattan. If a restaurant isn't up to par (and in this town, word gets around in no time), it won't last long anyway.

Living in areas with a lot of shopping options, like Midtown, Chelsea, Soho and Tribeca, can also mean a lot of noise. So, if you're looking to have it all—shopping, restaurants, a built-in social circle, and peace and quiet—you may be disappointed. If you're lucky enough to find this paragon of apartments, plan on paying through the nose for it.

New York will be a blast if you have a lot of disposable income. If you're on a middle-class budget, decide either to skimp on your rent and travel a bit for what you want, or go for the super apartment and

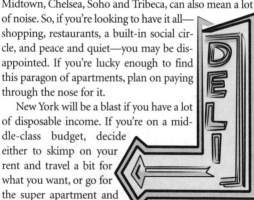

WWW.ZANYS.COM
Find a NYC apartment now!

know that you won't have as much money to spend in your new neighborhood as you perhaps hoped. Or, better yet, you could always get a better-paying job to afford it all!

STORAGE

IF YOU HAVE TOO MUCH STUFF FOR THE PLACE YOU'RE LIVING IN, YOU HAVE THREE OPTIONS: SELL SOME, GIVE IT AWAY OR FIND SOMEPLACE ELSE TO PUT IT. PACKRATS WHO DON'T HAVE A PARENT'S GARAGE THEY CAN THROW STUFF INTO DO THE NEXT BEST THING: THEY FIND A COMMERCIAL STORAGE SPACE.

◆◆◆◆◆◆◆◆

New Yorkers have come to rely on storage companies to house their valued non-essentials, either in between apartments or even after they move in. Storage facilities offer private padlocked rooms for reasonable monthly fees. Best of all, most of these companies will provide a moving truck to pick up your stuff free of charge. You're usually required to transport your goods to and from the truck into your private locker, but sometimes a friendly truck driver will lend a hand.

Storage units range in size from small closets to spaces large enough to hold three bedrooms' worth of junk. Larger units are more expensive. Once your goods are safely packed away, you can seal your locker with your own heavy-duty padlock, which enables you alone to access your possessions any time the storage facility is open. Many facilities offer 24-hour access, but others have limited hours when you can retrieve your possessions. Consider your needs carefully when choosing between the various storage facilities. Often, you can barter your way

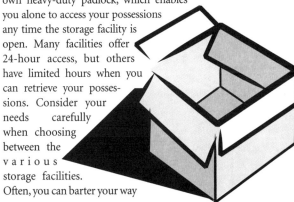

to bigger discounts by threatening to go to a competitor.

When you decide on a storage company, you'll be required to sign an agreement. Read the details carefully,

"In New York City, one suicide in ten is attributed to a lack of storage space."

JUDITH STONE

because in many cases you are forgoing your rights to the property if it is destroyed by fire, water damage or theft. If you want to insure the contents of your locker, you'll usually have to pay an additional monthly fee for insurance, since few homeowners' or renters' policies cover items in commercial storage. It's advisable to put true valuables, like jewelry, cash and artwork, in safety deposit boxes rather than in storage lockers. You pay for convenience, so you can often save money by going to a storage facility that's far away from home. If you don't need to retrieve your possessions frequently, consider storage lockers in the outer boroughs.

Like landlords, storage facilities charge monthly for their services. If you decide to charge your locker on a credit card, the facility can automatically deduct the rental fee from your account. Even if you decide to pay by check, most facilities require a credit card number upon signing an agreement. If you fall behind on your payments, the facility takes over the locker and everything in it. Anything left inside is then auctioned off—so keep up those payments!

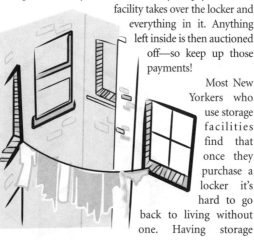

Most New Yorkers who use storage facilities find that once they purchase a locker it's hard to go back to living without one. Having storage capacity in this city is an addictive pleasure. Many lockers are filled to the brim by people who can't stop buying, even when their apartment is full or overflowing. Storage facilities are happy to help these packrats.

STUDENTS

WHETHER YOU'RE A STRUGGLING CO-ED OR A PAINTER WAITING TO BE DISCOVERED, YOU'LL HAVE SPECIAL APARTMENT NEEDS THAT ARE WORLDS AWAY FROM THOSE OF ALL YOUR FRIENDS WHO ENDED UP ON WALL STREET. FIRST AND FOREMOST IS RENT. SINCE MONEY WON'T BE FLOWING FOR A WHILE, IT'S BEST TO FIND A PLACE THAT IS AS CHEAP AS POSSIBLE. OTHER CONCERNS DEPEND ON WHETHER YOU'RE HITTING THE BOOKS OR THE KEYBOARD.

Many students find that their schools provide the most affordable quarters in the city, mainly because they're subsidized by astronomical tuition fees. Others, particularly students at schools in high-rent districts like Hunter, New York University or Columbia, look for more affordable housing off campus. Although there are significant benefits to moving off campus, not least of which is going it on your own, there are also many drawbacks.

First off, many students find that their performance in school drops in proportion to how far they live from campus. Off-campus students aren't able to interact with other students as easily on a regular basis, and must therefore rely on their own self-discipline to  complete their studies. If you do decide to live off campus, it's advisable to find a place within walking distance of school. Other factors to consider are the additional financial burdens and logistical headaches you'll incur, such as utility bills and broker's fees, that aren't an issue in student housing. In all, most students find that campus life is a better value, though not necessarily more enjoyable, than off-campus life.

If you've decided to share an apartment with a fellow student or friend, there are a few things you should know. Unlike sharing a tree house, sharing an apartment is a major responsibility and, contrary to your first instinct, best friends often make the worst roommates. As a young student with little or no established credit, it's unlikely you'll be able to sign a lease without a cosigner such as a parent. In apartment-share situations, it's best that everyone has a cosigner in case anyone defaults on paying their share of the rent. If only one person acts a cosigner, then she will be responsible for covering the entire portion of unpaid rent.

Other issues to settle up front include shared expenses such as utility and telephone services. To protect yourself, split the responsibility and put every tenant's name on all bills. This is your right in New York, and you should do it when you first have the services installed. This safety measure protects individual tenants from being liable for an entire bill. Money can make people do strange things—you never know when someone might jump ship. Don't assume that just because someone is your friend that they'll always have the courtesy to pay bills on time.

> "If there is one city I should pick to live in, it would be New York. It is a city where I walk down the street and feel anything is possible."
>
> **MARIA SCHELL**

Another major student concern is peace and quiet. Whether you do your studying at a library or not, it's essential that your apartment be quiet enough to at least permit a good night's sleep. Students who have chosen to live off campus must be especially careful not to rent a noisy apartment. Once the school year begins, the last thing you want to have to do is look for a quieter place. Remember that standard leases require landlords to provide a place that is "reasonably quiet." Other special needs that students have might include access to music or art studios. If you need such facilities, inquire about basement spaces in larger apartment buildings. Some landlords have extra unused space that they can offer to tenants in their buildings free of charge, or for a nominal fee.

STUDIOS FOR ARTISTS

ASTRONOMICAL RENTS AND THE GREAT DEMAND FOR RESIDENTIAL SPACE HAVE COMBINED TO PUSH NEW YORK ARTISTS FURTHER AND FURTHER TO THE PERIPHERY OF THE GALLERY CENTERS IN DOWNTOWN MANHATTAN. AS SUCH, IT'S RARE TO FIND YOUNG ARTISTS ABLE TO AFFORD MANHATTAN STUDIOS ON THEIR OWN. IF YOUR BURGEONING ART CAREER IS SUPPORTED BY A GENEROUS BENEFACTOR, YOUR BEST BET FOR A LARGE STUDIO SPACE IS IN NEIGHBORHOODS LIKE CHELSEA, SOHO, TRIBECA AND NOHO. OTHERS WHO CAN'T AFFORD SUCH LUXURIES ARE WISE TO SCOUR THE EAST VILLAGE, CHINATOWN, HARLEM AND WASHINGTON HEIGHTS FOR WORKSPACE.

Many artists have elected to look in Brooklyn and Queens for spaces large enough to live and work in. Neighborhoods like Dumbo, Williamsburg, Prospect Heights, Long Island City, Astoria and Greenpoint offer terrific deals for both young and established artists. Currently, even modest studios rent for at least twenty five dollars per square foot. When considering studio spaces, make certain to check that there is adequate natural light and that water, heat and bathroom facilities are in good shape. By law, it's illegal to rent a space without giving a tenant access to a working bathroom. Also ask about safety concerns in the building. Do you plan to weld? What happens if you wreck the walls or spill paint on the floor? These are the kind of answers you should get in writing before signing a lease.

TYPES OF BUILDINGS

IN YOUR SEARCH FOR A PLACE TO LIVE, YOU WILL COME ACROSS A FEW DISTINCTIVE STYLES OF ARCHITECTURE IN NEW YORK CITY. EACH HAS ITS OWN LIST OF PLUSES AND MINUSES.

◆◆◆◆◆◆◆◆

BROWNSTONES

These elegant brown-faced buildings can be found in many of Manhattan's older neighborhoods. The term "brownstone" is often used loosely to describe any building with a stoop (a short flight of steps up to the main doorway). True brownstones, though, are set apart from limestone-faced buildings by the color of stone used in the facade. Often, as time and weather erode the facade, the outer layer must be entirely replaced or refinished.

These buildings are coveted for their architectural style and ample space. On intact brownstones you're likely to find appealing features like trim, large windows, backyard gardens, high ceilings, brick walls and hardwood floors. In general, brownstones offer a warmer atmosphere than other, more modern buildings.

> "Do you know New York stifles me? It makes me so unhappy. There are so many things I want, and so many things I cannot afford to have. I don't see how people ever have money enough to live here."
>
> **DOROTHY GISH**

Brownstones were originally built as single-family dwellings. As New York's population grew and demand for housing outpaced the supply, many were converted into multi-family dwellings. When searching the classifieds for a brownstone, look for the abbreviation "flthru," which means they're looking for someone to rent the entire floor of the building at once.

Some brownstones have been divided into two single-person studios on each floor. Basement apartments, usually accessed underneath the stoop, lack good sources of natural light, but almost always come with garden access in the rear. First floors, otherwise known as parlor floors, tend to have the highest ceilings, but don't divide up well because adjacent rooms are not private enough. First floors weren't originally designed to serve as bedrooms, so they don't divide well.

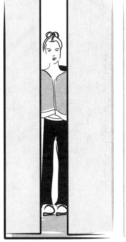

Second and third floors are ideal for enjoying the views and natural light. One downside to brownstones is that with only a handful of tenants in each building, landlords aren't required to have a live-in superintendent on the premises. This means maintenance issues might be harder to deal with. Another drawback to brownstones is the security liability they might pose. Usually brownstones have two locked doors to the outside—an exterior door that remains open and a private, locked door in the vestibule. Some buildings in particularly unsafe neighborhoods lock both doors at all times. Rarely are they equipped with electronic buzzers or surveillance cameras like those in many apartment buildings. In general, people who prefer their apartment to be private and charming choose to accept the drawbacks that come with renting in a brownstone.

OTHER ROWHOUSES

The second most common materials for New York City rowhouses are wood and brick, although the interiors of these building are usually quite similar to brownstones. Wood rowhouses were once the city standard, but their tendency to go up in flames soon made stone the favored building material. Many New York row-houses were faced with beautiful red brick, but over time this exterior has been inexplicably covered by aluminum siding.

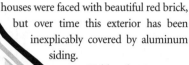

Unlike brownstones, some brick rowhouses were built as multi-family dwellings from the start. Others were originally built for one family, and have subsequently been converted into multi-family dwellings. The former, naturally, tend to be more practical and roomy. Expect all rowhouses to be walk-ups with either three or four flights of stairs. When inspecting these old buildings, look for signs of structural wear like cracking walls, tilted floors and loose railings. Landlords frequently neglect their responsibility to keep their building up to code.

Rowhouses are ideal for couples or families who don't mind the intimacy of the relatively tight quarters. Roommates and apartment-sharers are better suited to larger tenements or high-rises.

HIGH-RISES

People who prefer to live in skyscrapers know who they are. These large buildings, anywhere from ten to 45 stories high, have many features that would never be found in small apartments. Most have doormen, who are there not only for security but also for the convenience of residents. Doormen aren't limited to holding the doors open for you—they can also hail taxis, carry luggage and receive groceries and laundry (see "Doormen").

If you demand a lot of creature comforts, then high-rises are your best choice. In most you'll find sophisticated security measures like surveillance cameras, underground parking, pools, health facilities, central air-conditioning, live-in superintendents, trash removal, laundry rooms and bicycle storage areas. Most of all, tenants enjoy high-rises because of their terrific views of the city. More modern high-rises even have roof-top sundecks. All buildings in New York over six stories high are required to have an elevator.

The main drawbacks to living in a high-rise are the lack of privacy and charm that rowhouses offer. Most high-rises have strict policies regarding noise, so if you plan on entertaining guests regularly, especially boisterous ones, expect complaints from neighbors and doormen. Tenants who violate noise policies can be evicted from the building.

> "Single-family homes in New York generally come in two price ranges: expensive and unbelievably expensive."
>
> **MICHAEL DECOURCY**

High-rise apartments are often lacking in charm. Many come pre-furnished, or have rules governing the amount of changes you can make to your home. Wall-to-wall carpeting, windows that can't open and featureless hallways are often par for the course. Try to meet your neighbors before you move in. If you're incompatible, the adjoining walls can start to feel awfully thin.

APPRECIATION

Amerada Hess Corp. **LINDA BOLNICK** • American Express **DEBORAH HICKEY, ANN NOWAK** • American Express Tax and Business Svcs. Inc. **SCOTT EDISON** • American International Group Inc. **BARBARA RUBEL, PATRICIA SIBRINSZ** • Arthur Andersen **STEPHANIE HALPERN, BARBARA HUTNYON** • AXA Financial/Equitable Cos. **TINA MERCIER** • Bank of New York Co. **KAREN PURTELL, COURTNEY INTERSIMONE** • BBDO, NY **ANTHONY OTTRANDO** • BDO Seidman **PAT DEGNAN** • Bear Stearns Cos. **JANE KELLY, JODI MILLER-CASCADE** • Bristol-Myers Squibb Co. **GAIL WILLIAMS** • Chadbourne & Parke **LAURIE MALLACH, BERNADETTE MILES** • Chase Manhattan Bank **PATRICIA DROZOWSKI, ROBIN CHESNEY, SHIRLEY BERRY-HERTZOG** • Citibank Fiserv **BETSEY MESSINA** • Cleary Gottlieb Steen & Hamilton **JANET SIKIRICA** • Clifford Chance Rogers & Wells **CAROLINE OLDOR, PATRICIA MORONEY** • Columbia University **CHUCK MINTZ** • Columbia University, Real Estate Housing Office **MARTHA McANDREW** • Coudert Brothers **MARY SIMPSON, SUSAN BURACZEWSKI** • Cravath Swaine & Moore **LISA KALEN** • David Berdon & Co. **LISA CALICK** • Davis Polk & Wardwell **BONNIE HURRY** • Deloitte & Touche **EDDA ZURKOFF, JANE SEBOK** • Deutschebank **ROBIN GANS, GINA ESPOSITO, JACQUELINE MURRAY** • Dewey Ballantine **WILLIAM DAVIS, KISHA NUNEZ** • Donaldson Lufkin & Jenrette Inc. **LIZ MARTINEZ** • Edelman Public Relations Worldwide **LAILANI SALCEDO, ROBIN SKLAR** • Ernst & Young **DAN BLACK, ANGIE CERCONE, NANCY GERESSY** • Fried Frank Harris Shriver & Jacobson **JOSIE GANEK, ALLISON CAULFIELD** • Goldman Sachs Group Inc. **ANDREW WALKER** • J.P. Morgan & Co. **CANDYCE GOLIS, CHRIS KOSZTA, DIANE MIGLIONICO** • Kirkland & Ellis **MARY VAUGHAN** • KPMG Peat Marwick **SHARON LOSE, EDNA AULT** • LeBoeuf Lamb Greene & MacRae **STEPHEN DiCARMINE, BARBARA DENT** • Lehman Brothers Holdings Inc. **BRENDA LEVIS, SUSAN MURPHY, BLAKE BEATTY, JENNIFER MURPHY, CANDACE DARLING, LEIGH LANIER, DEBORAH SCHEPPE** • Morgan Stanley Dean Witter & Co. **PATRICIA PALUMBO, TRACY RUSSELL, ANN MARIE DINEEN, LINDA FISHER** • Pfizer Inc. **RANDALL DECKER** • Porter Novelli **EILEEN BENWITT** • Pricewaterhouse Coopers **AMY VAN KIRK, MARK FRIEDMAN, LISETTE MANCI** • Saatchi & Saatchi **LINDA TORRESSEN** • Schulte Roth & Zabel **AMBER GRAVES** • Shearman & Sterling **LILY NG, MARY MULLIGAN** • Simpson Thacher & Bartlett **KRYSTYN REZA, DEE PIFER** • Skadden Arps Slate Meagher & Flom **ADRIANNE WEISSMAN, CAROL SPRAGUE** • Sullivan & Cromwell **LINDA BLAIR, MARIA ALKIEWICZ** • The MI Group **ROB DAVIS** • Time Inc., Rockefeller Center **HENRY LESCAILLE, ROBERT NESBITT, BERNARD PALMER, JOANNE BRISSON, LINDA CHANG** • Time Warner **KAREN MANGIONE** • White & Case **ALI IANNUZZO, DANA STEPHENSON** • Young & Rubicam, NY **LISA GILL, STEPHEN McGARRY**